LEGAL PLURALISM IN THE HOLY CITY

Legal Pluralism in the Holy City *is a ground-breaking contribution to the study of co-existing and intersecting legal systems in contemporary Jerusalem, within the context of the raging national conflict in the city and in surrounding Palestine. It provides Shahar with a vantage point from which he contributes to the theory of legal pluralism in a subtle way. I have no doubt this book will be an important read for both academics and practitioners interested in law-in-action, legal pluralism, Islamic law and the Israeli-Palestinian conflict.*

Baudouin Dupret, CNRS, France, and Centre Jacques-Berque, Morocco

With convincing detail and insightful analysis Shahar demonstrates the resilience and creativity of Jerusalem's Muslim courts. Never avoiding the political realities or fieldwork challenges, he clarifies with originality and telling examples the intertwined jurisdictional, organizational and humanitarian issues facing the Muslim courts in Israel and, by implication, throughout the Muslim world.

Lawrence Rosen, Princeton University, USA

Shahar gives us a detailed ethnography of a complex set of legal fields, including an Israeli shari'a court in West Jerusalem and two non-Israeli shari'a courts in East Jerusalem. Through detailed accounts of everyday life in the court and illustrative cases, he traces processes of inter-court competition, women's demands for law reform, and innovations undertaken by the shari'a judges. An important contribution to legal ethnography and the social study of Islamic law.

John R. Bowen, Washington University in St. Louis, USA,
author of *Can Islam be French* and *Blaming Islam*

Shahar, a rare combination of anthropologist and Islamologist, offers fresh perspectives on application of Islamic and Israeli law in the shari'a court in West Jerusalem and its interaction with the Family Court and the Palestinian and Jordanian shari'a courts in East Jerusalem. The study, based on participant observations and court cases, is indispensable for researchers in socio-legal history, Islamic law, and legal pluralism.

Aharon Layish, Hebrew University of Jerusalem, Israel

Cultural Diversity and Law

Series Editor:
Prakash Shah, School of Law, Queen Mary University of London, UK

Around the world, most states are faced with difficult issues arising out of cultural diversity in their territories. Within the legal field, such issues span across matters of private law through to public and constitutional law. At international level too there is now considerable jurisprudence regarding ethnic, religious and cultural diversity. In addition, there are several layers of legal control – from communal and religious regulation to state and international regulation. This multiplicity of norm setting has been variously termed legal pluralism, inter-legality or inter-normativity and provides a fascinating lens for academic analysis that links up to cultural diversity in new and interesting ways. The umbrella of cultural diversity encompasses various population groups throughout the world ranging from national, ethnic, religious or indigenous groupings. This series particularly welcomes work that is of comparative interest, concerning various state jurisdictions as well as different population groups.

Also in the series

Muslim Families, Politics and the Law
A Legal Industry in Multicultural Britain
Ralph Grillo
ISBN 978-1-4724-5121-7

State and Legal Practice in the Caucasus
Anthropological Perspectives on Law and Politics
Edited by Stéphane Voell and Iwona Kaliszewska
ISBN 978-1-4724-4690-9

Declarations of Interdependence
A Legal Pluralist Approach to Indigenous Rights
Kirsten Anker
ISBN 978-1-4094-4737-5

Between Cultural Diversity and Common Heritage
Legal and Religious Perspectives on the Sacred Places of the Mediterranean
Edited by Silvio Ferrari and Andrea Benzo
ISBN 978-1-4724-2601-7

Legal Pluralism in the Holy City

Competing Courts, Forum Shopping, and Institutional Dynamics in Jerusalem

IDO SHAHAR
University of Haifa, Israel

Routledge
Taylor & Francis Group
LONDON AND NEW YORK

First published 2015 by Ashgate Publishing

Published 2016 by Routledge
2 Park Square, Milton Park, Abingdon, Oxfordshire OX14 4RN
711 Third Avenue, New York, NY 10017

First issued in paperback 2016

Routledge is an imprint of the Taylor & Francis Group, an informa business

British Library Cataloguing in Publication Data
A catalogue record for this book is available from the British Library

The Library of Congress has cataloged the printed edition as follows:
Shahar, Ido, 1969– author.
Legal pluralism in the Holy City : competing courts, forum shopping, and institutional dynamics in Jerusalem / by Ido Shahar.
pages cm. – (Cultural diversity and law)
Includes bibliographical references and index.
ISBN 978-1-4094-1052-2 (hardback)
1. Islamic courts—Jerusalem.
2.Palestinian Arabs—Legal status, laws, etc.—Jerusalem. 3. Forum shopping—Jerusalem. I. Title.
KML158.75.S53 2015
340.9095694'42--dc23

2015004239

ISBN: 978-1-138-70162-5 (pbk)
ISBN: 978-1-4094-1052-2 (hbk)

To Tamar, Talia and Roee

Contents

List of Figures and Tables *ix*
List of Abbreviations *xi*
Acknowledgments *xiii*

1 Introduction 1

PART I HISTORICAL AND FORMAL LEGAL CONTEXT

2 Shari‘a Courts in Palestine and Israel: A Socio-Historical Review 15

3 Shari‘a Courts in Israel: The Legal Setting 29

4 Establishment of the Shari‘a Court in West Jerusalem 41

PART II A COURT IN MOTION: ETHNOGRAPHIC PORTRAIT

5 The Site 51

6 The Cast of Characters 61

7 Organizational Routines 77

8 Doing Ethnography in the Shari‘a Court in West Jerusalem: Some Reflexive Notes 85

PART III THE WEST JERUSALEM SHARI‘A COURT AND THE FAMILY COURT

9 Breaking Shari‘a Courts’ Monopoly in Jurisdiction 95

10 Shari‘a Courts’ Response to Competition 107

11 Forum Shopping: Where to File a Maintenance Suit 123

PART IV A TALE OF THREE COURTS AND ONE CITY

12 Three Shari'a Courts in Jerusalem 137

13 Forum Shopping between Shari'a Courts 151

PART V CONCLUDING DISCUSSION

14 Israeli Shari'a Courts as Pluralistic Organizations: A New Institutional Perspective 167

15 Empirical and Theoretical Implications 177

Appendix 1: Shari'a Court Fees 191

Appendix 2: Form for Court Petition 193

Appendix 3: Fatwa by the Mufti of Jerusalem 195

Bibliography *199*
Index *221*

List of Figures and Tables

Figures

4.1	Number of Files Adjudicated by the Israeli Shari‘a Court in West Jerusalem, 1988–2004	48
6.1	Jerusalem Maps—Palestinian and Israeli Neighborhoods in Metropolitan Jerusalem (2000)	62
7.1	Types of Files in the Shari‘a Court in West Jerusalem by Year	78
7.2	Types of Files in the Shari‘a Court in West Jerusalem by Year (Percentage)	79
7.3	Layout of the Courtroom	80

Table

10.1	Number of Files Opened in Israeli Shari‘a Courts, 2001–2004	110

List of Abbreviations

EI2	*Encyclopaedia of Islam*, 2nd edition, Leiden: E.J. Brill, 1965–2005
HCJ	(Israeli) High Court of Justice
ISC	Israeli Shari‘a Court in West Jerusalem
MK	Member of Knesset (Israeli Parliament)
NII	(Israeli) National Insurance Institute
NIS	New Israeli Shekel
OCHA	UN Office for the Coordination of Humanitarian Affairs in the Occupied Palestinian Territories
OLFR	Ottoman Law of Family Rights (1917)
PNA	Palestinian National Authority
SCA	(Israeli) Shari‘a Court of Appeal
SMC	Supreme Muslim Council

Acknowledgments

I owe many thanks. First and foremost, I wish to acknowledge the generous assistance and goodwill of the many people whom I met in the shari‘a court of West Jerusalem during my years of research. Qadi Ahmad Natur, former president of the shari‘a court of appeal, granted me initial permission to conduct fieldwork in the court, and former Qadis Ziad ‘Asliyya and Muhammad Rashid Zibdi literally opened the court's doors to me and accorded me wide access to the court's activities. The court's staff provided most valuable assistance and support, and made my visits to the court not only fascinating but also pleasurable. A tremendous debt of gratitude is due to all those who conversed with me—court staff, lawyers, *shar‘i* advocates, marriage registrars, arbiters, and mediators, as well as litigants and occasional visitors to the court—who shared with me their personal stories, ideas, and views. I feel this book is a tribute to their generosity and trust!

This book had a long "incubation period" and germinated slowly through countless discussions and exchanges with more people than I can mention here. Still, some colleagues and friends, whom I list in no particular order, deserve special thanks: Dror Ze'evi, Brinkley Messick, Aharon Layish, Moussa Abou Ramadan, Iris Agmon, Menny Mautner, Assaf Likhovski, Immanuel Sivan, Gordon Woodman, Cilia Fassberg, Yuksel Sezgin, Lynn Welchman, Keebet and the late Franz von Benda-Beckmann, and Yossi Rapoport. All of them made valuable comments throughout the years, which contributed immensely to the fruition of this project. I am particularly indebted to Ursula Wokoeck, who copy-edited the book, for her valuable suggestions that went far beyond language and style issues. I also thank the editors at Ashgate Publishing, Alison Kirk and Alex Buckley, and the editor of the series, Prakash Shah, for believing in my project and for seeing it through.

The various phases of field research and writing were generously supported by the following grants and institutions: The Kreitman Foundation and the Haim Herzog Center for Middle East Studies supported my field research with generous grants. Further grants at the Hebrew University (the Golda Meir Fellowship) and at Tel Aviv University (the Yonathan Shapiro Fellowship) provided financial support for additional field research. The first draft of the book was completed during my year as post-doctoral fellow at the Centre for Socio-Legal Studies at the University of Oxford. A second draft was completed upon my return to Israel, when I spent a year at Ben Gurion University of the Negev with the assistance of the Center for Absorption in Science. Lastly, the Rector of the University of Haifa, the Dean of the Faculty of Humanities and the Research Authority at the University of Haifa provided me with generous financial support in the preparation of the manuscript for publication.

Some portions of the book previously appeared in the following essays, and I am grateful to the publishers for granting me permission to use them here: Forum Shopping between Civil and Shari'a Courts: Maintenance Suits in Contemporary Jerusalem, in *Religion in Disputes: Pervasiveness of Religious Normativity in Disputing Processes*, edited by K. Benda-Beckmann, F. Benda-Beckmann, B. Turner, and M. Ramstadt, London (2013), 147–64; A Tale of Two Courts: How Organizational Ethnography Can Shed New Light on Legal Pluralism. *Political and Legal Anthropology Review*, 36, 1 (2013), 118–37; Legal Pluralism Incarnate: An Institutional Perspective on Courts of Law in Colonial and Postcolonial Settings. *Journal of Legal Pluralism*, 65 (2012), 133–63.

Last but not least, my deepest gratitude is reserved to my family: my parents, Dalia and Avi, who supported me from afar when I struggled with fieldwork dilemmas and writing blocks; my life-partner, Tamar—the keenest critical reader I have ever met—who shared the ups and downs of this long project from its early stages to its completion; and my children, Talia and Roee, for their patience and support during the long years of research and writing. This book is dedicated to them.

Chapter 1
Introduction

It was a routine morning in the Israeli shari'a court in West Jerusalem, a few months before I completed my fieldwork there. I was sitting in Qadi Muhammad Rashid Zibdi's courtroom,[1] observing how he calmly manages one case after another, when all of the sudden a burst of loud, threatening jumble of Arabic and Hebrew words disrupted the tranquility of the court. All the heads in the room turned toward the door: the loud voice seemed to be coming from the nearby waiting room, where some sort of incident was apparently developing. Qadi Zibdi announced an immediate break and left the courtroom to see what was going on outside. I followed him. It turned out that a few minutes earlier a young prisoner had been brought to the court by two guards of the Israeli Prison Authorities. As we entered, the guards were making desperate efforts to prevent a large crowd of family and friends from approaching, touching, and hugging the prisoner.

Since the situation was clearly becoming tense—one of the guards already had his hand resting on his gun holster—Qadi Zibdi was quick to intervene: raising his voice above the tumult, he asked the crowd to calm down immediately. When order was regained, he turned to the guards and told them in Hebrew that there is no need to be so harsh, after all, these people have not seen their relative for a very long time. The senior guard replied that there are certain rules he will not allow to be violated, but Qadi Zibdi insisted that everyone must cool off right away. It was at this point that the prisoner's lawyer intervened in the conversation, stating that he has not had an opportunity to speak with his client and that he therefore requests several minutes in privacy with him.

Qadi Zibdi replied that this is a very reasonable request; he asked the guards to unlock the prisoner's handcuffs (thus leaving only his feet chained) and to allow him some private space on the green sofa in the corner of the court's waiting room. Reluctantly the guards carried out Qadi Zibdi's orders, and it was not long before the prisoner, who was sitting "privately" with his lawyer, was once again encircled by excited family members. Qadi Zibdi returned to his courtroom to proceed with the hearings, but I remained outside, watching the prisoner, the guards, and the excited crowd.

Standing beside me was an employee of the shari'a courts administration, who also heard the hullabaloo and came to watch the happening. Amused by the drama unfolding in front of us, the man told me in Hebrew:

---

1 All names mentioned in the book are pseudonyms, except for the names of presiding qadis.

> You know, this sort of thing could only happen here. In the civil courts the prisoners never have a chance even to talk to their relatives and friends, let alone touch them. They [the prisoners] enter the courtroom through a special secured entrance and are strictly separated from the audience. Here, by contrast, several weeks ago, a prisoner was brought to the court by four Prison Authorities guards, who were also escorted by eight police officers from an elite squad. He [the prisoner] has two daughters and a wife, but the guards didn't let him touch them. Things went on like this, but eventually Qadi Zibdi exploded and told the guards that it can't go on like this. He insisted that they take off the prisoner's handcuffs, and informed them that in the next hearing the prisoner will sit with his wife for a whole hour. And indeed, this is exactly what happened: in the next visit the prisoner and his wife sat with the qadi privately in his chambers.

This event, which I recorded in my field diary on May 17, 2004, illustrates the unique duality that characterizes the Israeli shari'a court in West Jerusalem: on the one hand this court is an integral part of the Israeli legal system, administered by the Israeli Ministry of Justice, and on the other hand it is a Muslim-Palestinian arena, where Palestinian solidarity is expressed and celebrated; on the one hand it is a mechanism of control, which Israeli authorities deploy to strengthen Israeli rule in Jerusalem, and on the other hand it is a mechanism of resistance, which East Jerusalemite Muslims deploy to undermine Israeli dominance in the city.

The comparison my interlocutor made between the Israeli shari'a court in West Jerusalem and the Israeli civil courts operating in the city—that do not treat Palestinian prisoners as benignly—highlights another prominent feature of this court: the fact that it operates parallel to several other courts of law, all of which have jurisdiction in matters pertaining to the personal status of Muslims. Due to the peculiar political circumstances in Jerusalem, no less than three other legal institutions, in addition to the Israeli shari'a court, deal with personal status matters of Muslims in the city: the Israeli family court in West Jerusalem, the Jordanian shari'a courts in East Jerusalem, and the shari'a courts of the Palestinian National Authority (PNA) on the outskirts of the city. In other words, the West Jerusalem shari'a court operates in an environment characterized by substantial *legal pluralism*—an environment where several competing judicial systems exist side by side.

How does its complex and turbulent environment—characterized by both political and legal pluralism—affect the Israeli shari'a court in West Jerusalem? How does this environment affect the individuals whose cases are brought to this court? These are two of the major questions addressed in this book. In the chapters below, I present an organizational ethnography (see e.g., Van Mannen 1979, Rosen 1991, Bate 1997, Yanow 2009) of the Israeli shari'a court in West Jerusalem. While I aim to provide a rich portrait of this organization, I do not study it in isolation; rather, I show how it has been shaped, over time, by its intricate relations with its pluralistic environment. It is these relations, I contend, that have turned it into an especially dynamic and versatile organization.

Although legal pluralism is unusually conspicuous in the case in focus—namely, the case of the Israeli shari'a court in West Jerusalem—it is far from being a rare phenomenon. Quite to the contrary: research into legal pluralism has grown exponentially in recent decades, showing that multiple legal and normative orders often exist side by side, in the same social field. This book therefore tackles a ubiquitous socio-legal phenomenon and seeks to contribute to its theoretical understanding. More specifically, the book sets forth a new approach—an organizational approach—to legal pluralism. Unlike many other theoretical approaches to the phenomenon, this approach does not focus on the relations between abstract bodies of law under conditions of legal pluralism, but rather on the relations between different courts of law as organizations. In situations of legal pluralism, courts applying different bodies of law serve the same population and consequently affect one another in direct and indirect ways. These mutual effects have implications for these courts' rulings as well as for individual litigants whose cases are brought before them. While the suggested organizational approach to legal pluralism is not meant to replace existing approaches, it does seek to add a more grounded, practice-based, and "materialistic" perspective on the phenomenon. By combining legal pluralism with organizational analysis, I contend, we can address a level of analysis that has rarely been tackled by students of legal pluralism to date, and shed new light on a well-studied phenomenon.

Legal Pluralism: An Organizational Approach

In a nutshell,[2] the notion of legal pluralism evolved as a counter-hegemonic perspective to the dominant perspective of "legal centralism," the idea that "law is and should be the law of the state, uniform for all persons, exclusive of all other law, and administered by a single set of state institutions" (Griffiths 1986a: 3). In opposition to this monopolistic and state-centric view of state law, "legal pluralist" thinkers postulate that: (a) "not all the phenomena related to law and not all that are law-like have their source in government" (Moore 1986: 15); and (b) "there is a plurality of law in all social arenas" (Tamanaha 2000: 298).

A salient characteristic of intellectual fashions is that they seem to be suddenly there. The same is true of legal pluralism. What was virtually unrecognized as a discernible analytical concept before the 1970s was, toward the end of that decade, the hottest dish in the buffet of socio-legal concepts. Anthropologists of law, but also sociologists and historians of law and lawyers with a social-scientific orientation, were studying instances of legal pluralism everywhere: in the past and in the present; in tribal societies, in nation states, and in international law; in post-colonial states and in the industrialized West (see Merry 1988).

2 For useful overviews of studies of legal pluralism, see Griffiths (1986a), Merry (1988), Woodman (1998), F. von Benda-Beckmann (2002), Benda-Beckmann and Benda-Beckmann (2006), Berman (2009).

In light of legal pluralism's attractiveness for large audiences of various academic disciplines, it is not surprising, perhaps, that the concept lacked an agreed-upon definition. While some writers referred to it in prescriptive terms, as an ideology that aims to ameliorate our perception of law,[3] others referred to it in descriptive terms, but still were unable to agree whether we deal here with a theory/a doctrine/a paradigm/a perspective, or simply with a particular state of affairs. If scholars were unable to agree on the correct adjective to modify the term, needless to say that they found it extremely difficult to agree on the concrete meaning of legal pluralism and on its analytical constituents. For example, some writers spoke about the interaction of "bodies of law" (Woodman 1998), others about "systems of law" (Hooker 1975), "legal mechanisms" (Vanderlinden 1971), "concrete patterns of social ordering" (Galanter 1981), and so on. Similarly, writers used different terms to denote the social group within which an instance of legal pluralism may occur: "a corporate group" (Smith 1969), "an association" (Ehrlich 1936), "a subgroup" (Pospisil 1958), and "a semi-autonomous social field" (Moore 1973) are just a few examples of the wide variety of terms employed by scholars.

The concept also attracted some harsh criticism. Critics such as Brian Z. Tamanaha sought to "pierce the legal pluralism balloon," by revealing its "unstable theoretical foundation," so that "the momentum of the doctrine will break" (Tamanaha 1993: 202). Along with others (see e.g., Roberts 1998), Tamanaha's criticism generated a heated debate that focused mainly on conceptual and definitional matters. Proponents and opponents of legal pluralism were drawn to hairsplitting debates concerning the nature of the relations between law and government/state (for a review of these debates, see Woodman 1998): Can law exist independently of the state or of central government? Is it theoretically and analytically admissible to speak of non-state law? If so, what is the dividing line between state law and non-state law?

Nevertheless, despite the criticism, and despite its inherent conceptual vagueness, the study of legal pluralism has remained a vibrant area of socio-legal research for several decades. Over these decades, the themes and questions that occupied scholars of legal pluralism have changed considerably. The focus on legal pluralism in post-colonial contexts, which characterized the 1970s, gave way in the 1980s and 1990s to intensive research into legal pluralism in Western contexts. This focus was replaced in recent years by a rising tide of empirical studies focusing on legal pluralism in the context of globalization. This burgeoning line of research, which Merry (1988: 872) dubbed the "new legal pluralism," examines the interrelations between transnational, national, and local legal orders

3 Sack and Aleck (1992), for example, state that: "Lawyers and non lawyers must accept the plurality of 'law' and learn to handle it constructively—in theory as well as in practice …," so that we can achieve "a switch from legal positivism and its bias in favor of an increasing centralization, unification and uniformization of 'law' to legal pluralism" (Sack and Aleck 1992: xx1).

(see e.g., Benda-Beckmann, Benda-Beckmann, and Griffiths 2005, Tamanaha 2007, Berman 2009, Michaels 2009, Twining 2010). These developments reflect a process of elaboration and consolidation of this field of research. A mature body of literature, rich and comprehensive both theoretically and empirically, has emerged in recent years and has made legal pluralism truly a key concept in contemporary socio-legal research.

And yet, despite the maturity of this field of research, I contend that both opponents and proponents of legal pluralism have failed to notice a substantial shortcoming in the literature: the lack of attention to the organizational level of analysis. Apart from a few notable exceptions (see e.g., Moore 1973, Benda-Beckmann 1981, Spiertz 1991, Santos 2006) researchers have rarely examined legal pluralism from an organizational perspective and have rarely noticed that legal pluralism involves not only a plurality of normative orders but also a plurality of legal organizations that operate side by side in the same social field. These organizations interact and affect one another in complex ways: they may compete with one another, support one another, imitate one another, or distinguish themselves from one another. They may share some resources—both material and symbolic—and compete over others. They may or may not share personnel, and their staff may maintain friendly or hostile relationships. The web of interrelations between courts under conditions of legal pluralism affects court rulings, as well as individual litigants who maneuver among "competing" courts. While all this is of interest to students of legal pluralism, it has hardly received their attention to date.

Compared with some other traditions of legal scholarship, the study of legal pluralism is rather socially-grounded and "materialistic;" it pays considerable attention to the embeddedness of the law in everyday practices and in social and cultural arrangements. And yet, in this book, I argue that scholars have not gone far enough in examining legal pluralism as a socially-embedded, practice-based phenomenon. Again and again, discussions of legal pluralism drift towards explorations of abstract "normative orders," "legal systems" or "bodies of law," and the relations between them. All too often, scholars' attention is diverted from the manifestations of legal pluralism in day-to-day life and in concrete organizational settings, such as courts of law. This problematic tendency was identified almost three decades ago by Merry (1988), in her seminal essay "Legal Pluralism:"

> [t]he concept of legal pluralism can press too quickly toward analyses of systems to the neglect of variations in particular local places […] Thinking of legal pluralism seems likely to get us out of the courtroom and the lawyer's office, but once outside, legal pluralist analyses could lead away from detailed examinations of particular local places. (Merry 1988: 791)

In this book I contend that an organizational perspective on legal pluralism can do much to "ground" the phenomenon in social, cultural, political, and economic reality. It can help us see legal pluralism not only in idealistic terms, as a set of relationships among abstract normative orders, but also in materialistic, practice-based terms—or, as Merry (1988) put it, it can help us bring courtrooms, lawyers' offices, and "local places" back into the study of legal pluralism.

In the chapters below, the suggested organizational approach to legal pluralism is elaborated and brought to life through an extended study of the Israeli shari'a court in West Jerusalem. This court is studied as an organization—with its own organizational hierarchy, organizational culture and organizational routines, its own salaried employees, and its own material and symbolic resources. Furthermore, it is studied in the context of its relations with other courts that operate in its vicinity and serve the Muslim population, namely, the Israeli family court in Jerusalem, the PNA shari'a courts, and the Jordanian shari'a courts in the city.

I suggest that an organizational perspective on legal pluralism directs our attention to three sets of questions. The first set of questions, already mentioned above, has to do with the interrelations between courts of law that apply different bodies of law to the same population, asking, for example: do these courts "compete" over litigants? Do they compete over economic resources? Do they compete over legitimacy and prestige, and by what methods? Do they coordinate their decision-making processes? Are there personal acquaintances between their staffs? How do these contacts influence the courts' judicial policies and decisions?

A second cluster of questions has to do with the strategies deployed by individual litigants in situations of legal pluralism, when they are required to choose among two or more available courts. This form of behavior, known as *forum shopping* (see Garner 2001: 590), has received but scant attention in the extant literature on legal pluralism (a notable exception: Benda-Beckmann 1981), perhaps due to this literature's focus on abstract bodies of law rather than on courts as concrete organizations. What courts do individual litigants perceive as accessible to them, and why (these may not be the same as the courts available to them de facto)? What are litigants' considerations when they choose among alternative legal forums? Can parties in a single dispute appeal to more than one court simultaneously, and if they do so, what are the consequences? How does litigants' "forum shopping" affect the various courts and their judicial policies?

Lastly, an organizational approach to legal pluralism draws our attention not only to the relations between equivalent courts serving the same population, but also to the relations between each of these courts and the *organizational fields* (DiMaggio and Powell 1983) to which they belong. For example, the Israeli shari'a court in West Jerusalem operates in two organizational fields simultaneously: the Israeli state-law organizational field and the Palestinian-*shar'i* organizational field. These fields include not only courts of law but also other kinds of organizations, such as government ministries, educational institutions, religious authorities, and non-governmental organizations. Each of these fields has not only distinct legal traditions but also distinct institutional and administrative logics, and each exerts a different set of pressures on the Israeli shari'a court in West Jerusalem. In the language of organization theory, the dual belonging to two different organizational fields turns this court into a *pluralistic organization* (Kraatz and Block 2008).

While courts that operate under conditions of legal pluralism do not necessarily belong to more than one organizational field—some may belong to one field only—this is often the case. This raises another, third set of questions: how does the operation in two or more organizational fields influence courts and their decisions? How do such courts cope with the often contradictory demands from the different fields? How do they maintain their legitimacy in both fields? What legal and organizational cultures do such courts develop? These and similar questions will be addressed in the following chapters, and particularly in Chapter 14.

Combining these three topics of investigation provides us with a comprehensive *organizational perspective on legal pluralism.* To develop this new perspective, I draw on theories and analytical constructs from the field of *organization studies* (e.g. Scott and Davis 2007, Perrow 1986). Organizations—especially formal, bureaucratic ones—are a prominent feature of industrial and post-industrial societies, and as such, they have become the focus of a thriving field of academic research known as organization studies or organization theory. This is an interdisciplinary field that brings together sociology, psychology, economics, political science, and other disciplines, all of which have relevancy to organizations and organizational processes. Legal scholarship, too, has some important overlaps with organization studies (see e.g., Powell 1996, Suchman and Edelman 1996), but the specific phenomenon of legal pluralism has not yet been addressed from an organizational perspective. This book aims to fill that lacuna.

Structure of the Book

This study is an interdisciplinary project. It combines history and ethnography, diachronic and synchronic perspectives; it examines relatively broad, macro-political processes as well as micro-level interactions; and it is based on participant observations in the studied court (conducted in the years 1998–2000 and 2001–04) as well as on textual and legal analyses of court cases and rulings. The structure of the book reflects its interdisciplinary character. In the following, I provide a brief preview of the book's chapters and of the main arguments presented in each of them.

The book is divided into five parts. Part I, "Historical and Formal Legal Context," consists of three background chapters that outline the recent history of shari'a courts in Palestine/Israel and describe the evolution of legal pluralism in these courts' environment. The first one (Chapter 2), "Shari'a Courts in Palestine and Israel: A Socio-Historical Review," begins with a brief description of the shari'a court system in the Ottoman Empire and of the *millet* system, which constituted a unique form of intra-state legal pluralism. This is followed by a review of the transformations that the shari'a court system in Palestine underwent during the late Ottoman period and under the British Mandate (1917–48). Chapter 2 concludes with the founding of the State of Israel in 1948 and the establishment of a shari'a court system as part of the Israeli state apparatus. Altogether, the chapter shows that despite the far-reaching transformations in the status of shari'a courts in Palestine/Israel under different political regimes, legal pluralism has always been a prominent feature of these courts' environment.

Chapter 3, "Shari'a Courts in Israel: The Legal Setting," presents the legal framework governing the operation of shari'a courts in Israel, the material and procedural laws they apply, and their jurisdiction. Chapter 4, "Establishment of the Shari'a Court in West Jerusalem," focuses the discussion even further and describes the founding of the organization that stands at the center of this book. The chapter recounts how, following the occupation and annexation of East Jerusalem in 1967, the Israeli authorities initially tried to co-opt the Jordanian shari'a courts that operated there, and therefore refrained from establishing an Israeli shari'a court in the city. It was only after these efforts at co-optation had failed that Israeli authorities decided to establish an Israeli shari'a court in West Jerusalem. This chain of events shows, I contend, that the establishment of the Israeli shari'a court in West Jerusalem was no less a political act than a legal-administrative one, and that the operation of this court cannot be understood without consideration of the political context that brought it into existence.

Part II, "A Court in Motion: Ethnographic Portrait" shifts from the socio-historical and legal reviews to an ethnographic portrayal of the Israeli shari'a court in West Jerusalem, based on my six years of fieldwork in this court. It consists of four chapters, each of which sheds light on a different aspect of the court's operation. Chapter 5, "The Site," describes the court as a "hybrid organization" that combines diverse cultural, administrative, and legal influences. The chapter shows how this hybridity finds expression in the court's spatial and temporal arrangements, as well as in its legal culture. Chapter 6, "The Cast of Characters," presents the various actors that take an active role in the social interactions in the court. The court's "clientele"—that is, the Muslim litigants who appeal to it and attend it occasionally—are described, as well as several groups of "repeat players" (Galanter 1974: 97) in the court, such as the court's personnel, legal councilors, and marriage registrars (*ma'adhuns*) appointed by the court.

Chapter 7, "Organizational Routines," provides a close look at the day-to-day operation of the court. The routines for handling cases of various types are described, as well as the routines of the court's secretariat, archive, and typists. Finally, the last chapter in this part (Chapter 8), "Doing Ethnography in the Shari'a Court in West Jerusalem: Some Reflexive Notes," discusses the challenges and difficulties I faced during my fieldwork. I describe the various phases of my research and discuss problems, such as limited access to data sources, my identity as an Israeli Jew studying a Palestinian site, and the occasional reluctance of court visitors to cooperate with my research.

Part III, "The West Jerusalem Shari'a Court and the Family Court," consists of three chapters that deal with the relationship between these two courts. Since both courts belong to the Israeli legal system, I consider their concomitant functioning as a case of intra-state legal pluralism (Woodman 1999), that is, legal pluralism that occurs within the boundaries of a single state apparatus. Chapter 9, "Breaking the Shari'a Courts' Monopoly in Jurisdiction," tells the story of a controversial initiative in the Israeli parliament (the Knesset) to restrict the exclusive jurisdiction of Israeli shari'a courts by according civil family courts with parallel jurisdiction in some matters relating to the personal status of Muslims. Despite vehement opposition to the legislation amendment, and despite the efforts of shari'a court officials to prevent it, it eventually passed in the Knesset in November 2001. As a result legal pluralism has intensified, as far as Muslims in Israel are concerned: in most matters of personal status, Muslims are henceforth allowed to resort either to shari'a courts or to family courts, and this choice is anything but trivial.

Chapter 10, "Shari'a Courts' Response to Competition," analyzes the reactions of Israeli shari'a courts, and of the West Jerusalem shari'a court in particular, to the encroachment of their jurisdiction by family courts. It is argued that Israeli shari'a courts responded by trying to compete with family courts, that is, by trying to attract more litigants and to prevent potential litigants from appealing to family courts. Accordingly, attempts were made to remove bureaucratic obstacles and to turn the West Jerusalem shari'a court into a more "user-friendly" organization. In addition, legal reforms were promoted with the aim to improve the status of women in Israeli shari'a courts. Legal modifications (mostly procedural) were introduced in order to achieve more favorable rulings for women, and thus to reduce the danger that this large constituent of the courts' "clientele" will abandon them in favor of the now accessible family courts.

Like the previous chapter, Chapter 11, "Forum Shopping: Where to File a Maintenance Suit," also deals with the consequences of legal pluralism and of the competition between courts, but tackles this issue from a different perspective: that of individual litigants who must decide which legal forum to appeal to. The analysis focuses on a specific, very common dilemma: the dilemma of Muslim women in Jerusalem who seek a maintenance order and have to choose whether to appeal to the Israeli shari'a court in West Jerusalem or to the Israeli family court in the city. Empirical examples and excerpts from interviews with legal councilors (lawyers and *shar'i* advocates) show how complex and value-laden this choice is. They also show that on many occasions, litigants are not fully aware of the implications of their choices, and their decisions are therefore ill-informed.

Part IV, "A Tale of Three Courts and One City," consists of two chapters that explore the relations between the three shari'a courts in Jerusalem: the Israeli, the Jordanian, and the Palestinian shari'a courts. Since each of these courts belongs to a different state (or state-like) legal system, the relations between them constitute a case of inter-state legal pluralism (see Woodman 1999). Chapter 12, "Three Shari'a Courts in Jerusalem," begins by presenting some background information on the Jordanian and the Palestinian shari'a courts in Jerusalem. Subsequently, the chapter reviews the history of the relations between the Israeli shari'a court and the other shari'a courts. It is argued that the relations between the courts have developed over the last decade from mutual antagonism to relatively close cooperation and interdependency.

The chapter elaborates on the process that led to this "change of heart." I contend that a central feature of the relations between these courts is the radical difference between them in terms of the types of capital they possess. Of the three courts, the rulings of the Israeli court are the only ones that are officially enforced by Israeli authorities, and they are therefore more economically valid. However, the Israeli court possesses much less symbolic capital (Bourdieu 1986) than its counterparts. This inherent asymmetry between the courts downplays the competition between them, and lays the ground for cooperation, which is based on capital exchange.

Chapter 13, "Forum Shopping between Shari'a Courts," directs attention, again, to the point of view of individual litigants. It examines litigants' complex considerations when they decide which shari'a court to appeal to, and shows that litigants, too, perceive the relations between these courts as complementary rather than competitive. The chapter presents numerous empirical examples of active cooperation between the courts and between their staffs, to the benefit of Muslim Jerusalemite litigants. However, the chapter also highlights some frictions and tensions between these courts, which also bear effects on litigants.

The book's final Part V, "Concluding Discussion," includes two chapters. Chapter 14, "Israeli Shari'a Courts as Pluralistic Organizations: A New Institutional Perspective," builds on data provided in the preceding chapters to extend and elaborate the organizational perspective on legal pluralism. Whereas the previous chapters focus on the relations between courts—as organizations—under conditions of legal pluralism, this chapter analyzes the relations between these courts and the *organizational fields* to which they belong. The chapter draws on *new institutional* theory, which is one of the prominent theories in organization studies (e.g. Meyer and Rowan 1977, DiMaggio and Powell 1983, Powell and DiMaggio 1991, Scott 1995, Greenwood, Oliver, Sahlin, and Suddaby 2008), to argue that Israeli shari'a courts—and the West Jerusalem shari'a court in particular—belong simultaneously to two organizational fields: the Israeli state-law organizational field, and the Palestinian-*shar'i* organizational field. Due to this complex positioning in two different organizational fields, these courts are exposed to opposing pressures and expectations, which in turn leads to the emergence of an organizational culture that is especially versatile and dynamic. The chapter focuses on two judicial reforms enacted in Israeli shari'a courts in recent years and shows that what looks at first sight as a manifestation of incoherent judicial policy, is in fact a perfectly coherent response to opposing pressures originating in the two organizational fields.

The final chapter, Chapter 15, "Empirical and Theoretical Implications," integrates the findings of this research by discussing the entire organizational network of the Jerusalemite courts under study—that is, the Israeli shari'a court, the Jordanian shari'a court, the Palestinian shari'a courts, and the Israeli family court. This concluding chapter examines the impact of legal pluralism from several perspectives. First, it highlights the consequences of legal pluralism in the context of the Israeli–Palestinian national struggle in Jerusalem; then it discusses the implications of legal pluralism for gender relations among Muslims in contemporary Jerusalem; and lastly it examines the effects of legal pluralism on each of the courts in the studied organizational network.

This chapter re-visits the two objectives of the book: first, to provide a rich picture of an intriguing court and a profound situation of legal pluralism, marked by exceptional political, legal, and cultural tensions; second, to develop and apply a novel, organizational perspective on legal pluralism, conceptualizing legal pluralism as a set of relations between courts of law as organizations.

PART I
Historical and Formal Legal Context

Chapter 2
Shari'a Courts in Palestine and Israel: A Socio-Historical Review

The Israeli shari'a court in West Jerusalem is but one institution within a system of shari'a courts in Israel, shaped by its predecessors, the Ottoman and the Mandate legal systems (Layish 1965: 50, Eisenman 1977: 328–9, Naveh 1997: 58). To better understand the operation of this contemporary shari'a court, we must first examine the rich social and legal history that has shaped it. This chapter begins with a review of the shari'a court system in the late Ottoman period, followed by a description of the evolution of this system in Mandate Palestine. It then proceeds to examine the establishment of the shari'a court system under Israeli rule.

Late Ottoman Period

One of the most significant features of the Ottoman legal system was the *millet* regime, which was largely preserved in Palestine/Israel after the Empire had collapsed. The *millet* system of the Ottoman Empire was a "personal status regime" (Galanter and Krishnan 2001: 271), under which some non-Muslim religious minorities (Jewish and several Christian denominations) were granted a certain degree of religious and cultural autonomy. These religious communities were allowed to establish their own autonomous courts, applying religious law and adjudicating personal status matters of members of their respective communities (see Ursinus 1993). In other words, the *millet* system produced a state of "classic" legal pluralism (Merry 1988), in which different groups in the population were allocated to different tribunals.

Shari'a courts, however, were not part of the *millet* system: they were state courts that exerted authority over all subjects of the Ottoman Empire—Muslims and non-Muslims alike. As demonstrated by Amnon Cohen in his studies of the records of shari'a courts in Jerusalem in the sixteenth to nineteenth centuries, Jews and Christians were obliged to attend shari'a courts on many occasions. Surprisingly perhaps, sometimes they willingly chose to appeal to shari'a courts, even in matters over which their own communal courts had jurisdiction (see Cohen 1984, 1994, Cohen et al. 1993–2003, Qattan 1999, Shaham 2006, Marglin 2013).[1]

1 While Jews and Christians were able to choose between two different tribunals and could therefore manipulate the legal system to their advantage (since each tribunal applied a different legal code), Muslims were obliged to appeal to shari'a courts.

Under Ottoman rule, shari'a courts and the qadis officiating in them gained unparalleled power. Unlike earlier rulers of Muslim states, who lived quite contentedly with a legally pluralistic system consisting of several sub-systems of law,[2] the Ottoman sultans invested efforts in unifying the legal system in the Empire. For this purpose, they promulgated comprehensive and detailed regulations of secular criminal law and procedure, and gave order to assemble them in the form of codes, known as *kanun-name* (Heyd 1973: 2). Qadis, but also governors and other "secular" judges, were then ordered to administer justice in accordance with both the shari'a and the statutes of the *kanun* (ibid.: 216).

As noted by Haim Gerber, the *kanun* mentions explicitly—and repeatedly—the role of the qadi in applying these statutory regulations (Gerber 1994: 63). The qadi was to issue rulings according to the shari'a and/or the *kanun*, which in turn would be carried out by Ottoman officials (*ahl al-'urf*). The *kanun-name* repeatedly stressed that without prior decision by a qadi, no member of the military class could impose any punishment, not even a small fine, on ordinary people (*ri'aya*) (Inalcik 1991: 5). Thus, according to Gerber, the promulgation of the *kanun* and the unification of the Empire's legal system weakened other judicial institutions, while increasing the power of qadis presiding in shari'a courts.[3]

This state of affairs prevailed also in Ottoman Palestine, where qadis and shari'a courts enjoyed broad powers and jurisdiction. So salient was their social and political position, that some writers concluded that they practically ruled the towns where the courts resided (e.g. Abir 1975: 292, Shaw 1977: 46). Although this may very well be an overstatement (see Doumani 1985: 158), it is clear that qadis were key players in the religious, social, and political fields in Ottoman Palestine between the sixteenth and nineteenth centuries.

Such was, more or less, the situation in Ottoman Palestine until the second half of the nineteenth century. By that time, Ottoman government embarked on an extensive centralization project, known as the *tanzimat*, in the course of which some Western administrative mechanisms were adopted. These top-down introduced reforms left their imprints on every aspect of the social and political life in the Empire (Davison 2000). The judicial system, in particular, underwent profound changes: new "regular" tribunals (*nizami* courts), each consisting of

---

2 There is widespread agreement among scholars of Islamic law that ever since the early Muslim dynasties of the Umayyads and the Abbasids, the judicial authority of the qadis was concurrent with that of other legal functionaries such as the inspector of the markets (*muhtasib*), the chief of police (*ra'is al-shurta*), and the officer in charge of complaints (*sahib al-mazalim*). Moreover, already at this early stage, broad areas of the law—such as penal law, taxation, constitutional law, law of war (and to a lesser extent the law of contracts and obligations)—were excluded from the jurisdiction of shari'a courts (Schacht 1964: 77; see also, Shahar 2008b).

3 See also the admiring words of Joseph Schacht, who states that the Ottoman Empire gave the shari'a "the highest degree of actual efficiency which it had ever possessed […] since early Abbasid times" (Schacht 1964: 89).

several instances and specializing in specific legal fields (civil, criminal, and commercial), were established (Rubin 2011), and new Western-inspired codes were drafted. "Western" ideas of accessibility to the law, of state liability, and of equality before the law became fundamental tenets of the modern Ottoman legal discourse (see Findley 1980, 1991, Agmon 2006, Rubin 2011).

All in all, the legal reforms resulted in a profound transformation in the mode of operation of the shari'a courts. In the new, modernized legal system, penal and (many) civil cases, which previously fell under the jurisdiction of shari'a courts, were now referred to the *nizami* courts. Shari'a courts in the Ottoman Empire were thus virtually transformed into family courts, with jurisdiction in matters of personal status and endowments (*waqf*).[4] This field of the law was perceived by Ottoman reformers and by Western scholars alike as the "core" or the "heart" of the shari'a, and it was therefore the last to be codified (see Messick 1993: 61–2).

Yet, even before the codification of personal status law, shari'a courts in the Ottoman Empire were profoundly transformed. First of all, some sections of the *Majalla*, the newly drafted civil code,[5] were applied in shari'a courts as early as 1876. In addition, as part of the reformers' efforts to modernize, standardize, and centralize the legal system, both the position of qadis and the administrative routines in shari'a courts were dramatically altered. Among other things, a new college for training qadis was founded in Istanbul (1855), and qadis were appointed by the central government, rather than by officials in the provinces or districts (see Akiba 2003, 2005). Furthermore, new regulations and instructions were issued with regard to qadis' terms of service, the division of labor in court, the fees to be charged from litigants for diverse legal services, and the recording and archiving procedures (Agmon 2004, 2006).

The most dramatic transformation took place, however, shortly before the collapse of the Ottoman Empire. On October 25, 1917, while the British were making their final advance in Palestine, a comprehensive personal status law, known as "The Ottoman Law of Family Rights" (OLFR),[6] was promulgated together with

4 Shari'a courts had exclusive jurisdiction over all Muslims—Ottoman subjects and foreigners—in all matters of personal status and *waqf*. In their capacity as state courts, they also had jurisdiction over non-Muslim Ottoman subjects in some matters of personal status—such as guardianship and succession—unless the parties belonged to the same religious community and had agreed among themselves to be tried before the religious court of their community.

5 The *Majalla*, promulgated by the Sultan in 1876, was drafted between the years 1869 and 1876. It was based on the principles of the Hanafi school of law, but it did not always incorporate the dominant opinions of this school. Rather, of all the opinions advanced by Hanafi jurists, the code incorporated those deemed "most suited to the conditions of the times," in accordance with the principle of the eclectic method (*takhayur*). Furthermore, in its division into numbered books, sections, and articles, the *Majalla* clearly reflects Western influence. On the *Majalla*, see Onar (1955), Meron (1970), Liebesny (1975: 46–70), Findley (1991).

6 In a monograph on the Ottoman Family Law of 1917, Agmon (in progress) explains convincingly why the term "Ottoman Law of Family Rights" is in fact an inaccurate

a code of procedure for shari'a courts.[7] In their search for legal rules "more suited to modern times," the Ottoman drafters of the code incorporated regulations derived not only from the Hanafi school, but also from the other three orthodox schools of Islamic law (this legal technique is called *takhayyur*).[8] Moreover, they employed what Schacht characterized as "an unrestrained eclecticism:" they integrated not only opinions from the four schools, but also turned to the past and adopted any opinion, from any historical period whatsoever, that served their purposes (this technique is called *talfiq*, see Schacht 1964: 106).

The OLFR was therefore a revolutionary code of Islamic family law. Indeed, as shown by Messick (1993), the adoption of a Western mode of codification was not merely a matter of pouring Islamic content into a European form. Rather, it was a fundamental change in the underlying logic of the shari'a: statutory laws, promulgated by the sultan, replaced the traditional "jurists' law;" abstract, analytical categorizations replaced the analogical, case-oriented mode of reasoning; and a fixed code replaced the open-ended argumentation of shari'a jurisprudence (see Messick 1993: 56).[9]

The OLFR was revolutionary on another level as well: the Ottoman reformers who drafted it apparently intended it to serve as a general personal status law, applicable to every citizen of the Empire, whether Muslim, Christian, or Jewish (Agmon, in progress). Thus, of the 157 articles that make up the OLFR, almost 30 deal with specific issues relating to Jews and Christians. Furthermore, Article 155 states that any provision of the law that is not specifically excluded (by this law) will apply to non-Muslims as well; and Article 156 states that the jurisdiction of "spiritual leaders" (i.e. non-Muslim religious personalities) in matters of marriage, divorce, and alimony is thereby annulled. In other words, it appears that the

---

translation. She contends that the word "*huquq*" in Arabic and Ottoman meant both "laws" and "rights," but in the context of this law—which deals with the regulation of family life rather than with families' rights—the correct translation should be "Family Code." However, since the term "Ottoman Law of Family Rights" is very common in the literature, I chose to continue using it. I thank Dr Agmon for sharing her work in progress with me.

7 For a more detailed discussion of the Ottoman personal status law, see Goitein and Ben Shemesh (1957: 214–33), Eisenman (1977: 113–28), Akif Aydin (2000), Tucker (1996).

8 Four recognized schools of law exist in Sunni Islam: the *Hanafiyya*, the *Shafi'iyya*, the *Malikiyya*, and the *Hanbaliyya*. These schools are named after their mythical founders and are all considered equally orthodox. Yet, the Hanafi school was the official school of Islamic law in the Ottoman Empire, which turned it into the most prominent school in the wake of the centralizing reform process in the nineteenth century.

9 And yet, the rupture between "traditional shari'a" and "modern," post-*tanzimat* shari'a-based codes should not be overstated. While codification in the Western sense is indeed a modern phenomenon, there is historical evidence that many of the processes that characterized the *tanzimat* reforms (e.g. attempts at centralization, unification, and standardization of the legal system, intervention of the state or of the ruler in the "jurists' law," etc.) were also apparent, in one form or another, in pre-modern Muslim states (see e.g., Jackson 1996, Findley 1980: ch. 5).

promulgation of the OLFR constituted a first step in a process that was intended to lead to the cancelation of the entire *millet* system and its replacement by a general family law. It is not surprising, therefore, that religious leaders—Muslims and non-Muslims alike—were united in their objection to this law (see e.g., Ortayli 1994 [1990]: 148, Yildirim 2005: 355).

The OLFR was never implemented in Palestine under Ottoman rule, but it was later applied by the Mandate regime to Muslims alone (see below). Its general character was thus undermined, and its main impact remains as a model of a codified Islamic family law. Since the reforms were not yet completed when the Empire collapsed, it was left to the Empire's successors—the colonial regimes and later the new nation-states that were established in the Middle East and North Africa—to pursue them in the direction they saw fit. As elaborated below, the British Mandate authorities chose to embrace some aspects of the reform and to reject others. The Israeli legislature followed suit.

Mandate Palestine

The British forces completed the occupation of Palestine in September 1918, but they started setting up the colonial administration even earlier (Jerusalem had been captured in December 1917). Based on their rich colonial experience, they devised a strategy for securing their rule in Palestine by political and legal means without alienating the religious communities, and especially the Muslim community (McTague 1983: 2–3, Kupferschmidt 1987: 17). As they did in other colonies, they sought to co-opt the local colonized elites (Hooker 1975: 56) and to incorporate religious/indigenous institutions into the new colonial administration. Since personal status matters were perceived as most sensitive in terms of cultural identity (see Chanock 1985: 145), colonial administrations were usually interested in incorporating religious/indigenous tribunals, dealing with these matters, into the colonial legal system. This policy, which was typical of colonial rule in general (see e.g., Bohannan 1957: 72, Gluckman 1965: 64, Sartori and Shahar 2012), is the main source of legal pluralism in post-colonial states until this very day (Hooker 1975, Benton 2002: 127).

In Palestine, however, the British colonial regime encountered an especially complicated situation: the *millet* system—an endogenous arrangement of legal pluralism that fitted perfectly with the British tradition of colonial law—was in the process of being canceled and replaced by a general family law (the OLFR). The Mandate authorities therefore faced a dilemma: on the one hand, they could apply the readymade, unified, and modernized family law drafted by the Ottoman reformers; on the other hand, they could retain the traditional *millet* system that had been operating for generations, and that was compatible with their habitual colonial policies.

Both options, so it seems, had pros and cons from the viewpoint of Mandate policymakers. The OLFR was a "Westernized" legal code. It was easy to use, clear, systematic, comprehensive, and relatively coherent. In addition, the Muslim population considered it a legitimate law, drafted by Muslims and based on shari'a law. At the same time, the promulgation of the OLFR was met by fierce opposition from Christian and Jewish religious leaders, who saw it as an attempt to subjugate their communities to Islamic law and to limit—if not cancel altogether—their religious and communal autonomy (Ortayli 1994 [1990]: 148). Given this complex state of affairs, it is not surprising that the British opted for a solution aimed at "having the cake and eating it too."

At first, the British issued a proclamation (No. 42, June 1918; amended, No. 81, November 1918) that re-established the Ottoman court system in all territories under British control. The proclamation stated unequivocally that the jurisdiction and procedures of the religious Muslim, Christian, and Jewish courts will remain as they had been before the promulgation of the OLFR. In other words, it was decided that the OLFR will not apply in Mandate Palestine, and that the *millet* system will remain intact. This initial proclamation was soon to be followed, however, by an ordinance (publicized on September 25, 1919) that differentiated between the Muslim community, and the Christian and Jewish communities. According to the ordinance, the OLFR was to be applied in Palestine, but *only* in shari'a courts, and *only* with regard to Muslims.

Contrary to the explicit intentions of the Ottoman reformers, the OLFR was not applied as general family law in Palestine under British rule, but as a codified Islamic personal status law, enacted only in shari'a courts. The Mandate legislature thus made sure to omit the articles in the OLFR that referred to non-Muslim communities (see Goadby 1926: 115, Vitta 1947: 149–50, Eisenman 1977: 155) and to revoke the jurisdiction of the shari'a courts over non-Muslims. This way, the status of the shari'a courts was practically equalized to that of other religious courts, and they were integrated into the *millet*-like system that was reinstituted by Mandate authorities.

The British were keen not to interfere with religious matters and not to imperil the delicate *millet*-like system they had introduced. Indeed, it appears that Mandate legislature hardly ever interfered in the material law of religious courts in general, and of shari'a courts in particular.[10] The Palestine Order in Council (1922–47), which became the main mechanism for Mandate legislation, sought to preserve the autonomy of the religious courts as much as possible.[11] Still, the new political situation made some changes inevitable. The fact that Palestine was no longer under a Muslim sovereign, as well as the abrupt severance of the Muslim religious

10 When introducing reforms by means of criminal legislation, such as the ban on the marriage of minor girls and on polygamy, the Mandatory legislator provided "good defense" to Muslims and exempted them from panel sanctions (see Eisenman 1977: 307–12). Only in the field of succession did the Mandatory legislator intervene in religious law: the Succession Ordinance, 1923, sec. 21, made the Ottoman Law of Succession of 1913 applicable to *miri* property (see Layish 1965: 58).

11 Relevant articles in the Palestine Order in Council are: 47, 51–9, 64–7.

establishment from the Ottoman center in Istanbul, had several implications for shari'a courts.

First, the British government stepped into the shoes of the Ottoman Ministries of Justice and Awqaf, and "smoothly" took over the administration of Muslim religious affairs in Palestine (see Kupferschmidt 1987: 18). A Muslim clergy (*'alim*) was appointed as inspector of the shari'a courts, and new qadis were nominated—following consultation between the senior British judicial officer, the inspector, and the Muslim members of the civil court of appeal. Since it was no longer possible to appeal to the chief mufti (*Sheikh al-Islam*) or to the court of cassation in Istanbul,[12] a shari'a court of appeal was established in Jerusalem (1918).[13] The appellate court replaced the Ottoman institutions of appeal, and it therefore had competence to review any decision made by any shari'a court in Palestine since the date of the occupation (Kupferschmidt 1987: 18–19). The shari'a court of appeal had three members—a president and two permanent members (see M. Natur 1996: 126–31).

Second, following some disturbing religious riots during the Nabi Musa festivities in 1920,[14] the British sought to appease the Muslim community. After consulting Muslim leaders, they established the Supreme Muslim Council (SMC) in 1921 that took control over the management of all Muslim religious affairs in Palestine (Vitta 1947: 102–4, Kupferschmidt 1987: 18). The duties of the SMC included the appointment and dismissal of all shari'a court and *waqf* officials, including qadis, inspectors, muftis, and administrators of *waqf* property (*ma'murs al-awqaf*). The government's approval of such appointments/dismissals was needed, but still, the founding of the SMC awarded the Palestinian Muslim community unprecedented autonomy in the administration of their religious affairs. This extensive autonomy was later used (some would say abused) as a political lever.

Although the British intended the council to function as an administrative body, not a political one, the SMC gradually gained political influence and autonomy under the charismatic leadership of Hajj Amin al-Husayni (the Grand Mufti of Jerusalem and the president of the council since its establishment and until 1937). At first, the British acquiesced, but by 1937 the Peel Report had dubbed the SMC "an Arab *imperium in imperio*" and in order to regain control, the British dismissed al-Husayni. They did not appoint a successor for his position (Peled 2001: 6).[15]

---

12 This option was officially abolished by Article 9 or Proclamation No. 42 (1918).

13 See a notice on the establishment of this court on September 13, 1918 (*Official Gazette*, 1919–22: 14).

14 The Nabi Musa festival was the most important "folk" Islamic event in Palestine. It drew tens of thousands of peasants from all over the country to the shrine of Nabi Musa (Prophet Moses) near Jerusalem. In 1920 the event was accompanied by an outbreak of wide anti-British and anti-Jewish riots (see, Al-Kayyali 1970: 148–9).

15 For a comprehensive study of the SMC, see Kupferschmidt (1987); see also Porath (1974: 188–206).

We may conclude that Mandate legislation exerted considerable influence on shari'a courts in Palestine. True, the codified version of the shari'a applied in these courts—the OLFR—was drafted by Ottoman reformers and not by British colonial officers; but being new, it had never been implemented before and was turned from "abstract letters of the law" into a binding manual only by the Mandate authorities. Indeed, the jurisdiction of shari'a courts over non-Muslims was canceled, but it seems that their jurisdiction in matters of personal status of Muslims was actually wider than in late Ottoman times. The founding of the shari'a court of appeal in Jerusalem was certainly an important administrative and judicial act, which symbolized the process of localization undergone by the shari'a courts system under British rule. Furthermore, the major role played by the SMC in the political struggle against Zionism also improved the status of shari'a courts, as a symbol not only of Islamic values and identity, but also of Arab/Palestinian nationalism.

During the British Mandate, shari'a courts have also retained their privileged position relative to the Jewish and Christian tribunals. Their jurisdiction was broader,[16] and unlike the other courts, it derived directly from the British crown (see Naveh 1997: 60–61). Moreover, unlike the Christian and Jewish courts that had to be financially self-sufficient, the Mandate government continued to fund the shari'a courts and covered their considerable deficits. The Jewish community protested bitterly against this situation, but to no avail (Kupferschmidt 1987: 87–8).

British policy towards Islamic institutions in Palestine was therefore empowering: shari'a courts retained their privileged position; the British carefully avoided any legislation that might conflict with Islamic law; and the Muslim community gained broad autonomy in administering its religious affairs. This autonomy was reduced, however, in 1937, following the dismissal of Hajj Amin al-Husayni from his position as head of the SMC, and the transfer of control over *waqf* assets from the SMC to British officials.

Establishment of the Shari'a Court System in Israel

The Arab–Israeli war of 1948 and the formation of the State of Israel also marked the destruction of the Palestinian community. When the rumpus of war silenced and the armistice agreements between the Jewish state and its Arab neighbors were signed, the magnitude of the catastrophe (the *nakba*) that had struck the Palestinian community was finally realized: thousands of Palestinians were listed among the casualties; about 700,000 Palestinians fled the country or were expelled,

16 While the shari'a courts had exclusive jurisdiction in all matters pertaining to personal status of Muslims (as determined by Article 52 of the Palestine Order in Council), the articles referring to the Jewish and Christians tribunals (Articles 53, 54) determined that these courts will have exclusive jurisdiction only in some matters of personal status (marriage and divorce, alimony, probation of wills), and concurrent jurisdiction in other matters (e.g. guardianship, custody, maintenance).

and became refugees;[17] and approximately 450 Palestinian towns and villages, out of 550 that had existed in the area that became Israel, were completely destroyed (see Morris 1987: 1).

The 150,000 Palestinians that remained within the borders of the State of Israel found, virtually overnight, that they became a minority in the newly established Jewish state. This population comprised mostly peasants and urban workers, while the bulk of the community's elites—including members of the SMC, qadis, and other religious functionaries—were quick to flee the country when fighting began.[18] Consequently, the community's structures and institutions, including the Muslim religious establishment, were almost totally demolished.

Already during the war, Israeli policymakers looked for ways to gain control over the administration of Muslim religious institutions in the country. The sense of urgency that characterized their actions derived, as noted by Peled (2001: 18), not only from the wish to reinstate law and order and to restore Muslim communal life, but also from the unholy ambition of seizing the vast *waqf* resources. Thus, as early as August 1948, the Israeli Ministry of Religious Affairs re-established the shari'a courts in Nazareth and Acre. Concurrently, steps were taken to protect Muslim holy places and an initial list of Muslim *waqf* property was compiled (see Peled 2001: ch. 2).[19]

After the establishment of the State of Israel in 1948, Israeli policymakers followed in the footsteps of the British Mandate authorities and opted for the preservation of the *millet*-like system. Among other things, they maintained the exclusive jurisdiction of communal-religious courts in matters of marriage and divorce for members of their respective communities (14 such communities were recognized by the Israeli authorities). Consequently, Israel lacks until this very day a general law of marriage and divorce (Shachar 1995: 3, see also Eisenman 1977: 466).

Several reasons can explain the decision to maintain the *millet*-like system and its inherent legal pluralism instituted by the Mandate authorities. First, Israeli authorities were afraid—no less than the British authorities—of communal and religious unrest. A policy of keeping the status quo, especially in the sensitive domain of personal status, was therefore very reasonable.

---

17 The exact number of Palestinian refugees is hard to ascertain and is highly contentious, primarily for political reasons. Recent estimates, however, range between 700,000 to 750,000 (see Khalidi 2001: 13, n. 6, Morris 2001: 37).

18 Of all the muftis and qadis, who were employed by the SMC before the war, only one qadi—Shaikh Tahir al-Tabari of Tiberias—remained in the country (Kupferschmidt 1987: 62).

19 Indeed, within a few months Israel managed to seize almost all Muslim *waqf* property. This was achieved by proclaiming this property "absentee property" and by transferring it to the management of the "Custodian of Absentee Property" (see Lustick 1980b: 195–8, Saban 2000: 299).

Second, as contended by several commentators, the Israeli authorities sought to apply a policy of divide-and-rule with regard to the non-Jewish citizens of the state. To increase state control over the "Arab minority," they tried to divide this population into several legal-political categories (Muslims, Druze, Christians belonging to no less than nine denominations, Circassians, and Bedouins) and to treat each of these "communities" differently (see Kanaaneh 2002: 140, Pappé 2000: 642–3). The *millet*-like structure was a ready-made categorization system that served this purpose very well.[20]

Third and most important, Israeli policymakers were probably guided by considerations that had to do with internal tensions within the Jewish society in Israel. Specifically, the preservation of the *millet*-like system enabled Israeli policymakers to evade a clash between those parts of the Israeli public who view Israel as a Jewish (religious) state, and those who view it as a democratic (secular) state. The tension between these two opposing elements has been inherent to the Israeli polity ever since the state was established, and because Israeli policymakers lacked the will and/or the political power to resolve this conflict, they simply chose to leave the situation as is. In other words, they chose to preserve the status quo with regard to state–religion relations (Friedman 1995: 51–82).[21]

The price of this choice, however, was some reduction in the Israeli authorities' control over the Muslim-Arab minority. Moreover, the *millet*-like system reduced Israeli policy makers' "degrees of freedom" and limited their capacity to base their policies toward the Arab-Muslim minority solely on "state" (read: Jewish-Zionist) interests.[22]

A comprehensive, path-breaking account of the backstage of Israeli policy making toward Islamic institutions is provided by Peled in her book *Debating*

---

20 However, where the *millet* system failed to "deliver the goods"—as in the case of the Druze, who were not recognized by the Ottomans as a separate religious community—Israel did not refrain from creating a new judicial-religious category. As noted by Layish (1979: 15), the Israeli government's recognition of the Druze as a religious community (1957) aimed not only "to right a wrong originating in the legal intolerance shown to the Druze by Islam," but also "to reward the community for its readiness to integrate and to fulfill all the duties incumbent on Israeli citizens, including military service."

21 Moreover, Israeli policymakers, headed by Israel's first Prime Minister, David Ben Gurion, were interested in the incorporation of the ultra-orthodox Jewish community into the Zionist state. They believed that maintaining the status quo would permit devout Jews to participate in the life of the nation without seriously disadvantaging the non-orthodox majority (see Wald 2002: 106–8).

22 For a similar argument with regard to rabbinical courts in Israel, see Sezgin (2004). Writing within the tradition of clear-cut separation between state and society, Sezgin argues that the initial decision to preserve the *millet*-like system may have been "capacity-enhancing" from the point of view of the State of Israel, but later on it became "capacity diminishing" due to "changing cost–benefit structures and the relative balance of power between the state and social actors" (p. 221). For an elaboration of this perspective, and for a comparative discussion, see also Sezgin (2013).

Islam in the Jewish State: The Development of Policy toward Islamic Institutions in Israel (2001). Peled argues that "following years of interministerial debates, Israel adopted a fragmented policy towards Muslim communal institutions, which divided jurisdiction among several ministries with highly divergent agendas" (p. 2). Her well-documented account indicates that this policy was (and still is) characterized by ambiguity, indecision, and bureaucratic feuding.

Based on archive material that only became accessible in the late 1990s, Peled skillfully traces the development of Israeli policy toward Islamic institutions over the years. She describes Israeli policy as multifaceted and contradictory, rather than monolithic and pre-determined,[23] and claims that the roots of the inconsistencies in this policy are to be found in the inherent tension between "a benevolent approach emphasizing cultural autonomy for the Arab minority (both Muslim and non Muslim) and a preoccupation with control and security considerations" (p. 2; see also Rekhess 1991). Hence, while the government was willing to grant Muslim citizens broad autonomy in religious and cultural spheres, its policies were also designed to prevent any Muslim organization or institution from developing into a center of national leadership.

Israeli policy toward Muslim institutions, according to Peled, should therefore not be viewed as a simple logical extension of Ottoman and British Mandate arrangements (see e.g., Layish 1965: 58 for such a description), nor as a premeditated policy, designed to reduce the management of Muslim communal affairs in Israel to a bureaucratic arm of the Israeli state, and to co-opt the Muslim leadership (Peled 2001: 12, quoting Dumper 1994; see also Abou Ramadan 2008). Rather, Israeli policy toward Islamic institutions should be viewed as the sum total or the outcome of power struggles between conflicting ideologies, conflicting political agendas,[24] and conflicting ministerial and individual players. These power struggles and internal tensions have not come to an end during Israel's first decade; they still continue to unfold until this very day.

Irrespective of whether or not Israeli policymakers had a coherent, premeditated vision of how the administration of Muslim institutions in the Jewish state should look like, a few basic trends in the Israeli policy may be discerned in retrospect: First, by employing various methods and mechanisms, the state managed to seize almost all *waqf* property (see Lustick 1980a: 131, Dumper 1994: 30–34, Reiter 1989: 23, Peled 2001: 30). Second, haunted by the precedent of the SMC, the Israeli government was determined to prevent the emergence of any unified Muslim communal organization in charge of administering all Muslim institutions in

23 Peled notes that scholars of modernization and of Marxian schools of thought have in common the view that "Israeli policymakers have shared a monolithic grand vision concerning the Jewish state's proper policy towards its primarily Muslim Arab minority" (Peled 2001: 8). Her own research strives to rebut this pervasive view.

24 E.g. the conflict between the aspiration to gain control over the vast *waqf* real-estate resources, and in contrast, the ambition to highlight Israel's enlightened treatment of Muslim holy places (see Peled 2001: 3).

Israel and capable of mobilizing the community. Therefore the Israeli government employed a "multiple-layered" policy of "divide and conquer"—not only did it establish different organs to be in charge of the various Muslim institutions (*waqf*, shari'a courts, Islamic education, and Islamic holy places), it also divided the authority over these organs among several government ministries (see Peled 2001: 148–9). Third, in sharp contrast to the British Mandatory policy of fostering Muslim communal autonomy, the Israeli government sought to reduce this autonomy as much as possible. Unlike other religious communities (e.g. the various Christian communities, the Druze) that enjoy different levels of autonomy,[25] the state has prevented the development of an autonomous Muslim communal organization. Moreover, state policy toward Muslim religious institutions was designed to keep the ultimate control of these institutions in the hands of the state authorities and government ministries.

The most salient feature of Israeli policy towards Islamic institutions is therefore the quest for control (Peled 2001: 148–9; see also, Lustick 1980a). Undoubtedly, from the point of view of the Israeli authorities, the administration of Islamic institutions in general, and of shari'a courts in particular, was perceived as a mechanism of control and co-optation. And yet, to quote Edelman (1994: 78–9), "the ability of the Jewish political establishment to monitor the shari'a court system has not turned the qadis into pliant tools of the majority." Rather, the qadis were able to take advantage of their wide jurisdiction and to pursue a judicial policy that did not always accord with Israeli policymakers' intentions (see Layish 1975: 332–6. See also Chapter 10).

Shari'a courts therefore constitute statal arenas on the one hand, and Muslim communal arenas on the other. As such, they contribute both to the creation of communal identity and communal cohesion, and to the crystallization of particular patterns of relations between the state and the Muslim-Palestinian community. In a dialectical manner, the shari'a court system comprises a mechanism of state control and co-optation, but also a mechanism of resistance to state hegemony and control.[26]

25 See Abou Ramadan (2008). Abou Ramadan distinguishes three models of minority communal organization in Israel: the fully autonomous (characterizing the Catholics), the partial or semi-autonomous (characterizing the Greek-Orthodox and the Druze), and the non-autonomous (characterizing the Muslim community). Thus, in contrast to the common view among researchers, that the Muslim community in Israel has at least a restricted autonomy, Abou Ramadan claims that the Muslim community does not enjoy any measure of formal autonomy (for a similar view, see Karayanni 2003: 101–2). While Abou Ramadan's arguments may be valid from a strictly legal and formal point of view, it seems to me that he conveniently dwells upon formalities, while ignoring the level of actual socio-legal reality and practice. See discussion below.

26 A dialectical function of this sort is characteristic of many other "ethnic" or "religious" legal systems in post-colonial countries (see Merry 1990, Lazarus-Black and Hirsch 1994).

To conclude the discussion, it may be argued that despite Israeli efforts to restrict Muslim communal autonomy as much as possible, the preservation of the *millet*-like system in the field of personal status law has turned into a sort of "Trojan horse" within the Israeli legal system. Shari'a courts have operated from within this system to frustrate policymakers' intentions of eliminating any vestige of Muslim communal autonomy. Thus, while British Mandatory policy facilitated an empowerment of Muslim communal organization, Israeli policy resulted in a suppression of all the actors in the Muslim religious field on the state level, with the exception of shari'a courts and the presiding qadis. Consequently, the shari'a court system in present day Israel enjoys unparalleled centrality in this field (see Abou Ramadan 2008), and hence they constitute a complex socio-legal arena that cannot be portrayed in any one-dimensional manner.

Chapter 3
Shari'a Courts in Israel: The Legal Setting

In the following pages I briefly describe the formal legal setting, in which shari'a courts operate in present day Israel. Three related issues will be discussed: the legal framework; the material and procedural laws implemented in the courts; and their jurisdiction.

Legal Framework

As noted, the Ministry of Religious Affairs established shari'a courts in Nazareth and Acre as early as August 1948.[1] Another two courts were opened in Jaffa and Tayyibe in 1950, and a shari'a court of appeal, located in West Jerusalem, was established on January 1, 1953. During the first years of their existence under Israeli rule, the operation of shari'a courts was not regulated by Israeli law. The courts employed the OLFR and the Ottoman Law of Procedure for Shari'a Courts of 1917, as adopted and amended by the Mandate regime,[2] and the qadis were simply appointed by the bureaucrats of the Ministry of Religious Affairs.

During the early 1950s, the recently established shari'a courts were the subject of a heated ministerial feud between the Ministry of Religious Affairs and the Ministry of Justice. The two ministries were quarreling over jurisdiction, and meanwhile the legislation of a "shari'a courts law" was delayed (see Peled 2001: 62–3). As a result of the delay, rulings of shari'a courts were canceled in several cases by civil courts, on the grounds that they have no legal authority. This, of course, infuriated the qadis, who protested against the government's neglect of a matter of such importance for the Muslim community in Israel (ibid.: 63). Finally, the pressures on the government ministries bore fruit, and a draft law was prepared.

In December 1953, the Knesset passed the Shari'a Courts Law (Validation of Appointments), 5714–1953. The law granted post-factum recognition to all

1 In Nazareth the court was re-opened by the military governor at the request of the Muslim community, and only later was it attached to the Ministry of Religious Affairs (see Peled 2001: 26).

2 Article 11 of the Israeli Law and Administration Ordinance, No. 1, 5708–1948, stated that "the law which existed in Palestine on the 5th Iyar, 5708 (14th May, 1948), shall remain in force ..." By this ordinance the Israeli legislator adopted all the Mandatory legislation, including the articles in the Palestine Order in Council that refer to the operation of shari'a courts.

rulings issued by the shari'a courts in Israel since their establishment. It also confirmed previous appointments of qadis, and charged the Minister of Religious Affairs with the implementation of the law.[3] And yet, while the Shari'a Courts Law (Validation of Appointments) regulated the operation of existing shari'a courts, and legalized the rulings of the officiating qadis, it did not outline a procedure for making new appointments. A comprehensive qadis law that regulates all matters relating to the appointment of new qadis, was only legislated in 1961.[4] The Qadis Law defined a qadi as a judge in a shari'a court or in a shari'a court of appeal (Article 1), and stated who is eligible to be appointed as a qadi: a Muslim, who has "suitable training in shari'a law;" whose way of life and character befit the status of a qadi; and who is at least thirty years of age, and is married or has been married (Article 2).

The law further determined that qadis should be appointed by the state's president, upon the proposal of an appointment committee (Article 3). The committee has nine members: two qadis elected by the body of qadis for three years; the Minister of Religious Affairs (chairman of the committee), and another minister to be elected by the government; three Members of Knesset (at least two of them Muslims); and two lawyers, at least one of them a Muslim (Article 4).[5]

The Qadis Law also determined that the president of the shari'a court of appeal will be appointed by the Minister of Religious Affairs (Article 6(a)); and that a person appointed to be a qadi must pledge allegiance to the State of Israel (Article 7).[6] The rules for the administration of shari'a courts, and the sitting places and areas of jurisdiction of the shari'a courts, shall be prescribed by the Minister of Religious

3 It thus gave direct authority over the shari'a court system to the Minister of Religious Affairs, rather than to the Minister of Justice.

4 In addition to the Qadis Law, 5721–1961, two other laws of lesser importance have bearing on the operation of shari'a courts: The Religious Courts (Summons) Law, 5716–1956, grants religious courts (including the shari'a courts, of course) the power to summon prisoners to court; to compel summoned parties and witnesses to arrive at court; and to fine ("an amount not exceeding seventy five pounds") parties or witnesses, who refuse to give evidence, produce a document or answer a question—without a satisfactory explanation. The Religious Courts (Prevention of Disturbance) Law, 5725–1965, grants the religious courts the authority to order the removal or to compel by fine any person who disturbs court proceedings.

5 Although the law determined that there should be a Muslim majority on the committee (two qadis, two MKs, and one lawyer were to be Muslims—five members out of nine), there was no guarantee that this majority will be sustained. The committee was allowed to convene with a quorum of less than nine members, but no less than six members (Article 4(d)). Moreover, the chairman of the committee, who controlled its assembly and its schedule, was not a Muslim. As noted above, he was the Minister of Religious Affairs—usually, an orthodox Jew (see Saban 2000: 297, Kretzmer 1990: 167–8, Edelman 1994: 78).

6 According to Peled (2001: 136), this particular stipulation was hotly debated by Muslims both in Israel and in the Muslim World.

Affairs, following consultation with the president of the shari'a court of appeal, the body of qadis, and the Minister of Justice (Article 10(a), (b)).

With the new law confirmed by the Knesset, the Minister of Religious Affairs has appointed new qadis whenever the ranks of officiating qadis diminished. In 1963, the Minister of Religious Affairs issued regulations regarding the representation of litigants in shari'a courts by *shar'i* advocates (sing. *murafi' shar'i*), who are not lawyers. According to these regulations, a committee of three qadis will be in charge of examining the eligibility of *shar'i* advocates for representing litigants in shari'a courts. Ethical rules of the Bar were imposed on *shar'i* advocates as well.

More regulations were issued in 1968 with regard to shari'a court fees. These regulations detailed the sums of money to be charged for the various services provided by shari'a courts. The sums of money have been updated several times since then. In 1971, two new courts were opened in Haifa and Beer-Sheva; a court was opened in West Jerusalem in 1988,[7] and another one in Baqa al-Gharbiya in 2006. This brings the total number of regional shari'a courts operating presently in Israel to eight.

All in all, the administration of the shari'a court system by the Ministry of Religious Affairs has been characterized over the years by neglect and deprivation (see Peled 2001: 148). The shari'a courts were discriminated against in comparison with the rabbinical courts in terms of budgets, number of employees, and nomination of judges.[8] Under the administration of the Department of Muslim Affairs in the Ministry of Religious Affairs, the shari'a court system became a marginal and neglected arena within the Israeli legal system (Shahar 2000: 49). The qadis and other Muslim religious functionaries have often complained about the neglect, but paradoxically, they have also benefited from this lack of governmental attention. Due to its marginality, the shari'a court system has escaped close scrutiny by state institutions, and gained some additional degree of freedom. The fact that there was almost no supervision of shari'a courts' actions—except, perhaps, for a limited

7 The West Jerusalem court is the focus of this book. Its establishment will be discussed in detail in Chapter 4.

8 A clear example of this neglect may be found in the fact that between 1978 and 1996 the Ministry of Religious Affairs did not see fit to appoint a permanent qadi to preside at the Beer-Sheva shari'a court (see Shahar 1997: 13). For a broader discussion of discrimination against the Muslim minority in Israel in particular, and against non-Jewish religious institutions in general, see Adalah's report *Legal Violations of Arab Minorities in Israel* (March 1998). According to the report, "the budget of the Ministry of Religious Affairs shows the stark contrast between Jews and non-Jews, and the wide-scale discrimination against non-Jews. The Knesset Budget Law of 1998 allocates only 1.86% of the total (430 million US$) for the Muslim, Christian and Druze religious communities combined, although they comprise close to the [sic] fifth of the population. Thus, more than 98% of the total budget is allocated to support Jewish religious services and institutions."

judicial review of their rulings by the High Court of Justice (HCJ)[9]—enabled the qadis to create and maintain de-facto autonomy.[10]

Since 2001, however, state supervision over shari'a courts has somewhat increased. In September 2000, the Israeli government, headed by Prime Minister Ehud Barak, decided to annul the Ministry of Religious Affairs, and to disperse its responsibilities among other government ministries. This decision was never fully implemented, and was later canceled all together, but it affected the shari'a courts nevertheless: in January 2001, the shari'a court system was transferred, together with the Druze court system, to the responsibility of the Ministry of Justice.[11]

The transfer of shari'a courts to the Ministry of Justice was made in agreement with the shari'a courts administration, and with the active support of the president of the shari'a court of appeal, Qadi Ahmad Natur. Presumably, Natur believed that the reassignment would increase the status of shari'a courts within the broader Israeli legal system. Nevertheless, he did not anticipate that this would also result in greater attention and stricter supervision. Since the reassignment, several reforms have been initiated, and the level of governmental supervision of the shari'a court system has significantly increased.

The most important reform, however, was the amendment of the Qadis Law of 1961—at the initiative of Qadi Natur and several Muslim Members of Knesset. Amendment No. 10 to the Qadis Law passed in the Knesset in July 2002. The major changes that were introduced to the law referred to the requirements for nominees to the position of qadi: they were now required to have "high religious education in shari'a or in Islamic studies, to the satisfaction of the appointment committee members, or otherwise be lawyers, members of the Bar, who have practiced law for a period of no less than 5 years" (Article 2(a)(1)). In addition, nominees were now required to pass an exam (Article 2(a)(4)), composed by an examining committee comprising three members: the president of the shari'a court of appeal; a Muslim MK; and a person, who has been a qadi in the past, or has been an active lawyer for at least five years (Article 2(b)).

These changes were introduced in response to criticism as to the lack of adequate criteria for the eligibility to the position of qadi. According to the Qadis Law of 1961, appointees for the position of qadi in Israel were not obliged to have

9 Since shari'a courts are integrated into the Israeli legal system, their rulings are liable to judicial review by the High Court of Justice. Basic Law: The Judiciary (5743–1983), authorized the High Court to intervene and to quash a proceeding taken or a decision given by a religious court—shari'a courts included—if the religious court exceeded its authority, or acted contrary to "natural justice" (Article 15(d)(4)). See also HCJ 1842/92.

10 See also Report No. 46, of the State Comptroller and Ombudsman, 1995. This report disclosed severe findings with regard to the neglect, lack of control, and lack of supervision by the Ministry of Religious Affairs with regard to the shari'a court system.

11 See Prime Minister's statement on the transfer of authority from the Minister of Religious Affairs to the Minister of Justice, Knesset Plenum, February 21, 2001, http://knesset.gov.il/tql/knesset_new/knesset15/HTML_28_03_2012_09-20-03-AM/20010221@177-01FEB21@014.html [accessed 4/10/2015].

any formal education—not in the shari'a nor in any other field of knowledge. They were only required to have "suitable training in shari'a law," and to be characterized by "a way of life that befits the status of a qadi." Both criteria are defined in subjective terms, and are therefore totally obscure.

The fact that the requirements for the position of qadi were so minimal had indeed negative implications for the status of qadis in Israel (see Neuhaus 1991: 38, Reiter 1997: 208, Peled 2001: 121). During the 1990s, however, another problem emerged: the obscurity of the criteria for the selection of qadis resulted in multiple appeals against the decisions of the appointment committee. Nominees who were not chosen, as well as several civil society organizations, "flooded" the committee with "reservations" concerning its decisions. Several appeals against the committee were also submitted to the High Court of Justice. As a result, the appointment of new qadis, who were selected by the committee, was delayed for months and even years.[12]

Two other significant changes were introduced: First, the president of the shari'a court of appeal became a permanent member of the appointment committee. This means that only one additional qadi (instead of two, previously) will be elected by the body of qadis as a member for a period of three years (Article 4(a)). Second, the Minister of Justice replaced the Minister of Religious Affairs as chairperson of the appointment committee, and in all other matters relating to the procedure of qadi appointments.[13]

We may conclude that under the administration of the Ministry of Religious Affairs, the shari'a courts suffered neglect, but also benefited from a lack of supervision; while under the administration of the Ministry of Justice, some important, long-needed reforms were introduced, but governmental supervision tightened. Another notable change discernible in the last decade or so is the significant increase in the power of the shari'a court of appeal and of its president, Qadi Ahmad Natur. A manifestation of this process of centralization is undoubtedly

12 For example, the appointment of lawyer Dugan al-Ataune, who was elected by the appointment committee to the office of qadi of Beer-Sheva on June 2, 1996, was postponed until January 2001; while the appointment of Muhammad Zibdi—a school principal, who was elected to the office of qadi of Jerusalem in November 2000—was postponed until May 2001. In this last case, several organizations for equal rights for women also appealed to the High Court of Justice against the decision of the appointment committee, arguing that another candidate, a woman, who was much more qualified than the selected candidate (Zibdi), should have been appointed instead. They also argued for the importance of appointing a woman to the office of qadi, but the High Court did not see fit to deal with this fundamental question. In any case, the appeal was denied (see HCJ 891/01). For a critical view on "the extreme paternalism" displayed by the court in this ruling, see Abou Ramadan (2003a: 649).

13 The fact that the appointment of two qadis, who were selected by the appointment committee according to the amended Qadis Law, in July 2004, did not meet with any obstacles, testifies, perhaps, to the greater efficiency and perceived legitimacy of the new procedures.

to be found in Amendment No. 10 of the Qadis Law, which granted the president of the shari'a court of appeal far-reaching authority (see also Abou Ramadan 2003b).[14]

Material and Procedural Laws

The legal foundations of the material and procedural laws applied in present day Israeli shari'a courts are derived from the Ottoman codes: the *Majalla* (1876), the OLFR (1917), and the Law of Procedure for Shari'a Courts (1917). To these codes we should add the Mandatory procedural regulations of the shari'a court of appeal.[15] As discussed, the Ottoman codes were incorporated with some changes into the Mandatory legal system, and later on adopted by the Israeli legislator.

Since the Israeli legislature has generally refrained from intervening in the material religious laws (again, due to the sensitivity of religion–state relations in Israel and due to the "sacred" status quo), and since there is no Council of Muslim Jurists (*majlis ifta'*) in Israel, nor any other legitimate Muslim body of legislation, the Ottoman codes have remained in force in shari'a courts until this very day.[16] Nevertheless, the Israeli legislature was not indifferent to some elements of discrimination against women, which are inherent in both Jewish and Islamic law. The Knesset sought an alternative path, circumventing the need to interfere with material religious laws, while enabling the state to introduce normative and legal changes and to better the status of women.

The path taken was twofold. First, civil family laws were drafted and promulgated by the Knesset. These laws—for the most part, oriented toward achieving gender equality—were to be applied in both civil and religious courts, but were not meant to affect the jurisdiction of the religious courts. The second solution was to criminalize—by penal law—particular acts or behaviors that are sanctioned by the religious law. In line with this strategy, the Knesset legislated several material family laws: Age of Marriage Law, 5710–1950; the Women's Equal Rights Law, 5711–1951; the Capacity and Guardianship Law, 5722–1962; the Succession Law, 5725–1965; the Spouses (Property Relations) Law, 5733–1973; and the Prevention of Violence in the Family Law, 5751–1991.

---

14 As a matter of fact, Article 24(c) of Amendment No. 10 stated that the "head" of the shari'a court of appeal—as he was titled in the Qadis Law of 1961—will henceforth be titled the "president" of the shari'a court of appeal.

15 A proclamation regarding the establishment of a shari'a court of appeal (in Jerusalem), was issued on October 10, 1918; another proclamation, issued on August 1, 1919, determined the rules of procedures for this court (see Goitein and Ben Shemesh 1957: 281).

16 The Israeli legislature formally abolished the *Majalla* in 1984 (Abolishment of the Majalla Law, 5744–1984). However, Article 2 of this law states explicitly that the abolishment is not meant to affect the laws applied by the shari'a courts in Israel. Thus, the *Majalla* still applies in these courts until today (see Meron 2001: 14).

The Women's Equal Rights Law (5711–1951), for example, states that: "A man and a woman shall have equal status with regard to any legal act; any provision of law which discriminates, with regard to any legal act, against women as women, shall be of no effect" (Article 1). Article 3(a) of the law determines that: "Both parents are the natural guardians of their children; where one parent dies, the survivor shall be natural guardian;" Article 8(a) amends the Criminal Code Ordinance, by abrogating the "good defense" that was given to Muslims with regard to the ban on polygamy[17]; and Article 8(b) added a paragraph to the criminal code, stating that: "Where the husbands dissolve the marriage against the will of the wife […] the husband is guilty of a felony and shall be liable to imprisonment for a term not exceeding five years."

The articles cited above stand in direct contradiction to several principles in Islamic law, as prescribed by the *Majalla* and the OLFR. First, according to the *Majalla*, the father is the legal (natural) guardian of his children, while the mother is not a legal guardian, but may be appointed to that position (*Majalla*, Article 974). Second, a man may divorce his wife—with or without her consent—simply by saying that she is divorced (OLFR, Articles 102–9), while a woman needs to buy her divorce from her husband (*khul'*), or to appeal for a judicial dissolution of the marriage (OLFR, Articles 119–30). Third, while a man may be married to up to four wives at the same time, a woman may only marry one husband at a time (OLFR, Article 14).

These examples clearly amount to discrimination against women, as understood by the Israeli legislature, and demonstrate the contradictions between Israeli civil law and religious Islamic law. They also demonstrate how the legislator criminalized acts such as polygamy and repudiation of a wife without her consent.[18] Notably, since the religious law itself was not amended, such acts have become liable to both criminal prosecution and civil suits, while still valid and approved by the religious law.

The Israeli legislature, however, made sure that any civil law that refers to matters of personal status will include articles safeguarding the jurisdiction of religious courts, and ensuring the ability of litigants to choose adjudication according to their communal religious law. Thus, Article 7 of the Women's Equal Rights Law (5711–1951) prescribes that "all courts shall act in accordance with this law; a tribunal competent to deal with matters of personal status shall likewise act in accordance therewith, unless all the parties are eighteen years of age or over, and have consented before the tribunal, of their own free will, to have their case

---

17 The Mandatory legislator, who banned polygamy, provided "good defense" to Muslim men against this charge, by stating that the ban on polygamy does not apply to non-Jews whose personal law permits polygamous marriage (Criminal Code Ordinance, 1936, Article 181(c); see Layish 1975: 72–3, n. 3).

18 Another "traditional custom" that was banned and criminalized is the marriage of minors. According to Article 2 of the Age of Marriage Law (5710–1950): "A person who marries, or solemnizes, or assists in solemnizing marriages of a girl under 17 […] is liable to imprisonment of up to two years, or a fine, or both."

tried according to the laws of their community." Similar articles are found in other civil family laws as well.[19]

The Israeli legislature's strategy with regard to personal status laws resulted in the creation of a complex matrix of heterogeneous bodies of law, which combine—in a rather discordant way—religious and civil laws. As stated in the website of the shari'a courts system,[20] in addition to the Ottoman codes, the courts implement the following Israeli civil laws: The Succession Law, The Spouses (Property Relations) Law, The Prevention of Violence in the Family Law. To these laws we may add: The Age of Marriage Law, The Women's Equal Rights Law, and The Capacity and Guardianship Law. Two additional non-formal sources of law, frequently employed by qadis, are the "Code of Qadri Basha" and a treatise by the famous Hanefi scholar Ibn 'Abidin.[21]

The relations between these highly diverse sources of law are far from being well-defined.[22] Rather, they are characterized by ambiguity and equivocality, and qadis thus employ the various sources of law at their disposal in a non-systematic way. The qadis' judicial policy emerges from ad-hoc decisions, directives given by the shari'a court of appeal, and High Court of Justice rulings specifically directed toward shari'a courts. Nevertheless, principal questions of jurisdiction of religious and secular laws are still unresolved, and the shari'a courts' rulings are therefore characterized by inconsistencies and a lack of uniformity (see Abou Ramadan 2003b, 2006a, 2006b; see also, Layish 1975: 335).[23]

To conclude, the material and procedural laws applied in shari'a courts are diverse, and the relations between them are of an ambiguous nature. As socio-legal

19 See e.g., Article 13(a), 13(b) of the Spouses (Property Relations) Law, 5733–1973, and Article 155(a) of the Succession Law, 5725–1965. In this last case, a written consent of all the interested parties is required.

20 There had been talks about opening a website for more than three years (personal communication with Qadi Natur). The actual inauguration of the website was delayed, nevertheless, until May 2005.

21 Qadri Basha was an Egyptian jurist, who compiled a semi-official code of personal status laws, entitled *Kitab al-Ahkam al-Shar'iyya fi al-Ahwal al-Shakhsiyya, 'ala Madhhab al-Imam Abi Hanifa al-Nu'man.* The code was published (1875) by the government press, but was never officially enacted (see Cuno 2015: ch. 5). Ibn 'Abidin was the greatest Hanefi jurist of the nineteenth century. His book *Radd al-Muhtar 'ala al-Durr al-Mukhtar* (1236–1820/1), together with Qadri Basha's book, serve qadis in cases of a lacuna in the Ottoman codes. The use of these sources, however, is a matter of personal discretion of each qadi (see Layish 1975: 3, Sha'shu'a 1981: 16–19).

22 In fact, the only matter of personal status in which a clear-cut demarcation between religious and civil laws exists is succession (see Layish 1975: 4).

23 It appears that the habit of issuing rulings that contradict civil legislation is not at all unique to qadis, but rather characterizes judges in other religious tribunals as well. On the disregard of the *Dayyanim* (Jewish judges) in the rabbinical courts toward civil legislation, as well as toward High Court of Justice rulings, see Hacker (2003: 166–7, n. 64). On the disregard of qadis toward Israeli legislation, see Chapter 10.

institutions, these courts may be described as "hybrid institutions," employing norms and values originating from very different social philosophies. This "norm pluralism," or in John Bowen's terms (2003: 257) "value pluralism," is manifested in the courts' rulings, and especially in the discourse of the shari'a court of appeal (that is discussed below). The inconsistencies and the internal contradictions in the administration of the law by shari'a courts may indeed seem problematic and conspicuous from a legal point of view (see e.g., Abou Ramadan 2008). Nevertheless, from a sociological point of view, these internal contradictions are instructive and revealing—not only with respect to the "hybridity" of the courts, but also with respect to their contentious location at a nexus between laws, societies, and cultures.

Jurisdiction

As mentioned, the Mandate legislator reinstated the Ottoman *millet* system with some changes. The backbone of this system was the exclusive jurisdiction of religious courts in matters of personal status of the members of their respective community. However, the definition of "personal status matters" diverged between Muslim courts and all other communal courts: while in the case of all the other courts, matters of personal status were defined by Article 51 of the Palestine Order in Council (1922–47), for Muslim courts, they were defined by Article 52, with reference to Article 7 of the Ottoman Code of Procedures for Shari'a Courts (1917).

During the Mandate period, as well as under Israeli rule (until November 2001),[24] the shari'a courts thus exercised broader jurisdiction than any other religious courts. The reason for this situation was twofold: first, matters of personal status were defined more inclusively by Article 7 of the Ottoman Law of Procedures for Shari'a Courts (1917) than by Article 51 of the Palestine Order in Council (1922–47).[25] Second, Muslim courts were accorded exclusive jurisdiction in *all* matters of personal status (Article 52), while the other courts were accorded exclusive jurisdiction in *some* matters, and concurrent jurisdiction in others (Articles 53, 54 of the Palestine Order in Council, 1922–47. See, Bentwich 1926, vol. 1: 14).

The jurisdiction of the shari'a court of appeal was defined by Mandatory regulations issued on October 10, 1918, and on August 1, 1919. The appellate shari'a court was authorized to rule in appeals on all final judgments of shari'a

24 That was when Amendment No. 5 of the Family Court Law, 5755–1995, passed in the Knesset, and granted family courts concurrent jurisdiction over Muslim litigants, similar to the jurisdiction they had already with regard to litigants belonging to other religious communities (see discussion below, and in Chapter 9).

25 For example, Article 7 of the Ottoman Law provided these courts with jurisdiction in all matters relating to the administration of *waqf* property, whereas Article 51 of the Order in Council did not provide similar jurisdiction to non-Muslim religious courts.

courts of first instance, and on non-final judgments relating to issues of jurisdiction. Article 7 of these regulations stated that rulings concerning minors, incompetent litigants, and *waqf* institutions must be reviewed by the shari'a court of appeal, even if no appeal had been submitted. The execution of such rulings should be delayed until their confirmation by the appellate court (see Naveh 1997: 62–3).

The Mandate laws that were adopted by the Knesset thus defined a very broad jurisdiction for shari'a courts—a jurisdiction that was also confirmed by several civil court rulings (see e.g., HCJ 1/62, 250/83). Nevertheless, this broad jurisdiction has been reduced systematically and consistently by the Israeli legislature, gradually bestowing concurrent jurisdiction to civil courts, in matters that were previously under the exclusive jurisdiction of shari'a courts.

The first restriction of the jurisdiction of shari'a courts resulted from the Absentee Property Law (5710–1950), which passed in the Knesset on March 30, 1950. Article 1(a) and (e) of this law stated that until the appointment of new *waqf* committees (since members of the previous committees had fled the country during the 1948 War), the administration of *waqf* property is under the exclusive jurisdiction of the Custodian of Absentee Property. By this act of legislation, shari'a courts were deprived of their jurisdiction over nearly all *waqf* property in Israel.[26]

Further restriction of the jurisdiction of shari'a courts resulted from the Age of Marriage Law (5710–1950), that raised the minimum age of a bride to 17, and of a groom to 18. This was basically in line with Article 4 of the OLFR (Goitein and Ben Shemesh 1957: 293). But unlike the Ottoman and Mandatory legislators, the Israeli legislator sealed the loophole that enabled a qadi to permit the marriage of a boy aged 12–18, and of a girl aged 9–17, provided that they pass a test of puberty.[27] Instead, Article 5 of the Age of Marriage Law empowered civil courts—not religious courts—to permit the marriage of a girl under 17 years of age, in particular circumstances.[28] Although civil courts (since 1995, family courts) are authorized to permit such a marriage, the marriage itself is performed by religious courts, or by a marriage registrar appointed by a religious court.

The Succession Law (5725–1965) downgraded the jurisdiction of shari'a courts in matters of successions, wills and testaments from exclusive to concurrent. Not only did this law grant civil courts jurisdiction over these matters, it also gave them priority over religious courts: jurisdiction is to be transferred to the district court (since 1995, to the family court), unless all the parties concerned have signed a written consent to be adjudicated by the religious court (Article 151(a)). Still, if

---

26 The High Court of Justice dealt twice with the issue of the jurisdiction of shari'a courts over *waqf* property, and in both cases the court ruled that the exclusive jurisdiction remains in the hands of the Custodian of Absentee Property (see HCJ 282/61, 6452/1996).

27 In the case of a girl, the consent of the guardian was also required. These provisions were based on Articles 985–9 of the *Majalla* (see Layish 1975: 14–15).

28 The civil court may approve such a marriage in case of pregnancy, or if the court is convinced that "special circumstances" justifying such a permission exist.

the parties include a minor, or a person declared legally incompetent, his/her rights of succession according to the religious law must not be below his rights according to the Succession Law (Article 155).

Unlike the Succession Law, the Spouses (Property Relations) Law (5733–1973) did not accord civil courts jurisdiction in matters of personal status that were previously under the exclusive jurisdiction of religious courts. Instead, this law compelled religious courts to act in accordance with it, "in a matter dealt with by this law […] unless the parties have agreed before such court to litigate in accordance with religious law" (Article 13(b)). Thus, the Spouses (Property Relations) Law intervened in the material law implemented by religious courts, but did not downgrade their jurisdiction.

However, the most significant restriction of shari'a courts' jurisdiction has only occurred quite recently. Amendment No. 5 to the Family Court Law, passed by the Knesset on November 14, 2001, downgraded the jurisdiction of the Muslim and Christian religious courts from exclusive to concurrent in all matters of personal status, except for marriage, divorce, and *waqf*. This act of legislation has equalized, in effect, the jurisdiction of Muslim and Christian courts with that of rabbinical courts (the amendment will be discussed in detail in Chapter 9).

Lastly, it is important to note that Israeli legislation has also broadened the jurisdiction of shari'a courts in some matters. Court Regulations (Suspension of Leaving the Country), 5717–1957, granted shari'a courts—like any other court, for that matter—the jurisdiction to issue an order preventing a litigant from leaving the country. Likewise, The Prevention of Violence in the Family Law (5751–1991) granted shari'a courts the jurisdiction to issue a "protection order," preventing a litigant from entering an apartment in which a family member dwells; from being in a particular proximity to a family member; from harassing a family member; and from preventing a family member from using a property, even if he/she has a right in this property (Article 2). In recent years, qadis have made extensive use of these orders of protection (see the discussion in Chapter 10).

We may conclude this historical and socio-legal review of the operation of shari'a courts in Palestine and Israel, by pointing to the conspicuous dynamism of these courts. In total contradiction to popular views of shari'a courts as archaic, unchanging institutions, we have seen that these courts have undergone profound and continuous transformations during the last 150 years, or so. These transformations derive from historical developments in the socio-political environment (e.g. the move from Ottoman rule, to British Mandate, to Israeli rule), and they relate to every aspect of these courts' functioning: the legal framework under which they operate; the material and procedural codes the courts apply; and their jurisdiction. As we will see below, this dynamism at the legal and political levels also corresponds to conspicuous institutional and organizational dynamism that characterizes these courts. This type of dynamism will be described and analyzed in the following chapters.

Chapter 4
Establishment of the Shari‘a Court in West Jerusalem

Periodization and framing, of course, are key features of any historical narrative. The story of the Israeli shari‘a court in West Jerusalem as I choose to tell it, begins 30 years before its establishment, and involves complex and multi-faceted relations with several other legal institutions. Of these institutions, the most important one, undoubtedly, is a shari‘a court run by the Jordanian Ministry of Awqaf, that continues to operate in East Jerusalem until this very day. The ongoing interrelations between the Israeli and the Jordanian shari‘a courts will be examined more systematically in Chapter 12. Here I will discuss how the very fact that a "foreign" shari‘a court was functioning in occupied East Jerusalem, played a major role in the decision to establish a rival Israeli court in West Jerusalem.

Our story begins in 1947. The United Nations Partition Plan of 1947 provided for the establishment of separate Arab and Jewish States in what was Mandatory Palestine. Jerusalem was to be administered by a Trusteeship Council as a *Corpus Separandum*—an international zone under the supervision of the UN (Cattan 1981: 7–9, Mazzawi 1997: 239–47). Nevertheless, when the 1948 War ended, the Jewish state had managed to gain territories beyond those assigned to it in the Partition Plan; the Arab state was not established at all; and the rest of Mandatory Palestine, which was not taken over by the Jewish state, was captured by Jordan (the "West Bank") and Egypt (the Gaza Strip). The armistice agreement between Israel and Jordan signed in April 1949 divided Jerusalem between the two states: the Western part was to be controlled by Israel, and the Eastern part (the Old City) by Jordan.

West Jerusalem was almost exclusively Jewish, with only several thousand Arabs who remained under Israeli control, dwelling in several urban neighborhoods (e.g. Beit Safafa) and in some semi-urban villages (e.g. Abu Gosh).[1] Jerusalem was declared the "eternal capital" of the Jewish state, and Israel was anxious to establish in the city as many state and government institutions as possible. As mentioned in Chapter 2, a shari‘a court of appeal was established in Jerusalem in 1953. However, a first instance court was not established, and the West Jerusalemite

1 According to Palestinian sources, 37 of the 41 Palestinian villages surrounding West Jerusalem were destroyed, and 80,000 Palestinians were driven out of or fled from the West Jerusalem area in the wake of the war. See, http://www.un.int/wcm/content/site/palestine/pid/11594 [accessed: 10/12/2014].

Muslims came thus under the jurisdiction of the Jaffa shari'a court (some 40 miles away from Jerusalem).

At the same time, Jordan was enacting Jordanian law in East Jerusalem and the West Bank. In April 1950 the Jordanian Assembly passed a resolution that formally unified the two banks of the Jordan River into one state, the Hashemite Kingdom of Jordan. The integration of the two banks did not receive international recognition, but it was nevertheless enacted by the Jordanian government.[2] Palestinian residents of the West Bank and East Jerusalem thus came under Jordanian Law. They were also granted Jordanian citizenship, and (some) representation in parliament and government institutions.

Jordanian control over the West Bank and East Jerusalem was by no means unproblematic. The Hashemite Kingdom had to deal with a nationalist Palestinian opposition that saw the Hashemites as an occupying force, guilty—until proven innocent—of secret cooperation with the hated Zionist enemy (see Shlaim 1990: 432–4). Nonetheless, the devastation of Palestinian civil society following the *nakba*, the departure of large segments of the local Palestinian leadership, and the fear of further expansion of the Zionist state into the West Bank territories—all these factors resulted in a weakening of Palestinian opposition to Hashemite rule. A systematic policy of placing supporters in vital power positions, and at the same time replacing and distancing opponents (mainly the Hussaynis),[3] enabled King Abdullah of Jordan to secure his rule in the West Bank (see Wilson 1987: 244–8).

The Jordanian regime established civil or statute courts (*mahakim nizamiyya*) and religious courts (*mahakim shar'iyya*) in the West Bank.[4] The shari'a courts retained their jurisdiction over personal status matters of Muslims, but did not regain any of their residual jurisdiction of Ottoman times. Qadis in the shari'a courts were appointed by the Jordanian Chief Islamic Justice (*Qadi al-Quda*), and the courts themselves were operating under the administration of the Ministry of Religious Endowments (*Awqaf*) in Amman. The courts were to apply the Jordanian Law of Family Rights (promulgated in 1951), which was modeled after the OLFR of 1917, but incorporated some reforms of Egyptian origin, and some provisions of indigenous inspiration. In procedural issues as well, the Jordanian Law of *Shar'i* Procedure (1959) remained quite close to the Ottoman Law of Procedure of Shari'a Courts (Welchman 2000: 50).

Shari'a courts of appeal were convened at first in both Amman and East Jerusalem, but in 1951 a law was passed providing for a single shari'a court of appeal located in Amman. A specific article of this law, however, provided that the shari'a court of appeal may convene in East Jerusalem as well, if the need arises (Welchman 1990: 108). Under Jordanian rule, Jerusalem thus lost the permanent

2 Only Britain and Pakistan recognized the annexation (see Welchman 2000: 47–8).

3 On the Hashemite authorities' efforts to reduce the influence of the Hussaynis in the religious Muslim establishment of East Jerusalem, see Reiter (1997b: 9), Kupferschmidt (1987: 258).

4 On the Jordanian legislation in this regard, see Welchman (2000: 48–50).

seat of the shari'a court of appeal, which had been situated in the city since the beginning of the British Mandate. Yet, a shari'a court of first instance was founded in East Jerusalem. This shari'a court served, in addition to the Muslim population of Jerusalem, some 20 neighboring villages (see Reiter 1997b: 11–13).

Such was the situation between 1948 and 1967: Jerusalem was physically divided into a Jordanian and an Israeli city; in the Western, Israeli city, a shari'a court of appeal was operating since 1953, but there was no shari'a court of first instance. The shari'a court of appeal was applying Ottoman codes, British regulations, and Israeli civil legislation. By contrast, a shari'a court of first instance was operating in the Eastern, Jordanian, part of the city, but there was no shari'a court of appeal. The court of first instance was applying Jordanian codes of family law and procedure.

The situation changed abruptly in the wake of the 1967 War. A few weeks after the end of the war, the Knesset passed a governmental amendment bill, Law and Administration Ordinance (Amendment No. 11) Law (5727–1967), that enabled the extension of the laws, the jurisdiction and the administration of the State of Israel to any area of "*Eretz Israel*" (Land of Israel), as designated by the government order. This amendment, together with Municipalities Ordinance (Amendment No. 6) Law (5727–1967), facilitated in effect the annexation of East Jerusalem, and the unification of Jerusalem under Israeli rule. Indeed, one day later, on June 28, 1967, the Israeli Minister of Interior issued an ordinance extending the municipal boundaries of West Jerusalem to include the former Jordanian city, as well as several villages on the outskirts of Jerusalem (Brecher 1978: 25–6). Israeli law was extended to the annexed area,[5] and the Palestinian residents of this area—a population of approximately 70,000[6]—were granted the legal status of "permanent residents" in Israel.[7]

Immediately after the occupation and annexation of the city, Israeli authorities (both military and civil authorities) began to negotiate with the Palestinian leadership in East Jerusalem, in order to achieve their cooperation with the new political order imposed by Israel. Nevertheless, local Palestinian leaders were afraid that cooperation with the Israeli occupiers—even in municipal issues—might legitimize the occupation, and therefore abstained from accepting any of the Israeli moves (see Farhi 1979: 6, Reiter 1997b: 6–7).

---

5 The annexation of East Jerusalem was condemned by the international community that maintains until this day that East Jerusalem is an occupied territory (see Mazzawi 1997: 248–57).

6 Layish (1975: 4–5) estimates the number of Palestinians within the expanded municipal borders of Jerusalem at 69,000; Schmelz (1981: 65) gives the figure of 71,000.

7 According to Israeli law, permanent residents of the State of Israel may carry an Israeli ID card, but they may not participate in elections to the parliament. They have freedom of access and work in Israel, and they are entitled to all the social benefits of citizenship (e.g. social insurance, health care, etc.). Yet, unlike full-fledged citizenship, permanent residency may expire if its holder stays abroad for more than seven years.

The first organized act of resistance to the occupation took place on July 24, 1967, a month and a half after the war had ended. A group of some twenty prominent Muslim personalities founded a body called "The Islamic Board" (*al-Hay'a al-Islamiyya*).[8] This body was designed by its founders to protect the sacred places of Islam, the *waqf* properties, and the shari'a courts system from Israeli intervention (Farhi 1979: 9–10, Maoz 1984: 86). The new body developed into the "Supreme Islamic Board in Jerusalem" (*al-Hay'a al-Islamiyya al-'Uliya fi al-Quds*) that took upon itself the administration of the shari'a courts system and the *waqf* properties in the occupied territories, in the absence of a Muslim sovereign (Welchman 2000: 53). Although the Board was first and foremost a local Jerusalemite body (see Kupferschmidt 1987: 260), several of its members were previously senior Jordanian functionaries, and it maintained a strong affiliation with the Hashemite Kingdom.

The Supreme Islamic Board in Jerusalem was not officially recognized by Israeli authorities, or by Jordan. Yet, Israel did not prohibit its operation,[9] and Jordan used it in order to finance and indirectly control Muslim institutions in the West Bank. With the tacit agreement of the Jordanian government, the Board established a shari'a court of appeal in the *Haram al-Sharif* (Temple Mount) compound in Jerusalem. This court was meant as a substitute for the shari'a court of appeal in Amman that was no longer accessible to residents of the occupied West Bank. The Board's chairman was appointed as acting *qadi al-quda* and president of the shari'a court of appeal. In his former capacity, he was also the head of the shari'a courts system in the West Bank, which continued to be administered by the Jordanian Ministry of Awqaf. Thus, qadis in the West Bank were appointed in Amman after a recommendation by the acting *qadi al-quda* in Jerusalem; their salaries were paid by the Jordanian authorities, and court fees were sent back to Amman via the acting *qadi al-quda*. Even the rulings of these courts were issued in the name of the Jordanian king (see Welchman 2000: 55–6, Bisharat 1989: 59).

The Jordanian shari'a courts in the West Bank thus retained almost complete autonomy vis-à-vis the Israeli military and civil administration, and the Israeli authorities seemed to have accommodated this arrangement (Welchman 1990: 94–5). In Jerusalem, however, things were more complicated. Unlike the rest of the territories occupied by Israel, that continued to be administered by a "temporary" military regime,[10] Jerusalem was annexed to Israel. Israeli authorities

---

8 This body should not be confused with the Supreme Muslim Council (*al-Majlis al-Islami al-'Ali*) that operated in Jerusalem during the British Mandate (see Kupferschmidt 1987: 260, Welchman 1990: 95, n. 3).

9 As a matter of fact, Israel's initial reaction to the challenge posed by the establishment of the Islamic Board was to expel four of its founders. Later on, however, Israel did not object to the existence of the Board, nor obstruct its operation (see Farhi 1979: 7).

10 Thus, the Palestinian population of the West Bank and Gaza Strip remained subject to the laws of the states that previously ruled these territories (Jordan and Egypt), as well as to Israeli military laws.

have therefore attempted to co-opt the Muslim religious establishment in East Jerusalem and to integrate it into the Israeli legal and religious systems. In return for the incorporation of the Jordanian East Jerusalem shari'a courts into the Israeli legal system, Israel was willing to go as far as granting the Islamic Board authority to appoint qadis autonomously (Welchman 2000: 60–61). Furthermore, Israel was willing to exempt qadis appointed by the Islamic Board from the obligation to swear allegiance to the State of Israel, as long as they agreed to operate under the aegis of the Israeli legal system (Benziman 1980: 109–11). Nonetheless, this far-reaching offer, from the Israeli point of view, was rejected by the Islamic Board that consistently refused to acknowledge the legitimacy of the Israeli occupation and annexation of East Jerusalem.

Frustrated with the fruitless attempts to co-opt the Muslim religious establishment in the city, Israel adopted another strategy. In August 1969, the Ministry of Religious Affairs issued instructions to the Israeli Execution Offices in the West Bank and in Jerusalem, not to execute the rulings issued by the Jordanian East Jerusalem shari'a courts.[11] This order had immediate consequences, since without execution there was no operative meaning to most court rulings. In any matter that required execution, Muslim residents of Jerusalem were therefore obliged to appeal to the Israeli court system—that is, to the shari'a court in Jaffa. Moreover, since all documents and rulings issued by the Jordanian shari'a courts in East Jerusalem were not recognized by Israeli courts, ministries, and agencies, Jerusalem's Muslims were compelled to travel all the way to the Jaffa court, even in trivial matters such as issuing a marriage certificate.

By implementing a policy of "passive non-recognition of the shari'a court system in Jerusalem" (Reiter 1997b: 13), Israeli policymakers were aiming to compel the Muslim population in annexed East Jerusalem to appeal to the Israeli legal system, and thus to acknowledge, at least implicitly, Israel's sovereignty in the "unified" city. Palestinian leaders, who were well aware of the symbolic implications of the Israeli policy, waged a campaign in local newspapers calling for a boycott of Israeli legal institutions (see Shehadeh 1980: 51, n. 16, Welchman 1990: 95–6). Nevertheless, Israeli policy has proved effective, and statistical data confirm that the number of appeals made by Muslims residing in Jerusalem to the Jaffa shari'a court increased steadily during the following years (see Reiter 1997b: 16).

During the early 1970s Israeli policymakers continued to vacillate between two opposing strategies: the attempt to co-opt the Jordanian courts system, or—in case this fails—the plan to establish an alternative, Israeli, shari'a court in the city.

11 On the protest of the Palestinian judiciary in the West Bank against this policy, see Welchman (2000: 54–5). As noted by Welchman (2000: 54. n. 92), there is some confusion regarding this order. While Meron (1982: 365) argues that it referred only to the East Jerusalem Courts, Shehadeh (1980: 21–2) contends that it referred to all shari'a courts in the West Bank. Nevertheless, it is clear that in effect, rulings issued by shari'a courts in the West Bank (other than the Jerusalem courts) were actually executed by the Israeli civil and military administrations in the West Bank (see Welchman 2000: 55, 64).

In January 1973 it was reported in a local Arabic newspaper (*al-Quds*) that Israeli authorities had decided to open a permanent branch of the Jaffa court in Jerusalem, and that the Jaffa qadi will head this branch. Two months later, however, it was reported in the same newspaper that the Israeli government had revoked this decision, and that it is now considering instead to recognize the decisions issued by the East Jerusalem courts (see Welchman 2000: 60–61). Eventually, neither of these strategies materialized during the next decade, and the situation remained as it was: the Jordanian courts in East Jerusalem continued to operate without Israeli recognition, and Muslim Jerusalemites were compelled to travel to Jaffa in order to receive executable rulings of a shari'a court.

In the meanwhile, the Jaffa shari'a court was having difficulties in dealing with the increasing number of appeals filed by East Jerusalemites (Sha'shu'a 1981: 24). Israeli authorities therefore resuscitated the plan to establish a shari'a court in Jerusalem. This court, it was decided, would not be a branch of the Jaffa court but rather constitute a new, independent court. In an article published in *al-Sha'ab* newspaper in February 1985, Sheikh Sa'ad al-Din al-'Alami, the then acting *qadi al-quda* and chairman of the Supreme Islamic Board, called on the Israeli authorities to reconsider their decision, and to recognize instead the rulings and documents issued by the East Jerusalem courts. Al-'Alami's arguments echoed previous Palestinian protests against the non-recognition of the East Jerusalem courts; and likewise, his plea was ignored by the Israeli authorities. Still, it took the Ministry of Religious Affairs three more years to accomplish the task and establish a shari'a court in West Jerusalem. The inauguration of the court was announced on Israeli Radio on April 5, 1988 (see Welchman 2000: 61).[12]

We may conclude this overview of the developments that led to the establishment of an Israeli shari'a court in West Jerusalem, by pointing to the fact that this institution was established as part of a political struggle over sovereignty in the city of Jerusalem. Due to these unique circumstances, a distinctive situation of legal pluralism developed in Jerusalem, as two courts—each belonging to a different state legal system—operate simultaneously in the city, serving the same population in similar cases.

Within this environment of legal pluralism, the position of the newly-established Israeli court was dubious: The court was initially perceived by the Muslim population in East Jerusalem as representing the Israeli occupation of the city. As such, every appeal to this court was liable to be viewed as a symbolic recognition of the Israeli annexation of East Jerusalem. Indeed, as I was once told by a former qadi, Ziad 'Asliyya: "Had they [Israeli policymakers] known what a fine service this court provides to the State of Israel, they would have built it of gold."[13]

12 Curiously, a record of this governmental act appeared in the Official Acta (*Yalkut HaPirsumim*) only on January 1, 1989 (see *Yalkut HaPirsumim*, 5749–1989, 3624: 1762).

13 Qadi Ziad 'Asliyya made this comment while complaining about the neglect of shari'a courts by the Ministry of Religious Affairs (conversation with Qadi Ziad 'Asliyya, March 12, 1999).

In addition to the problematic identification of this court with Israeli rule, many Jerusalemite Muslims—and in particular, *shar'i* advocates and lawyers—tend to view the court as "contaminated" by Israeli civil legislation, and thus as not a "proper" shari'a court. As observed by Welchman in the late 1990s (2000: 64), the laws applied by this court are viewed as "non-shar'i both in content and by dint of being issued by a legislature not empowered to issue rules for shari'a courts, besides the issue of illegal annexation."

Thus, it may be argued that East Jerusalemite Muslims have good reasons not to attend this court, and indeed, in the first years after its establishment, the number of files opened in it remained relatively small. Yet, the officiating qadis have nonetheless managed to turn this court into a legitimate institution, by various tactics (discussed below) designed to enhance the court's legitimacy, and more importantly, by providing good services that help the Muslim-Palestinian population cope with the hardships inflicted by Israel. For Muslim residents in Jerusalem, the Israeli shari'a court has come to be recognized as one of the single Israeli institutions that do not necessarily aim at making their lives in the city miserable. As I was told, for example, by a "veteran" litigant, who due to personal misfortune found himself coming and going regularly to Israeli courts and institutions: "Here [in the shari'a court] at least you have the feeling that they genuinely want to help you. They listen to your problems, and they try to find solutions. Not like the 'Jewish institutions' [*al-mu'asasat al-yahudiyya*], which merely want us [i.e. the Palestinians] to disappear from al-Quds [Jerusalem]."[14]

Attesting, undoubtedly, to the increasing legitimacy of the Israeli shari'a court among Muslim residents of East Jerusalem, is the systematic growth in the number of cases adjudicated by this court in recent years (see Figure 4.1). It is therefore reasonable to conclude—and this is certainly my impression, based on dozens of encounters and conversations with litigants in this court—that the current attitude among the Muslim population toward the court is equivocal: it is perceived as a symbol of Israeli rule in the "unified" city, and at the same time as a valuable mechanism that may help Palestinians to persevere in the face of hardships inflicted by the Israeli authorities.

14 Conversation with 'U.A.Y., February 22, 2005. This man has lost his son, who died in the middle of a seemingly simple operation in 2001. The son, who was married to a wife originally from Jordan (Irbid), has left two young children. Since the widow did not have an Israeli ID card, the Ministry of Interior Affairs refused to extend her permit to stay in Jerusalem. 'U.A.Y. was therefore entangled in various and simultaneous procedures in various Israeli institutions: in the district civil court (where he sued the hospital in which his son died); in the Israeli shari'a court, where his wife was asking for custody—in agreement with their daughter-in-law—over their minor grandchildren (in order to prevent the deportation of the children in case their mother will be deported); in the National Insurance Institution; and in the Ministry of Interior Affairs. Unfortunately I lost track of this affair and I do not know how it ended.

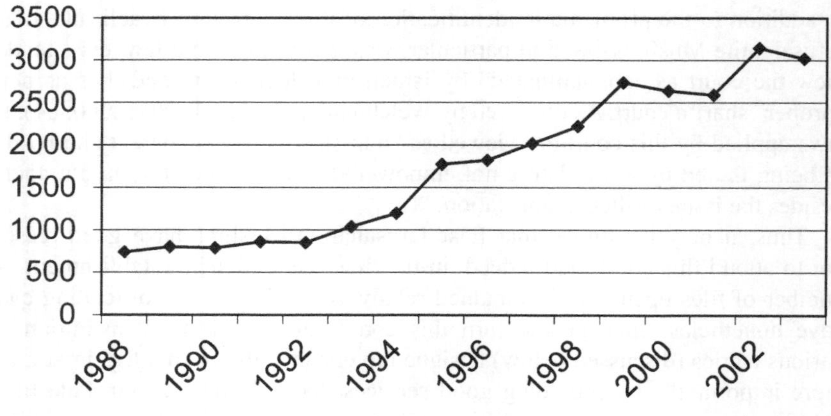

Figure 4.1 Number of Files Adjudicated by the Israeli Shari'a Court in West Jerusalem, 1988–2004

Conversely, from the point of view of Israeli policymakers, the shari'a court constitutes a powerful tool of co-optation of Muslim Palestinians in Jerusalem. And yet, due to its de facto autonomy, this court also operates occasionally to undermine Israeli policies in Jerusalem (see Shahar 2013). Thus, there is no wonder that the attitude within the Israeli governmental and legal systems toward this court may be described as equivocal. As I was told, for example, by a senior attorney working in the office of the Attorney General, "we treat the verdicts issued by the shari'a courts as insignificant."[15] Indeed, there are many cases in which rulings of the court are not executed by the Execution Offices and various governmental institutions (as will be discussed further in Chapter 12).

In the next part we turn to an ethnographic portrayal of the West Jerusalem shari'a court. This will allow for a closer, more elaborate examination of the general socio-historical themes that have been discussed thus far.

15 Interview with M.I., April 4, 2000.

PART II
A Court in Motion: Ethnographic Portrait

Chapter 5
The Site

My first encounter with the shari'a court of first instance in West Jerusalem took place in January 1998, when I visited the shari'a court of appeal that was located in the same building. I had an appointment with Qadi Ahmad Natur, the president of the shari'a court of appeal, and was having troubles finding my way. Although I had obtained the exact address of the court—right at the beginning of Jaffa Street, a central street in (Jewish) West Jerusalem—locating it turned out to be a challenging task. No sign whatsoever—neither in Arabic nor in any other language—indicated the existence of a court in this place. Eventually I identified an old, tall, one-story building with cracked walls and a neglected front entrance, and mustered the courage to knock on the heavy, bare door. I was welcomed by a friendly clerk who, following my explanation in stammering Arabic that I came to meet Qadi Natur, pointed out that this is actually the shari'a court of first instance. Nevertheless, he cordially led me through several internal doors to the section of the building that was occupied by the shari'a court of appeal.

The purpose of this initial visit was to ask for Qadi Natur's permission to conduct fieldwork and participant observations in the shari'a court of first instance, as part of my MA project. My numerous attempts to gain access to the Jordanian shari'a court in East Jerusalem had failed (for details, see below), and I was quite skeptical about my chances of getting a positive response from Qadi Natur. Still, this time I was equipped with a letter of reference from Prof. Aharon Layish, my teacher at the Hebrew University, who had also been one of Qadi Natur's teachers.

Natur, a man of about 45, neatly shaven and dressed in a three part suit, was curious about my research. He was rather hesitant—not to say suspicious—when I told him that I am an anthropologist, more interested in the social interactions in the court than in its purely legal aspects. I therefore emphasized that I will safeguard the anonymity of the litigants I encounter during my research. Finally, Qadi Natur gave me his initial consent to conduct fieldwork in the court of first instance, although he stressed that I will also need to obtain the consent of the qadi presiding in the court.

I left the meeting disappointed, feeling that there is little chance that I will ever be given access to this court. I assumed that Qadi Natur is using the same method as the Jordanian court officials that I approached—namely, shirking responsibility and letting someone else take difficult decisions (such as granting an anthropologist access to a court). I was surprised, therefore, when two weeks later I received a phone call from his office manager, informing me that I was granted permission to conduct my research in the court of first instance. She told me to coordinate my presence in the court with the presiding qadi at that time, Sheikh

Ziad ʻAsliyya (which I did immediately by phone), and two days later I began my fieldwork. For me this was the beginning of a long relationship, which continues to unfold until this very day.

In this and the following chapters of Part II, I present a (thick) description of this socio-legal institution based on my 15 years of acquaintance with it. It begins with a more grounded discussion of the tense political environment within which the court operates, followed by a discussion of the court's physical arrangements, and of its hybrid organizational characteristics.

The Court as a Site of Political Struggle and Cultural Dynamism

The old, decrepit building that I first visited in 1998 was the residence of the West Jerusalem shariʻa court, ever since its establishment 10 years earlier. This tall, narrow stone building—located in a backyard on Jaffa Street, next to the shariʻa court of appeal and to the shariʻa courts administration (*idarat al-mahakim al-sharʻiyya*), which operated there since the 1950s—was supposed to be a temporary residence. Yet as is usually the case in Israel, to quote a famous maxim, "nothing is more durable than a temporary arrangement," and the court remained in this place for more than 11 years, until September 1999, when it finally moved to a new location.

On the day of my first arrival to this "temporary" residence, there were no hearings held in the court. My impression was therefore of a quiet, dusky, mildewed place with a calm, intimate ambiance, in sharp contrast to the hubbub of the city center. It had only four rooms: a courtroom (5×8 meters), the qadi's chambers (4×4 meters), a small room—almost a niche—for two typists, and a tiny little kitchen. Nevertheless, on hearing days, as I was soon to learn, this quiescence was replaced by crowdedness and noise. Dozens of visitors—litigants and their escorting family members, lawyers, and *sharʻi* advocates—all squeezed into the small building, generating a hectic yet curiously still intimate atmosphere. It appeared that the growing number of files opened and processed each year—especially since the mid-1990s (see Figure 4.1)—resulted in a deluge of visitors beyond the court's capacity to handle.

As I was told by Qadi ʻAsliyya, the crowdedness is the reason why many litigants and their companions prefer waiting in the yard outside, until their names are called up by the court crier, inviting them to enter for their session. This was, of course, inconvenient when the weather was inclement. A more severe problem, though, was that such a gathering of Arabs in the middle of Jewish Jerusalem was bound to attract some extra attention by security forces. Israeli border police made it a habit to visit the place occasionally and to perform humiliating security checks on court comers.[1] Things got even worse when Jerusalem's central bus station was

1 On the habit of the Israeli border police to occasionally harass Arabs in the Western, Jewish part of Jerusalem, see Romann and Weingrod (1991: 69).

relocated to the vicinity of the court (due to a renovation of its previous location), and the harassment by the nervous policemen became a matter of daily routine. It became so disturbing, Qadi 'Asliyya told me, that he decided to transfer all of the court's hearings to his personal chambers, so that people can await their turn in what was previously the courtroom, and hence avoid standing in the yard outside.

This anecdote illustrates many of the court's characteristics: its neglect by Israeli authorities; its functionaries' efforts to turn it into a "user-friendly" institution that caters for the needs of Jerusalemite Muslims; and of course, the highly strained political context of the Israeli–Palestinian conflict that reveals itself in almost every aspect of the court's operation.[2]

Indeed, the turn of the century was particularly tense in Jerusalem. Those were the years that followed the assassination of Prime Minister Yitzhak Rabin (November 1995), when the Oslo peace process was already facing some serious difficulties and impediments, but was still presumably progressing toward a permanent status agreement that would put an end to the conflict between the two struggling peoples. Jerusalem, one of the key issues in the Israeli–Palestinian conflict, was the focus of heated public debates and elaborate political strategies pursued by both parties. Each side was trying to secure its interests in the city and to strengthen its position before the negotiations over the permanent settlement will commence. Israeli policymakers were preoccupied with securing the "Jewish character" of the city and were willing to perform various legal and political manipulations to achieve their goal.[3] In a similar vein, the Palestinian National Authority (PNA) tried to establish strongholds in Jerusalem, mainly by infiltrating and taking control of various institutions in the Eastern part of the city, such as "The Orient House" and the religious Muslim establishment, previously controlled by Jordan (see Amirav 2003).[4]

During my first two years of fieldwork in the Israeli shari'a court, the implications of the Israeli–Palestinian national struggle were evident in almost every case tried by the court. Indeed, the effects of this political context on the court's operation became one of the central axes of my MA thesis (Shahar 2000). The thesis analyzed the West Jerusalem shari'a court as an arena of struggle, where two power systems intersect: Palestinian–Israeli power relations in Jerusalem after the occupation and

---

2 Numerous sources deal with the issue of the Israeli–Palestinian national struggle in Jerusalem (see e.g., Benvenisti 1976, 1983, 1995, 1996, Benziman 1980, Kraemer 1980, Romann and Weingrod 1991, La Tendresse 1995, Muslim 1996, Friedland and Hecht 1996, Sabella 1997, 'Abd al-Jawad 1998, Bollens 2000, Klein 2001, Khamaisi 2001, Dumper 2002, Amirav 2003, 2009, Khamaisi and Nasrallah 2003, Misselwitz and Rieniets 2006, Pullan et al. 2013).

3 For example, the municipal borders of Jerusalem were redefined in order to leave large Arab neighborhoods outside the municipality, and thus reduce the number of Arabs in Jerusalem (see Choshen and Assaf-Shapira 2005).

4 There were even attempts to take control of the Jordanian shari'a courts operating on the Temple Mount (see Sharga'i 1999: B6).

annexation, on the one hand, and gender relations in the Palestinian community, on the other. Following Hirsch (1994), I tried to show that just like the Kenyan shari'a court in Mombasa studied by Hirsch, the West Jerusalem shari'a court plays a paradoxical role within both power systems, the national and the genderial: on the one hand it constitutes a site of hegemony and control, and on the other hand a site of empowerment opening up possibilities for resisting hegemony.

Furthermore, employing Foucault's conceptualization of power and resistance as fluid, unstable, and mutually constitutive (Foucault 1979: 93–5, 1982: 202–10), I analyzed the intersection of these two systems of power relations. I argued that in some instances, legal strategies deployed by women represent resistance to male hegemony, but at the same time serve to reinforce Israeli domination over the Palestinian population in East Jerusalem. In several cases of family disputes, for example, wives argued that the fact that the marital home provided to them by their husbands is located outside the Israeli municipal borders of Jerusalem causes them damage (*darar*). The location of the house made them liable, they stated, to the sequestration of their Israeli ID cards[5]—undoubtedly, a most serious damage to their well-being.[6] They claimed that in light of the (potential) damage, the marital home provided cannot be considered a proper *shar'i* house, and hence they are perfectly justified in leaving it. This argument was usually accepted by the qadi, who tended to reject obedience suits (*ta'a zawjiyya*) in such cases and to grant the wives maintenance payments.[7] Yet, as many furious husbands told me,

5 As mentioned, Israeli authorities searched for ways to reduce the number of Palestinians living in Jerusalem. Since Palestinian residents of annexed East Jerusalem were granted a status of "permanent residents," rather than full-fledged Israeli citizenship, their ID cards—and hence their right to reside in the city (and in Israel)—could be sequestrated if they move the "center of their lives" to places outside Israel for a period longer than seven years. The Ministry of the Interior, in collaboration with Jerusalem's municipal authorities and the National Insurance Institute (NII), therefore started between 1995 and 1999 systematically to sequestrate ID cards of Palestinian Jerusalemites who did not reside within the Israeli municipal borders of the city. This policy that came to be known as "the quiet deportation" (see B'Tselem Report 1997, 1998, Zink 2009), eventually led to opposite, unintended consequences, since tens of thousands of Palestinians—much more than the actual number of people whose ID cards had been sequestrated—returned to the city out of fear of losing their Israeli ID cards (see Klein 2001: 264–70).

6 Notably, an Israeli "blue" ID card entails material benefits such as freedom of work and movement in Israel, Israeli social insurance, and health care. These benefits are so considerable, that East Jerusalemite Palestinians are willing to invest much effort in trying to obtain a blue ID card and avoiding its sequestration (see 'Abed Rabho 2012).

7 Article 73 OLFR states that "a woman must obey her husband, within the limits of what is allowed by the law." A woman is also obliged to move to her husband's house after their wedding (Article 71), unless the house does not constitute a proper *shar'i* house (*maskan shar'i*). If a wife leaves the marital home without her husband's permission and without *shar'i* justification, and then refuses to return, the husband can file an obedience suit (*ta'a*). If the court rules in the husband's favor, but the wife still does not agree to return to her husband's house, the court will declare her a "recalcitrant wife" (*nashiz*), and she loses

this argument was definitely problematic from a national Palestinian point of view, not only because of the high value it attaches to an Israeli ID card, but also because it endorses the Israeli definitions of Jerusalem's borders, which were set as part of the Israeli attempt to restrict Palestinian presence in the city.

It may be concluded, therefore, that from a political point of view, the Israeli shari'a court is a "Janus-faced" institution (Comaroff 1994: ix): one face promotes the Palestinian national cause in Jerusalem, and the other serves Israeli hegemony; one face promotes gender-equality, the other maintains patriarchal norms (see also Shahar 2004). Furthermore, this duality applies to the court's cultural and organizational aspects as well. Indeed, the Israeli shari'a court in West Jerusalem is undoubtedly an "institutional hybrid," interfusing Israeli laws with Ottoman codified Islamic law; patriarchal conceptions with notions of gender equality; and a Palestinian identity with an Israeli one.

A good example of such a mixture may be found in the procedure of oath. Taking an oath (*half yamin*) is a well-known legal procedure in Islamic law, which may be used in various circumstances. A famous maxim states that "the burden of proof (by testimony) lies upon the one who makes the allegation, and the oath belongs to him who denies" (*al-bayyina ala al muda'i wal-yamin ala man ankar*).[8] Thus the *Majalla* determines (Article 1742) that in case the plaintiff is unable to substantiate by evidence his/her claims against the defendant, the defendant may take an oath of innocence and win the case. However, if the defendant refuses to take an oath, then this right is transferred to the plaintiff, who may then take an oath and thereby substantiate the truthfulness of his/her claims, and thus win the case.

Many cases in the Israeli shari'a court in contemporary Jerusalem are decided after the defendants or the plaintiffs substantiate their claims by taking an oath. In such cases, Qadi 'Asliyya used to direct the man or woman taking an oath to put their right hand on the holy Qur'an, and to repeat after him: "I swear by God that I say the truth, the whole truth, and nothing but the truth" (*Uqsimu bi-allah, inni aqul al-haqq, kull al-haqq, wala shay' ghayr al-haqq*).[9] This procedure thus constitutes an interfusion of legal traditions—combining the Islamic method of swearing in (*tahlif*) a litigant as a way to prove his/her claims, with a Western formula.[10]

---

her rights to maintenance payments. However, if the wife manages to prove that the marital home is not a *maskan shar'i*, or that her husband has maltreated her or has failed to deliver the dower, the court will rule in the wife's favor and oblige the husband to pay maintenance.

8 For a general discussion of the mechanism of oath in Islamic law, see Brunschvig (1960: 1151b).

9 Notably, when an oath is taken, all the people present in the courtroom stand up in respect of this scared act.

10 Article 1743 of the *Majalla* states that a litigant must swear "in the name of God the Almighty." Apart from this, there are no particular instructions for swearing an oath. On the extensive use of the oath swearing mechanism in other shari'a courts, see Hill (1979), and Rosen (1989).

To use another analytical concept, the shari'a court in West Jerusalem may be described as a "liminal" institution, positioned "betwixt and between" cultures, communities, and bureaucratic traditions. Its liminality translates, however, into social action that is best conceived as reconciling and "soothing." The socio-legal interactions in court do not exacerbate cultural and political frictions, but rather mitigate them. Unlike other Israeli courts, which may be viewed from a Palestinian perspective as "harsh alienating places" (Hajjar 2005: 81), the shari'a court in West Jerusalem maintain its "familial" and communal character; its formal bureaucratic traits are moderated by an informal, user-friendly atmosphere.

Stemming from this hybridity/liminality is cultural generativity or cultural creativity,[11] which also characterizes this court's operation. As argued by many postcolonial writers, cultural hybridity should not necessarily be viewed as flawed.[12] It is not always a case of the oppressor obliterating the oppressed, or the colonizer silencing the colonized. Rather, hybridization may be viewed in terms of cultural strength—as a dynamic process of cultural production that "gives rise to something different, something new and unrecognizable, a new area of negotiation of meaning and representation" (Bhabha 1990: 211).

This hybridization, however, is obviously a demanding process. A description of one significant event—the relocation of the court from the old temporary building to its permanent new location—nicely illustrates the processual aspect of this hybridity.

Moving to a New Location

In September 1999, after more than 11 years of operation in an old, inappropriate building, the court was finally moved to a new location in the Jewish neighborhood of Giv'at Sha'ul.[13] In contrast to the previous building, which was an old Arab house, predating the Israeli period, the new residence is in a new, modern building, typical of the functional office buildings of the 1990s in Israel. Also the shari'a court of appeal and the shari'a courts administration moved to that location and occupy, together with the shari'a court of first instance, a large section on the first floor of the building. In the vicinity of this complex are several other government offices, as well as some civil courts.

---

11 For a discussion of the cultural generativity of hybridization, see Ashcroft (2001).

12 Cultural hybridity usually refers to "the creation of new transcultural forms within the contact zone produced by colonization" (Ashcroft, Griffiths, and Tiffin 2003: 118).

13 As a matter of fact, Giv'at Sha'ul was built on the ruins of an old Palestinian village, called Dir Yassin. This village was engraved in the collective memories of the two peoples as the site of a massacre of Palestinian civilians perpetrated by a right-wing Jewish militia. More than 100 Palestinians were killed in this village by the "dissident" forces of the IZL (*Irgun Zva'i Le'umi*) in April 1948 (see Morris 1987: 113–15). It is noteworthy that Palestinian Jerusalemites in general, and visitors to the shari'a court in particular, still refer to Giv'at Sha'ul as Dir Yassin, until this very day.

In its new location, the court enjoys a much larger space. It consists of a modest courtroom of 5×8 meters, a waiting room of approximately the same size, the qadi's chambers equipped with a small bathroom and toilet, two rooms for typists, a secretariat, a small kitchen, and a small archive, with just enough room to store the files of the past three years. All the rooms are air-conditioned and furnished with new furniture—green lounge in the waiting room, wooden benches in the courtroom, and office armchairs for the personnel. In addition, the rooms are equipped with communication devices (phones and intercoms) and are fully computerized.

And yet, despite the obvious improvement in the working conditions, my impression was that the relocation to the new building brought about a conspicuous crisis—both in terms of the relations among the personnel, and in terms of the relations between the personnel and court comers (litigants, lawyers, etc.). Whereas the daily routines and human relations in the old building seemed to me rather good spirited and calm, I was surprised to find uptight nerves, sour feelings, and resentments among personnel and visitors, when I first visited the new building. The spatial division in the new building accentuated the hierarchy between personnel and visitors: the secretariat was now secluded and separated from the waiting room by a locked door and a transparent, rigid divider. The qadi's chambers and the typists' rooms, which were always accessible in the old building, were now located behind two closed doors, opened only from the inside, or otherwise by a buzzer pressed in the secretariat. Consequently, the informal relations between court personnel and court comers, that had been a salient characteristic of the court in the old building, were significantly reduced in the new building.

All in all, my impression was that the first six months in the new building were quite difficult, as was also confirmed by several people with whom I spoke. Neither the personnel nor the *shar'i* advocates and the litigants felt themselves "at home." People were having difficulties getting to Giv'at Sha'ul, which is far more remote from the Arab Eastern part of the city than Jaffa street, the previous site. During these months, when I happened to share an elevator with court comers, I often overheard them complaining about the troubles of traveling to the court and of finding it: one had to switch two busses on the way, and when one finally arrived at Giv'at Sha'ul, there were no Arabs who could show the way, nor anybody else who knew where the court was (the small metal sign at the entrance to the building, with the Arabic title "The Shari'a Court of Appeal," was only placed there in April 2002).

Coming out of the elevator, people were still confused: they encountered an armed guard (Jewish, of course) who stood next to a magnometer (metal detector) gate. They were then required to declare the purpose of their visit, hand over their handbag for inspection, and to go through the magnometer gate.[14] When they

14 An armed guard was also present in the old building, but there he sat inside the courtroom that—as mentioned—had become the waiting room. There was no magnometer gate in the old building.

finally entered the court—at last, an Arabic speaking environment—their body language conveyed considerable disorientation: they hesitated to approach the court personnel with questions, they sat uncomfortably on the green sofas, waiting impatiently for their hearing to begin; and as soon as the hearing ended, they hurried outside, often forgetting to sign or to collect important documents.

When I asked a litigant, who once approached me,[15] if he feels comfortable in this court, he answered: "Me? Comfortable? Here? Have you seen what's next to the qadi?"[16] When I shook my head in negation, he grabbed me by the hand, led me to the courtroom (which was empty at the moment), and, pointing to the Israeli flag hanging on a pole next to the qadi's chair and to the large Menorah sign (the national coat of arms of the State of Israel) on the wall above the chair, he said: "See this? How can I feel comfortable here?"

Indeed, a flag and a Menorah sign were present in the old building as well, but the Menorah was hanging on the wall of the courtroom that had turned, as mentioned, into a waiting room, and it was concealed by a filing cabinet; and the flag that stood on the floor next to the qadi's chair was almost unnoticeable. While the atmosphere in the old building, its appearance and its spatial arrangement had generally blurred the "Israeliness" of the court, in the new building this Israeliness was thrown in the face of court personnel and court comers. This anecdote illustrates the shift in the balance between "Israeli elements" and "Palestinian-Muslim elements" that accompanied the move to the new building. Since the balance was tilted in favor of the Israeli identity, Muslim-Palestinian Jerusalemites felt more alienated.

This situation did not last for long, however. Within a few months, a noticeable process of "Arabization" and "Islamization" had taken place: a large reproduction of al-Aqsa Mosque, several golden pictures of calligraphic writings, and a black-and-white picture of the Ka'aba in Mecca during Hajj time were hanging on the walls; everyone was smoking again, despite the greenish signs on the walls warning (primarily in Hebrew, and only in smaller letters in Arabic) that smoking

15 By that time, I was well acquainted with the court's staff and with its regular visitors (i.e. *shar'i* advocates, lawyers, marriage registrars, etc.), but not with first-time visitors. During those first months, however, I was often approached by first-time visitors with questions relating to court hearings or court routines. Certainly, these people—well aware of the differences in appearance between Jews and Arabs—could not mistake me for a Muslim Arab. Why then did they approach me with such questions? The answer is simple, and it was noted to me many times: recognizing me as a Jew, they thought that I was a man of authority. Their mistake is a clear indication of their disorientation. Such mistakes rarely happened in the old building, whose looks caused people to identify it as a Muslim-Palestinian site. In such a site, a Jew is most likely to be a guest, and not a man of authority. Such incidents, nevertheless, gave me an opportunity to talk with first-time visitors even before their hearings.

16 This man agreed to answer my questions only after he made sure who I was, and after he was assured by the clerk's aide that I was a "good" person (read: not an agent of the Israeli security services).

is forbidden;[17] more harmony was felt again among the personnel, who started to enjoy their improved working environment; *shar'i* advocates regained their joking habits with court personnel, and surprisingly, they began to conduct consultation and advisory meetings with their clients in the court's waiting room. The relatively spacious room, functionally furnished, air-conditioned and equipped with a relatively clean restroom, apparently offered much better conditions than their tiny offices in the Old City.[18] Even the qadi "restored old-time glory" and began to conduct personal meetings with litigants and their delegates in his chambers whenever he felt, as he once told me, that "intimate discussion with the parties may prove beneficial for solving the conflict between them."

Thus, several months after the court had moved to the new building, balance was restored, and the atmosphere seemed pleasant and harmonious again. Nevertheless, the endemic tensions characterizing this socio-legal institution were not resolved, of course. The shari'a court in West Jerusalem remained a hybrid institution, combining various national, legal, and organizational cultures. This inherent hybridity finds expression not only in the court's spatial arrangement, but also in the temporal dimension. As an Israeli governmental institution, the shari'a court does not work on Fridays and Saturdays—the official rest days in the Israeli public sector. The court also does not work during Jewish holidays and during the official court vacation, in August. However, since it is also a Muslim court, it does not operate on Muslim holidays (*'Id al-Adha, 'Id al-Fitr*) as well, and during the month of Ramadan it works only until noon.

Working in accordance with both Israeli and Palestinian/Jordanian timetables has other peculiar consequences, besides the numerous vacations. For example,

17 My impression is that almost all men smoke. Smoking in court is so common that the waiting room is always smoky. Even in the courtroom, everyone resumes smoking, as soon as the hearing ends and the qadi withdraws to his chambers, and no one protests. It is noteworthy, however, that smoking is first and foremost a masculine behavior. Only once have I seen a woman visitor smoking, and then one of the court's personnel approached her and told her that it was inappropriate for women to smoke in the court. Nevertheless, one of the court's typists also "committed the sin" of smoking from time to time. She never did it, however, when the court was crowded.

18 I had the opportunity of meeting some lawyers and *shar'i* advocates in their offices in the Old City in East Jerusalem. Except for one lawyer, who had a relatively spacious office, all the others settled for tiny ones. The reason for this, they told me, is the economic hardships many of them faced, as well as the enormous rise in rent prices in the Old City. Shortage in accommodation and office space in East Jerusalem, and in particular in the Old City (the commercial center of Arab Jerusalem), has been exacerbated by Israeli restrictions on construction in Arabic neighborhoods, and by the influx into the city due to the Israeli policy of "quiet deportation" (see note 5 above). On the housing shortage in East Jerusalem, see Khamaisi (2003, 2006). See also a special report on the "planning crisis" published by the UN Office for the Coordination of Humanitarian Affairs in the Occupied Palestinian Territories (OCHA 2009).

when daylight saving time ends in Israel at the beginning of September,[19] East Jerusalemites continue to live for another month according to "summer time" of Jordan and the Palestinian Authority. This time difference causes much confusion, which results in many people not showing up on time for their hearings. The qadi and the court's staff are well aware of the problem, and they tend to respond with leniency and to resume the hearing even if the litigants had already been announced absent. The same leniency is demonstrated towards litigants or advocates who explain that they were late for their hearing because they had been delayed by Israeli roadblocks.[20]

19 The issue of the summer time schedule is the subject of an enduring political debate between orthodox Jews and secular sectors in the Israeli society. Orthodox Jews, who have to wake up early during the month of Elul (roughly September) for prayers, prefer the summer time to end as early as possible, before Yom Kippur. The matter is usually settled by compromise.

20 Several roadblocks (*ma'abir* or *"mahasim"*—an Arabicized plural inflection of the Hebrew word *Mahsom*), tightly control the entrance from the West Bank to Jerusalem. These barriers enable Israel to control and restrict the entrance of Palestinians into Jerusalem, including Israeli Jerusalemites that found themselves on the "wrong side of the separation wall" built by Israel in recent years. On the road barriers and on the harm they inflict on the Palestinian population in the occupied territories, see: http://www.machsomwatch.org/.

Chapter 6
The Cast of Characters

Whereas the previous chapter has outlined the cultural and political frameworks within which the shari'a court in West Jerusalem operates, the present chapter aims to provide a detailed description of the various actors that take part in the social interactions unfolding in the court: the clientele of the court (i.e. litigants); the court's salaried personnel; lawyers and *shar'i* advocates; semi-official functionaries appointed by the court (e.g. mediators, marriage registrars). The discussion dwells not only on the sociological and demographical characteristics of each of these groups, but also on the interrelations that they maintain with other actors.

Litigants

It is hard to ascertain the exact number of people who are subject to the jurisdiction of the Israeli shari'a court in West Jerusalem. From an Israeli official perspective, the court has territorial jurisdiction in matters of personal status of Muslims living in the District of Jerusalem. At the end of 2004,[1] the Muslim population residing within the municipal borders of Jerusalem (including the annexed Eastern part) mounted to some 224,800 people (32 percent of the total population in the city).[2] In addition, the District of Jerusalem also includes some villages and semi-urban boroughs (e.g. 'Ain Nequba, Abu Gosh) with a population of several thousands. Thus, we may estimate that officially the shari'a court in West Jerusalem has territorial jurisdiction over roughly 230,000 Muslims.

In effect, however, the Muslim population that may choose to appeal to this court in matters of personal status is considerably larger. As mentioned, in the course of the annexation the borders of Jerusalem were designed on purpose to include as many Jews as possible, and to exclude as many Palestinians as possible from the city (see e.g., Benvenisti 1996: 136–68, Bollens 2000: 65–95). Consequently, several large Arab neighborhoods (e.g. Al-Azariyya, Al-Za'im,

---

1 This research refers to the years 1998–2005, during which my fieldwork was conducted.

2 According to the Israeli Central Bureau of Statistics, in 2004 the total population of Jerusalem was 706,300; 64 percent (458,300) were Jews, 32 percent (224,800) were Muslims, 2.3 percent were Christians (14,700), 1.5 percent (8,300) were religion-wise unclassified (see Jerusalem Institute for Israel Studies, *Statistical Yearbook 2004*, at: http://jiis.org/?cmd=statistic.32 [accessed: 10/14/2014]).

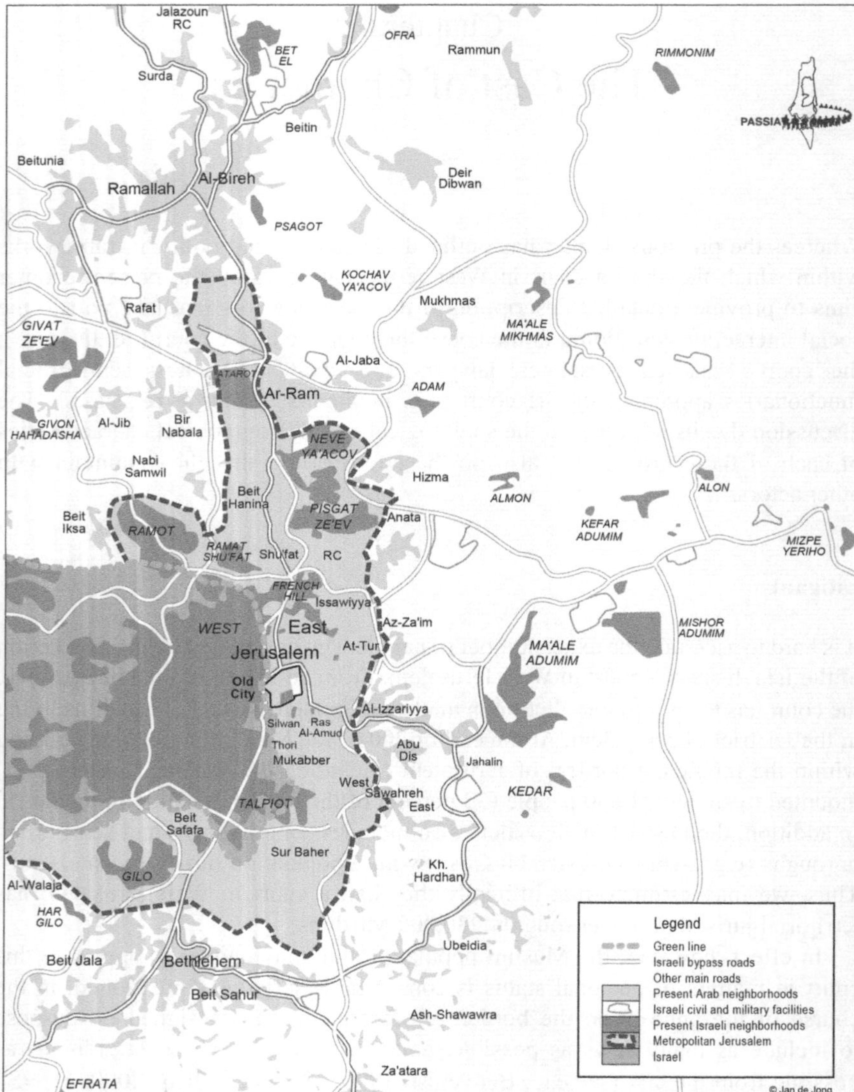

Planned settlements and settlements under construction have not been included e.g Har Homa

Figure 6.1 Jerusalem Maps—Palestinian and Israeli Neighborhoods in Metropolitan Jerusalem (2000)

Source: © The Palestinian Academic Society for the Study of International Affairs (PASSIA).

Dahiyyat al-Barid), which undoubtedly constitute part and parcel of the East Jerusalem urban fabric, have been left outside the city's Israeli municipal borders (see Figure 6.1). The residents of these neighborhoods may appeal to the Israeli shari'a court on various grounds: they may hold Israeli ID cards, or may wish to obtain such cards; or they may be married to spouses who hold Israeli ID cards. Whatever the reasons, according to my estimation, there are several hundred cases adjudicated in this court each year, which involve litigants from the mentioned neighborhoods or from the other cities or villages in the West Bank (primarily from the vicinity of Jerusalem—e.g. Ramallah, Bethlehem, Jericho, al-Khadr).[3]

Therefore, in order to calculate more accurately the "pool" of potential litigants who may appeal to the shari'a court in West Jerusalem, we need to add to the number mentioned above (230,000) approximately 50,000 Muslims residing in the Arab outskirts of Jerusalem, just outside the Israeli-defined municipal borders of the city.[4] Moreover, if we consider the Muslim population residing in the greater Jerusalem metropolitan area—that includes large Palestinian urban centers such as Ramallah and Bethlehem (see Bollens 2000: 112)—as potential litigants as well, then the number should rise by approximately 120,000 people. All in all, we may estimate that the pool of potential litigants who may appeal to the Israeli shari'a court is just a little below 400,000 people.

This is indeed a large population, and a highly diversified one. In terms of socio-economic characteristics, the Jerusalem metropolitan area is very variegated: there are some middle-class urban neighborhoods such as Sheikh Jarrah, American Colony, and Beit Hanina; some semi-urban neighborhoods such as 'Issawiyya, Arab al-Sawahrah, and Jabel al-Mukkabar; refugee camps such as

---

3 A clear indication of the "non-Zionist" rationale that guides the rulings of the shari'a court in West Jerusalem is the fact that such cases—even when both parties do not hold Israeli ID cards—are being dealt with by the court. Unlike other Israeli legal and governmental agencies that strictly observe a clear-cut differentiation between "Israelis" and "West Bankers"—and therefore, would refuse to deal with private legal matters of "West Bankers"—the shari'a court in West Jerusalem systematically ignores this differentiation. Thus, if two residents of Hizme, 'Anata or Al-Ram (Arab neighborhoods/villages in the vicinity of Jerusalem that were not included in Jerusalem after the annexation) wish, for example, to register their marriage in the Israeli shari'a court, to settle a marriage dispute or to issue an official testament, the court usually has no objections at all. As a matter of fact, even when an argument concerning the lack of territorial/material jurisdiction of the court is brought up by one of the parties (as often happens in such cases), the court generally tends to reject it (see e.g., ISC 260/1990, 215/1996, 171/2001). The shari'a court of appeal has done the same with several cases in which the appeal was based on similar jurisdictional grounds (see SCA 106/1994, 203/1997).

4 Bollens (2000: 112) relies on Palestinian sources in his estimation that the population of these neighborhoods amounted to 41,000 in 2000. By calculating a growth rate of 4.5 percent a year, we can estimate that by the end of 2004, the population of these neighborhoods stood at approximately 50,000 people. For a similar estimation, see Khamaisi (2003: 19).

Shu'afat refugee camp, and large rural habitats occupied by Bedouin tribes (see Figure 6.1). Thus, the population that comes to court is diversified as well: some people have university degrees, others can hardly read and write; some drive fancy cars, others come a long way by foot, since they cannot afford the bus ride; some women wear stylish modern—sometimes even daring—outfits, while others are veiled and covered from head to toe by *Jilbab*s.

Court Personnel

Occasional visitors to court—or, in Mark Galanter's (1974: 97) terms, "one-shotters"—come almost exclusively from East Jerusalem and the larger Jerusalem metropolitan area.[5] Most of these litigants hold Israeli, blue ID cards, but a substantial minority among them hold West Bank, orange ID cards. Like the one-shotters, the "repeat players" and the court personnel are mostly residents of East Jerusalem. The notable exceptions are the qadis and the chief secretaries, who are Palestinian-Israelis—that is, they are full-fledged citizens of Israel residing within the 1948 Israeli borders. All the qadis, who have presided in court since 1988, and all the chief secretaries came either from the *Muthalath* (the "triangle"), an area in Northern Israel, or from Jaffa. The Palestinian-Israeli identity of the high-ranking personnel in the court is of primary significance: it highlights their liminal role as mediators between the Israeli state and the East Jerusalem population. The Palestinian-Israeli population in general is often portrayed as a liminal group with a torn, ambiguous identity: they are both Palestinians and Israelis, and at the same time they are neither "real" Israelis nor "real" Palestinians (see e.g., Shafir and Peled 2002: ch. 4).[6] The hybrid, liminal positioning of the West Jerusalem shari'a court therefore owes much to the liminal identity of its senior staff.

The court staff during my years of fieldwork included the following persons—all names are pseudonyms, except for the qadis' names:

Qadi Ziad Taufiq 'Asliyya, a resident of the *Muthalath* in Northern Israel, who presided in court between the years 1994–2000.[7] He holds a degree in social work, and since 2001, also an M.A. degree from the shari'a faculty at the University of Hebron. His father, Sheikh Taufiq 'Asliyya, served as

5 Some cases (in my estimation, between 10 and 20) are transferred each year to this court from other shari'a courts in Israel. Such transfers occur when the qadi in the original location is acquainted with one of the litigants, or is required to excuse himself from handling the case for whatever reason.

6 For recent studies dealing with the identity of Israeli Palestinians, see Rabinowitz and Abu Baker (2005), Louer (2007).

7 Qadi 'Asliyya was preceded in the shari'a court in West Jerusalem by Qadi Zaki Mudlij, who presided in court in the years 1988–93, and was then appointed to the shari'a court of appeal.

president of the shari'a court of appeal. Qadi 'Asliyya is currently retired after another term of qadiship at the shari'a court in Haifa.

Muhammad Rashid Zibdi (Abu Muhammad), the presiding qadi in the years 2001–08. A denizen of Jaffa, who was a former schoolmaster and a school inspector in the Israeli Ministry of Education. He was in his mid-40s, and had no formal education in shari'a matters.

Ibrahim al-Ghol, chief clerk in the years 1997–2000. A graduate of the shari'a college in Baqa al-Gharbiyya (in Northern Israel). He was transferred to the shari'a court in Tayybe following a personal conflict with Qadi 'Asliyya.

Muhammad Jamil (Abu Zayd), acting chief clerk.[8] A veteran officer in the Jordanian army, about 55 years old, employed in the court since 1995.

'Izzat Ghandur (Abu 'Uday), aide to the chief clerk. In his early thirties, employed in the court since 1997.

Salih, the "court scribe," or actually the court computer operator, who is in charge of typing the protocols during the hearings. He is a practical electronic engineer,[9] in his mid-twenties, and employed in the court since 2002.

Siham—a typist. She is the most veteran employee of the court, working there since 1994. A colorful and somewhat eccentric woman in her mid-thirties.

Nadin, a typist, in her mid-twenties, working in the court since 2001.

Meir, a Jewish guard. Unlike other guards who served in this position in the past, Meir has become an amicable staff member. His post, nevertheless, is outside the court, in the corridor that leads to the first-instance court, the shari'a court of appeal, and the administration of the shari'a courts.

Except for the qadis and the chief secretaries, who are senior state employees, all the other staff members are employed by manpower agencies, and therefore do not have tenure. They are dismissed from their jobs and then immediately rehired each and every year by the Ministry of Justice (and until 2001, by the Ministry of Religious Affairs). As a result, their salaries and social benefits are very poor relative to the organized Israeli public sector. At the time Qadi 'Asliyya was presiding in court, the inequality between state employees (i.e. the qadi and the chief clerk) and employees of manpower agencies caused considerable tensions and grievances among the junior staff. Although the problem was not resolved, the tension seems to have faded away later on.

Throughout the years of the research (1998–2000, 2001–05), the division of labor among the court staff was far from constant. Rather, the role-definitions of the various staff members underwent considerable changes. Here are a couple of examples: the function of court courier (*mubashir*)—a traditional function in

8 No chief clerk was appointed after the transfer of Ibrahim al-Ghol to Tayybe. Abu Zayd is not eligible for the position of chief clerk since his Hebrew skills are very poor. And yet, he practically runs the court.

9 Graduate of al-Quds University in East Jerusalem.

shari'a courts that was also determined by Clauses 17 and 18 of the Ottoman Law of Procedures for shari'a Courts (1917)—was canceled by the qadi in January 2002. Being in charge of delivering rulings, habeas corpuses and summonses for litigants residing in Jerusalem, the carrier constituted not only a traditional function, but also a crucial one in the court operation. However, this arrangement was terminated, without much ado, by Qadi Zibdi, who discovered, as he told me, that "it simply didn't work: the courier could not cope with this job; there were piles of summons in drawers, which he didn't deliver, and hearings were postponed again and again due to deficient notifications." 'Izzat Ghandur (Abu 'Uday) who functioned as courier since 1997 was therefore moved to the position of aide to the chief clerk, and instead of relying on a courier to deliver the documents, the court started to use registered mail.[10]

This move was naturally accompanied by a new division of labor among the court's staff. At first, there were some frictions and a sort of turf war between various staff members, but within a couple of weeks, the new aide to the acting chief clerk, assumed full responsibility for maintaining and organizing the court's small archive: he was the only one, as he never failed to point out to me, that was allowed to enter the archive, to draw and to stow dossiers in it. This organizational transformation—which seems perhaps trivial, but in effect, changed the court's routines dramatically—was achieved not by orders from above, nor by a premeditated bureaucratic decision, but rather, by a simple organizational adaptation to changing circumstances and needs.

In April 2003 a social worker—a Palestinian-Israeli woman from Tayyibe (a Palestinian town at the center of Israel)—was recruited to serve in an "assistance unit" that was established in the court. She started working from 08:00 to 15:00 several days a week in the Jerusalem shari'a court, only to be transferred to the Jaffa shari'a court less than a year later (in February 2004). However, during the short period of her work at the Jerusalem court, she functioned more like an additional mechanism of dispute-resolution than a social worker: opponent parties were referred to her by the qadi, and she gained considerable prestige when she managed to reconcile several of them.[11] She was allocated a small office niche in

10 Nevertheless, since the Israel post ceased to work in many of the East Jerusalem neighborhoods (due to security problems during the second Intifada), the problem of postponed hearings on account of deficient notifications had not been solved. As an alternative recourse, the court asked the plaintiffs to deliver summonses to the defendant party by themselves. This method, as reported by Qadi Zibdi, proved highly efficient, and the number of delays due to deficient notifications decreased dramatically (conversation with Qadi Muhammad Rashid Zibdi, July 11, 2002).

11 Apparently, she was so successful in her reconciliation efforts that the manager of the shari'a courts administration told me (June 2004) that they decided to request a budget increase in order to establish assistance units at all shari'a courts in Israel. He noted that all they ask for is equalization of conditions with the family courts—which all have functioning assistance units, employing a regular staff of social workers, psychologists, and professional mediators. It took the Ministry of Justice six years to accomplish this

the typist's room, and there she conducted ad hoc dispute-resolution sessions with litigants who agreed to do so. In the short period that she worked in Jerusalem, her presence in court and her methods of intervention certainly changed the entire handling of marital disputes in the court. Similarly, when she was transferred to Jaffa, her sudden disappearance affected again the court's procedures, which nevertheless did not simply return to what they were before she arrived.[12]

To my mind, the fact that these two organizational transformations occurred within a period of more or less one year, indicates that the shari'a court in West Jerusalem constitutes, indeed, a highly dynamic institution—also at the organizational level. Changes and organizational transformations take place quite frequently in this court. Furthermore, it seems that these transformations occur without significant opposition from the court's staff and its "clients," who appear to adapt quite easily—and contentedly—to the frequent changes in the court's routines. As depicted in Chapter 5, it seems that the organizational culture of this court may be described as "prone to change:" an organizational culture that views changes in positive terms, creates very little barriers to change, and handles changes in a seemingly easy-going manner (see Holt et al. 2007).

Let us move now to reviewing the other repeat players in the court. They comprise three different groups: lawyers and *shar'i* advocates; marriage registrars (*al-ma'dhun*s); and mediators/arbitrators (*ahl al-khayr*, *muhakamin*) appointed by the court. Let us describe these groups one by one.

Lawyers and *Shar'i* Advocates

This is the largest and most important group of repeat players. The website of the Israeli shari'a courts listed some 187 lawyers and *shar'i* advocates, who are licensed to work and to represent litigants in the shari'a courts in Israel.[13] This is

---

equalization of conditions, and to pass a law to that effect: Religious Courts (Assistance Units) Law (5711–2011), passed in the Knesset on May 16, 2011.

12 For example, after the social worker was gone, the qadi himself started holding more and more "private" sessions of dispute resolution between parties in his chambers. As he explained to me, when he feels that there is a chance for reconciliation—but this chance is hampered by the lawyers or by family members who intervene in the dispute—he proposes to the disputing parties to meet him alone in his chambers. Since reconciliation is considered a blessing, he explained, he is more than willing to devote the necessary time and effort in order to achieve it. My impression was that such sessions increased dramatically in the weeks after the social worker stopped working in the court, and though it gradually decreased as time went by, it seems that it is still more frequent than it used to be before she arrived.

13 The list disappeared from the site in 2006, and reappeared in 2009 in a shorter version, containing only 58 names, out of which 24 are listed as Jerusalemites (see http://index.justice.gov.il/Units/BatiDinHashreim/MagreiMeida/Pages/Toanim.aspx [accessed: 10/15/2014]).

not a comprehensive list,[14] nor does it differentiate between lawyers and *shar'i* advocates,[15] but it constitutes a good starting point for an attempt to map the various categories of legal councilors working in the shari'a court in West Jerusalem.

Of the 187 lawyers and *shar'i* advocates listed by the administration of the shari'a courts,[16] 71 are registered as Jerusalemites. Of these, 31 are definitely repeat players, who appeared in court regularly during the six years of my participant observation. Seven others are repeat players but do not live in Jerusalem (five of them are registered in the West Bank, one in Lod, and one in Jaffa). Twelve others are "occasional players" in my terms, which means that they were listed in my field diaries, but less than five times. Of the 38 repeat players, three are women,[17] and five, as mentioned, are registered in the West Bank: three (including one woman) in Ramallah, one in Bethlehem, and one in Hebron.[18]

The list of legal councilors who regularly appear in court is therefore relatively small. Some members of this group appear in court almost every working day, and stay there for long hours. These people maintain close relationships—usually on friendly terms—with court personnel (mainly with the acting chief clerk and his aide). Thus, when they arrive at court, for example, they usually exchange kisses on the cheeks and hug each other, especially if someone was absent for some time. Legal councilors may bring small insignificant treats to the personnel (e.g. chocolate, cakes, pens), and the personnel may share with them—if they are in a particularly generous mood—coffee or tea, which they have prepared for

14 I personally know of at least two advocates who represented litigants during the years of my fieldwork in the West Jerusalem shari'a court and were not listed.

15 *Shar'i* advocates have usually no formal legal training. They are required to pass an examination administered by the Israeli shari'a court administration. Until 2005, no formal education of any kind was required in order to be eligible to take this exam. In 2005 the regulations were changed, and candidates for the role of *shar'i* advocates are now required to hold a B.A. from a recognized academic institution.

16 According to the aide of the director of the shari'a court administration, only advocates who paid the 2004 yearly fee are included in the list. In 2004, this fee amounted to 403.84 NIS (on shari'a court fees, see Appendix 1).

17 Women councilors thus constitute less than eight percent of this group. Moreover, the three women lawyers who do appear regularly in court occupy a relatively marginal position: they are not considered among the most successful advocates, and are viewed as "outsiders" by their colleagues.

18 Of course, there have been some changes during these six years in the list of legal councilors working in the shari'a court of West Jerusalem. According to my estimate, the number of repeat players has risen gradually from approximately 25 in 1998 to 35 in 2004. Throughout these years, a few councilors disappeared from court (due to sickness, death, or other reasons), and several—most of them young graduates of law schools—joined the club. Notably, about 30 councilors who are listed by the administration of shari'a courts as Jerusalemites do not appear in my diaries. It is possible, of course, that some of these councilors did appear in court, but I missed them, or otherwise failed to write down their names. Some of them probably reside in other locations and appear in other shari'a courts, and are only registered in Jerusalem; and surely, some may not be practicing.

themselves. There are, of course, instances of less amicability, in which certain advocates complain about maltreatment or partiality displayed by court personnel toward them, but these are rather rare occasions.[19]

Relations among the 38 legal councilors who are regular visitors in court are also generally characterized by friendliness and good humor. Advocates usually greet each other warmly when they meet, exchange jokes and anecdotes, and occasionally substitute for each other in court hearings. Nevertheless, during legal altercations, they tend to be extremely polemic and formalist and to provoke their fellow colleagues.[20] Thus, for instance, advocates often tease their opponents, arguing that they are ignorant of the law or lack proper legal expertise and education, and that their claims do not have any legal grounding.

Such stinging altercations, however, are actually manifestations of more profound tensions between members of this group of repeat players. These tensions are apparent between three subgroups: lawyers belonging to the Israeli bar, lawyers belonging to the Jordanian bar, and *shar'i* advocates.[21] The frictions between these subgroups are both professional and political. On the professional level, lawyers belonging to the Israeli bar are usually graduates of Israeli law schools; lawyers belonging to the Jordanian bar are commonly graduates of law schools in the West Bank or in Jordan; and *shar'i* advocates, as noted, typically lack any formal legal education. While lawyers with an Israeli license are usually Palestinian-Israelis with full Israeli citizenship, lawyers with a Jordanian license and *shar'i* advocates working in the Israeli shari'a court are usually residents of East Jerusalem.

Lawyers with an Israeli license are certainly more proficient in Israeli law than their colleagues, who have no Israeli legal training. Moreover, they can represent litigants in Israeli civil courts as well, a fact that grants them a significant advantage in the eyes of litigants. Yet, in terms of proficiency in shari'a, they have no advantage over their colleagues—the Jordanian lawyers and the *shar'i* advocates. While Israeli-licensed lawyers are allowed to work in Israeli

19 During the six years of my fieldwork in court, I have only witnessed two such events. Moreover, even these two cases have ended in a "*sulh*" (truce, conciliation) within a few days. From the councilors' point of view, staff members are too important to alienate; while from the point of view of staff members, maintaining a good, harmonious atmosphere in court is no less important. On the significant role played by clerks and court personnel in securing or preventing accessibility to justice, see Yngvesson (1988).

20 They would not hesitate, for example, to ask for a dismissal of the case if their opponent is more than ten minutes late. Likewise, they would usually object to any request for postponing a hearing when it comes from the opposing party. Nevertheless, councilors working in the shari'a court in West Jerusalem tend to combine, in a peculiar manner, a conflictual approach with an amicable, mediating posture. It is therefore difficult to categorize these councilors according to the classic types of "gladiator" and "mediator" lawyers (see Kressel, Hochberg, and Meth 1983, Gilson and Mnookin 1994).

21 Of the 38 legal councilors who are repeat players, 14 are members of the Israeli bar, 16 are members of the Jordanian bar, and eight are *shar'i* advocates.

civil courts, Jordanian lawyers are allowed, of course, to represent litigants in Jordanian and Palestinian courts. These courts are sealed for Israeli-licensed lawyers, primarily for political reasons: ever since 1967, the Jordanian Lawyers Association has refused to grant advocacy permits to any lawyer holding an Israeli license of advocacy. The excommunication of Israeli lawyers was part of the struggle against the occupation, and so was the boycott of Israeli legal institutions. Any lawyer who dared to appear in one of the civil courts that were administered by the Israeli Civil Administration of the Occupied Territories, was immediately excommunicated from the Jordanian bar (see Bisharat 1989: 58–60).[22]

As a result of this policy very few Jerusalemite lawyers became members of the Israeli bar (ibid.: 74). Nevertheless, the vacuum that was created by the refusal of Jerusalemite lawyers to work in Israeli legal institutions was quickly filled by Palestinian-Israeli lawyers, who came from towns and villages within the 1948 borders of Israel. These lawyers found good professional and economic opportunities in Jerusalem, and established their offices in the city. From the point of view of Jerusalemite lawyers (most of whom were members of the Jordanian bar), these Palestinian-Israeli lawyers encroached on their territory and thrived on their political sacrifice. As a lawyer with a Jordanian license told me:

> We suffered for years, refusing to bow before the occupation. And then what happened? Those lawyers from among the "Arabs of 48" (*'arab tamanyya wa'rba'yyin*) [Palestinians that remained in Israel after 1948] came and took our places. They earned a fortune, while we starved to death.
>
> *Q: So, what did you do?*
>
> What could we have done? We starved. Eventually we went and took the exam for *shar'i* advocacy (*murafa'a shar'iyya*),[23] and started to work here.
>
> *Q: And is it okay?*
>
> It's better than nothing.
>
> (Conversation with Y.H., January 12, 2004)

Although I have never witnessed a confrontation between Israeli-licensed and Jordanian-licensed lawyers that brought to the fore such grievances and tensions, there is no doubt that this political context molds the relationships between the two groups. On the surface, however, the competition between the legal councilors is more professional in nature. Surprisingly, several of the most successful councilors (in terms of court appearances) are neither Israeli-licensed nor Jordanian-licensed lawyers, but rather *shar'i* advocates without any formal legal training (one of them,

---

22 Notably, shari'a courts in the West Bank and in East Jerusalem were not boycotted. As described above, Israeli interventions in the operation of these courts were minimal, and since an affiliation with the Jordanian legal system has been maintained, the Jordanian bar allowed lawyers to continue working in these institutions (see Bisharat 1989: 59).

23 The lawyer refers to the exam administered by the Israeli shari'a court administration.

for example, is a former policeman; another was a schoolteacher). These people tend to charge lower fees from litigants, and they also have a good reputation as well-versed in the practicalities of the multiple legal institutions that operate in Jerusalem. They are, in fact, the busiest among the 38 legal councilors who are repeat players in court.

Marriage Registrars

Article 37 OLFR states that "the qadi who presides in the place of residence of one of the parties, or his deputy by specific authorization, must attend [the signing of] the marriage contract in person, conduct the marriage ceremony and register the marriage afterwards" (see Goitein and Ben Shemesh 1957: 295). The state's demand to be involved in a private issue such as the signing of a marriage contract is of course a characteristic of the modern era. Such requirements were made as a means of governing and controlling the population (Agmon 2004: 369), and they were promptly adopted by the modern nation-states that were established in the Middle East following the demise of the Ottoman Empire.

In contemporary Jerusalem, however, two such governing instruments operate simultaneously: marriage registrars appointed by the Jordanian shari'a court in East Jerusalem, and marriage registrars appointed by the Israeli shari'a court in West Jerusalem. As noted by Welchman (2000: 60), as early as 1970, long before the shari'a court in West Jerusalem was established, the Israeli shari'a court in Jaffa appointed two *ma'adhun*s to perform marriages in East Jerusalem. Welchman quotes an open letter, written by "an Arab son of Jerusalem," that was published in a newspaper. The letter writer complained about the burden of double recourse to Jordanian and Israeli *ma'adhun*s (ibid.: 59). The burden of double recourse is still on Muslim Jerusalemites, and yet the fact that a couple may choose to register their marriage with either a Jordanian or an Israeli appointed registrar is also enabling.[24]

Painstaking or enabling, one thing is sure: no qadi—Jordanian or Israeli—will willingly waive his prerogative to appoint marriage registrars.[25] From the qadis' point of view, the ability to appoint/dismiss *ma'adhun*s at will is very important. The position of marriage registrar is very profitable, since the *ma'adhun* charges fees for his services, independently of the court. It is therefore a desirable position, and a valuable asset in the hands of the qadi, who may appoint to the job whoever

24 The fact that both Israeli appointed and Jordanian appointed *ma'adhun*s work in Jerusalem is enabling because it makes possible, for example, to marry off minor girls (younger than 17 years of age). While Israeli law forbids such marriage, Jordanian law allows it. Thus, it is a common practice in contemporary Jerusalem to marry off minor brides (and sometimes grooms) with a Jordanian *ma'adhun*, and later on, when the couple reaches adulthood, to register their marriage in the Israeli shari'a court (see Shahar 2004: 204).

25 As determined by Article 37 OLFR, the qadi is authorized to appoint a special deputy for the purpose of performing marriage ceremonies.

he likes.[26] Thus, when the shari'a court in West Jerusalem was finally established in the late 1980s, the presiding qadi appointed several marriage registrars.

To be more specific, one of the tactics employed by qadis of the Israeli shari'a court in West Jerusalem as part of their quest for legitimacy among the local population—and surely, a very efficient tactic—was to appoint to the position of marriage registrars personages associated with the Jordanian Muslim establishment of the *waqf* administration and the *Haram al-Sharif* (see Shahar 2000: 74). These men were tempted, presumably by the material benefits of the job, and by agreeing to represent the Israeli court they lent their respectability to this court. Moreover, these same personages were also recruited at a later stage as mediators and arbitrators for the court (see discussion of these unique positions below).

In early 2006, the shari'a court in West Jerusalem employed seven marriage registrars, who were chosen by the qadis according to various political considerations, including an attempt to secure representation of different political factions in Palestinian society. Each of these *ma'adhun*s is authorized to perform marriages in a specific neighborhood of Jerusalem, and usually works parallel to a *ma'adhun* appointed by the Jordanian shari'a court. Over the years, some registrars were dismissed (usually due to reported corruption),[27] while others were appointed. Until 2003, the *ma'adhun*s had considerable presence in the court. First, they used to come to court regularly in order for the clerk to sign their marriage registries. They thus became repeat players in court, able to act as intercessors on behalf of one-shotters. Second, another reason for their coming to court was that they gradually began to serve as delegates for people who wanted their Jordanian marriage certificates (that were issued by a Jordanian *ma'adhun*) recognized by the Israeli shari'a court.

In cases, in which the marriage certificate was registered only by a Jordanian *ma'adhun*,[28] and a recognition of this document in the Israeli shari'a court was needed, the Israeli appointed *ma'adhun*s became providers of legal-bureaucratic assistance. Until 2002, the Israeli shari'a court had a very permissive policy in

26 The law—and this means both Ottoman codes, and British or Israeli legislation—does not indicate in any way, who may be appointed to the position of *ma'adhun*. This leaves the matter entirely to the qadi's discretion.

27 It appears that problems with corrupt *ma'adhun*s occurred during the Mandate period as well (see Kupferschmidt 1987: 86, n. 42).

28 Actually, the court clerk told me that the Jordanian and the Israeli marriage registrars often work in cooperation. The drill is rather simple: when a couple wishing to marry contacts either a Jordanian or an Israeli marriage registrar, this man advises them to register the marriage in both Jordanian and Israeli forms. He also explains to them that in order to save both time and money, they better perform this double registration at one and the same time. If the couple agrees, he informs his Jordanian/Israeli colleague, and the colleague comes to the office of the first registrar when the certificate is signed, in order to register the marriage in his own marriage registry. Nevertheless, sometimes, for various reasons, marrying couples register their marriages with a Jordanian *ma'adhun* alone, as discussed below.

such cases, and Jordanian marriage contracts were usually recognized without any difficulties. All a couple needed to do in order to obtain the recognition of a Jordanian marriage certificate was to deliver the original Jordanian documents together with a signed deposition, stating that the marriage is still intact, to pay a fee, and to file a petition. The Israeli shari'a court then almost automatically issued a declaratory judgment statement (*hujjat ithbat zawaj*), thereby recognizing the Jordanian marriage certificate.

Since the presence of the couple in court was not required for this procedure, many people used the services of Israeli appointed *ma'adhun*s in order to obtain the recognition of their Jordanian marriage certificates. The *ma'adhun*s took care of all the bureaucratic arrangements, and in return collected fees for their services. Some of these marriage registrars thus became significant repeat players in court, attending it almost every working day, and often remaining for long hours. Nevertheless, one influential group of people that certainly did not approve of this development was the legal councilors. Between 2002 and 2003 I heard numerous grievances concerning the marriage registrars, who are supposedly "robbing" the councilors of their livelihood by invading their field of action. It appears that these grievances did not fall on deaf ears: in September 2002 Qadi Zibdi decided that parties to *mu'amalat* cases (i.e. cases that do not involve litigation, but only formal recognition of a registered deed, a marriage or a divorce certificate), will henceforth be required to attend the court procedure in person. The formal reason for this decision was the disclosure of a couple of cases where certificates were forged, but to the minds of several of my interlocutors—legal councilors and marriage registrars alike—the move was intended to block the *ma'adhun*s from any involvement in such cases.[29]

Several months later, in February 2003, the shari'a courts administration issued special administrative regulations formally forbidding marriage registrars to file petitions on behalf of other people.[30] Thus, since 2003, marriage registrars were definitely much less present in court than before. Not only were they forbidden to act as delegates of other people in court, the shari'a courts administration also made sure that their presence in court will be limited. They are now allowed to come to court only on Thursday afternoons, in order to obtain the court clerk's signature on their marriage registries.[31] Likewise, they are forbidden to register marriages simultaneously with Jordanian *ma'adhun*s. Although less prominent in court than previously, marriage registrars are still repeat players: they attend the

29 Bearing in mind that *mu'amalat* cases constitute about half of the court's caseload (see Table 7.2), one can appreciate that this seemingly simple decision bore far-reaching consequences: hordes of new litigants stormed the court that naturally became even more densely crowded than before.

30 Administrative directive (*tawjih idari*) to marriage registrars, no date mentioned. I was given a hard copy of this document, which is not available online.

31 See administrative directive No. 12, no date mentioned. This document was uploaded in 2005 to the shari'a courts' website, but it is no longer available.

court at least once a week, and they may communicate with court personnel on behalf of other people in an informal manner (primarily by phone, but sometimes also in face-to-face conversations).

Mediators/Arbitrators

As noted by many observers of shari'a courts (e.g. Rosen 1989, Mir-Hosseini 1993: 61–2, Layish 1975: 106, 181), qadis often make extensive efforts to bring about reconciliation and compromise settlements between spouses.[32] Thus, qadis in Israeli shari'a courts make extensive use of Article 210 of the codex of Qadri Basha.[33] The article enables the qadi to refer disputing parties to semi-institutional mediation: whatever the classification of the dispute, the qadi may offer the parties to withhold legal litigation and to "give reconciliation a chance."[34] In addition, Article 130 OLFR, adopted from Maliki doctrine (see Meron 2001: 150), determines a procedure for an institutional use of arbitrators in "strife and discord" suits (*niza' wa-shiqaq*), enabling a judicial dissolution of marriages. Indeed, in present-day Israel—and apparently in other Middle Eastern countries as well (Botiveau 1993: 208–9, n. 39)—this procedure has become the prime mechanism for achieving judicial dissolution of marriages (see also Meron 2001: 150–51, Reiter 2009).

In my estimation, resort to such mechanism of arbitration/mediation occurs in more than 150 cases in the West Jerusalem shari'a court each year. This is indeed a substantial number of cases, and it reflects a growing involvement in the courts' procedures of another group of actors: "professional" arbiters, who are appointed regularly by the qadi, in order to try and reconcile disputing spouses. In this capacity, they meet the quarreling parties, together and separately, in neutral places and in their homes. They also visit the court occasionally in order to deliver their reports, to collect fees, or to take letters of appointment for new arbitration tasks.

Until 2002, this group included primarily employees of the Jordanian *waqf* administration (some of whom were also appointed by the Israeli shari'a court to

32 Goitein and Ben Shemesh (1957: 39–40) speculate that qadis' tendency to prefer conciliations and mutual agreements over issuing rulings emanates from an established tradition of avoiding the application of the holy shari'a for fear of distorting it. Whatever the reason, it is clear that a unique version of the "harmony ideology" (see Nader 1990) is also prevalent in shari'a courts.

33 On the informal code of Qadri Basha, see Chapter 3, note 21.

34 If the parties agree, two mediators are nominated, and informal mediation begins. In case reconciliation is achieved, the file is deleted from the court schedule; while if it fails, the parties return to legal litigation, to the exact stage in which it was previously halted. For files in the Israeli shari'a court in West Jerusalem, where such a procedure was employed, see e.g., ISC 104/2000, 162/2000, 110/2002, 2883/2003, 532/2004.

the position of *ma'adhuns*).[35] In this manner, these respected religious personalities (*shuyukh*) conferred their social prestige on the Israeli shari'a court. Furthermore, their incorporation into the court's daily routines definitely served to reinforce the informal elements in the court's organizational culture. Thus it helped turn the court into a popular legal institution—both in terms of its sheer popularity among Jerusalemite Muslims, and in terms of being "a people's place," rather than merely "a jurists' place."

35 Since 2002, there is a growing tendency, displayed by the current qadi, to appoint lawyers and *shar'i* advocates, instead of *waqf* employees, to the position of arbiters. It thus seems that the decision whom to appoint for this important position is also a matter of personal predilection of the presiding qadi. While Qadi Ziad 'Asliyya (presiding in court in the years 1994–2001) clearly preferred to nominate employees of the Jordanian *waqf* administration, and usually refrained from nominating legal councilors to this position, Qadi Muhammad Rashid Zibdi prefers to nominate councilors as arbiters. I have not spoken with either of them as to their considerations in appointing arbiters.

Chapter 7
Organizational Routines

Working days in the shari'a court of West Jerusalem begin early and end late. Abu Zayd, the acting chief clerk, usually arrives at court before 06:30,[1] and begins to prepare the court for the day. He takes out office accessories (e.g. court stamps, which are held in locked drawers), and piles up the dossiers for the day on the qadi's desk. Between 07:00 and 07:30 the qadi arrives from Jaffa by car (a fifty minutes ride).[2] By arriving so early to court, he told me once, he manages both to avoid the traffic jams at the entrance to Jerusalem, and to prepare himself for the day's hearings (by going over the files). By 08:00 the rest of the staff, including the Jewish armed guard, arrive at the court.[3]

Litigants and their companions are beginning to gather before the guard as early as 08:00. The court door is opened to the public at 08:30 sharp, and the crowd immediately pours in, approaching the court staff (primarily Abu Zayd and his aide, Abu 'Uday) with various questions and requests. Court hearings begin at 09:00 and end at 14:30, yet the timetable is very flexible and liable to constant changes. Thus I have often witnessed hearings that took place much later than 14:30. For example, on April 5, 1998, a hearing took place as late as 18:00 (Qadi Ziad 'Asliyya); and conversely, on July 8, 2002, a hearing took place as early as 07:45 (Qadi Muhammad Zibdi).[4]

Usually, the first hearings of the day are dedicated to cases that do not involve litigation (*mu'amalat, hujaj*)—mostly recognition of registered deeds

1 Abu Zayd lives in Shu'afat, a large Arab neighborhood in East Jerusalem, within the Israeli municipal borders of Jerusalem. It takes about half an hour to get by bus from Shu'afat to Giv'at Sha'ul—the neighborhood in West Jerusalem where the shari'a court is presently located.

2 He often drives to Jerusalem together with the assistant to the manager of the shari'a courts administration, who lives also in Jaffa.

3 I myself made an effort to arrive at the court as early as possible, for I found that morning hours, before the daily pressure begins, are the best time to hold relatively relaxed conversations with court personnel.

4 Such unusual hearings take place in special circumstances. However, the definition of "special circumstances" is rather broad and liberal. Thus, for example, the reason for holding a hearing before 08:00 on July 8, 2002 was that one of the lawyers representing a litigant in this case had another hearing that day at 09:30, in the Tel Aviv district court. Since hearings in this case were already postponed several times, the parties did not wish to postpone once more, and the qadi agreed. The protocol of the hearing was written by Abu Zayd, since none of the typists had yet arrived (see third hearing in ISC 721/2002).

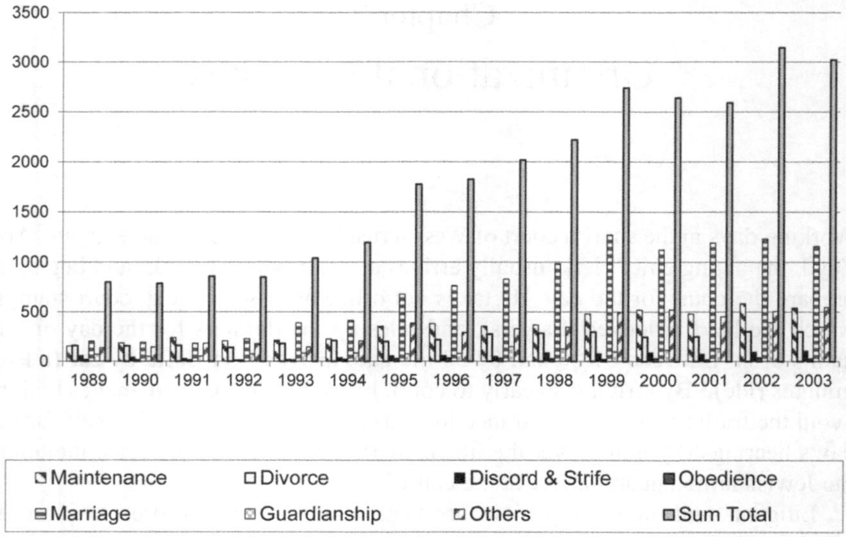

Figure 7.1 Types of Files in the Shari'a Court in West Jerusalem by Year
Source: based on data from The Shari'a Courts Administration

such as marriage and divorce certificates.[5] As mentioned above, many couples in Jerusalem register their marriages with a Jordanian *ma'adhun* rather than with an Israeli one. As a result, they later need to turn to the Israeli shari'a court and ask for the recognition of their marriage, so that other Israeli authorities will recognize it as well. Since these cases constitute mere procedural acts, which do not rob much of the court's time, the qadi tends to "clear the table" and to finish dealing with them in the morning. Later in the day, every time the court returns from its routine breaks, the first minutes are also dedicated to *mu'amalat*.

Yet, while the judicial burden on the court in these cases is perhaps negligible, the administrative burden due to the processing of such a file is not negligible at all. Since in recent years the registration of deeds has come to constitute more than 50 percent of the total number of the court files (see Figures 7.1 and 7.2), it

5 In classical *fiqh*, the term *mu'amalat* referred to those domains in Islamic law, which "preside over the relations of men among themselves." *Mu'amalat* were contrasted to *'ibadat*, which constitute "the ritual of Islamic law"—that is, the domains of law, which preside over the relations between the believers and God (see Bernard 1993). In the West Jerusalem shari'a court the term *mu'amalat* is usually evoked as a synonym to the term *hujaj*—that is, cases that do not constitute substantive lawsuits (e.g. the recognition of registered deeds or declaratory judgment).

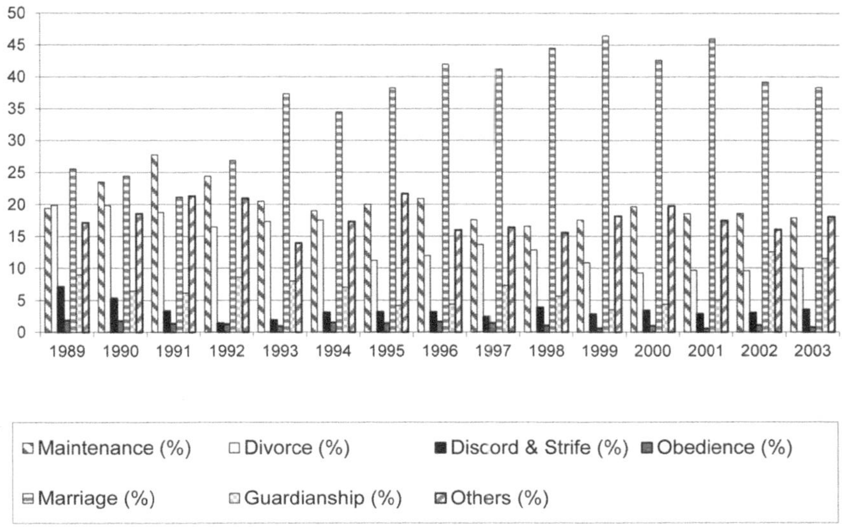

Figure 7.2 Types of Files in the Shari'a Court in West Jerusalem by Year (Percentage)

Source: based on data from The Shari'a Courts Administration

may be argued that the court's "notary function" has become more dominant in its operation, whereas its "judicial function" has decreased. In this respect, the Israeli shari'a court in West Jerusalem may be seen to resemble the shari'a courts of "classical" and medieval periods, that were presumably notary institutions to a great extent (see Tyan 1959: 78–9, Wakin 1972: 9–10).

The judicial element in court practices is manifested in substantive suits (*da'wa*, pl *da'wi*). Typical suits deal with matrimonial issues that fall under the jurisdiction of the court: divorce, dissolution of marriage, obedience, maintenance, dower, succession, custodianship and/or guardianship over minors, etc. Usually in such cases, one of the parties, aided by a lawyer or a *shar'i* advocate, files a suit against the other party.[6] Abu Zayd (the acting chief clerk) sets the date for the court session (usually three to four weeks ahead in order to allow the defending party to prepare him/herself). Then, Abu 'Uday (the assistant clerk) issues summonses for a specific day and hour, and either sends it by mail or otherwise gives it to the plaintiff or his/her delegate, for them to deliver it to the

6 As a matter of fact, approximately 70 percent of the suits are filed by women (see Shahar 2004: 196). This phenomenon is not unique, however, to the Israeli shari'a court. Several studies indicate that Muslim women tend to be more active than Muslim men in filing suits to contemporary shari'a courts (see e.g., Mir Hosseini 1993, Hirsch 1994).

defendant. On the set date, assuming that summonses were delivered and signed by the parties, and that no party was motivated to absent him/herself from the court session, the litigants probably attend court, accompanied by relatives and by their legal representatives.[7] After the qadi's desk is cleared from *mu'amalat*, hearings concerning substantive suits commence.

The spatial arrangement of the courtroom in the court's new residence is as follows: the qadi's desk is placed on a raised platform, at the far side of the room. To his left, at a separate table on the platform perpendicular to the qadi's desk, sits Salih—the court scribe (or rather, the court computer operator). On the floor in front and below the qadi's platform, two tables are positioned at right angles to the qadi's desk. These tables are two meters distance from each other, and are usually occupied by the legal representatives of the parties whose case is currently under consideration. Facing the qadi, several rows of wooden benches are arranged until the wall opposite to the qadi's podium. The litigants sit in the front row, and the spectators (relatives, friends, etc.) sit in the rear. There are also benches attached to the left wall of the hearing room. All in all, a small crowd of up to 25 people may sit on the wooden benches and observe the hearings (see Figure 7.3).

When a hearing is about to begin, the court scribe, Salih, opens a new MS-Word document (under the template which fits the case under consideration) and fills in the parties' personal details (names of litigants and legal representatives, places of residence, ID numbers, etc.).[8] His computer is connected to two monitors—one in front of him and the other facing the qadi and the parties' legal representatives. The qadi, as well as the legal councilors, can therefore observe what is being written, and ask for corrections if needed. Basically, Salih writes down a rather detailed—yet still partial—protocol: he only writes what either the qadi or the councilors dictate to him. All other altercations, which are not dictated, are simply ignored. Thus, there is a clear-cut distinction between "on the record" and "off the record" statements. Nevertheless, the qadi often reiterates and paraphrases things that were previously uttered "off the record," and thus transforms them into "on the record" statements.

The qadi may also act as translator on those rare occasions when the hearings, or parts thereof, are not held in Arabic. This may happen if one of the parties is not fluent in Arabic,[9] and in such cases it is usually Hebrew that substitutes for Arabic. Qadi Zibdi, who has perfect command of Hebrew, translates in such cases in real time from Hebrew to Arabic and vice versa. The court minutes, however, are always written in Arabic.

7 In the overwhelming majority of substantive cases, both parties hire attorneys to represent them.

8 Provided, of course, that it is the first hearing held in this case. If it is not the first hearing, the document is opened according to the file number.

9 Inter-religious marriages are not a common phenomenon, but they are not unheard of. Particularly prevalent in recent years are marriages between Muslim men and Jewish or Christian women, who recently immigrated from the former USSR republics to Israel. Such women usually need translation into Hebrew or Russian in order to follow the conversation.

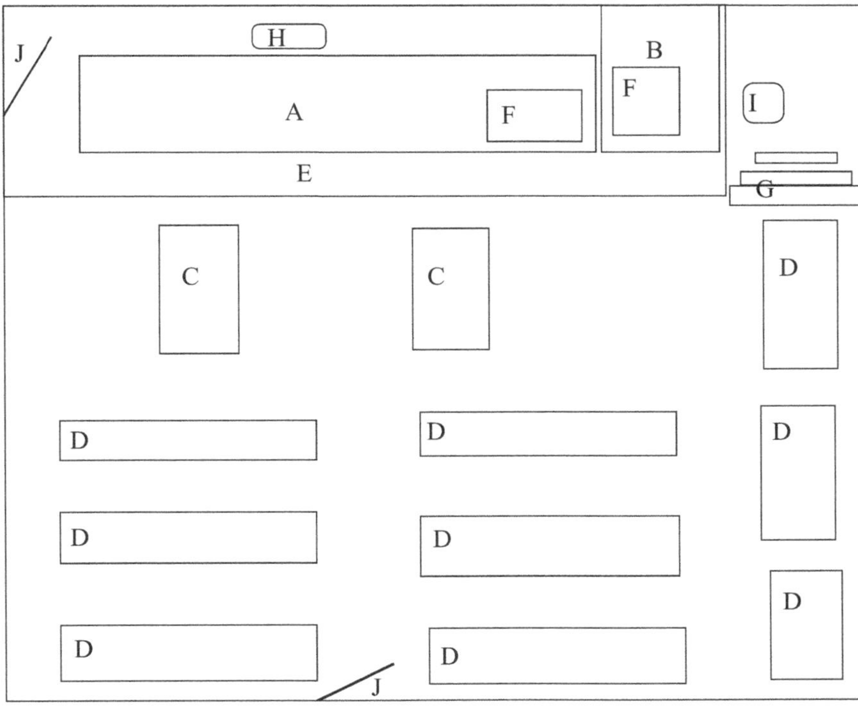

Legend: A = Qadi's desk; B = Scribe's desk; C = Lawyers' desks; D = Audience benches; E = Heightened platform; F = Monitors; G = Stairs; H = Qadi's chair; I = Scribe's chair; J = Doors

Figure 7.3 Layout of the Courtroom

Hearings commonly last no more than several minutes, with many hearings briefly postponed or delayed due to procedural reasons. Along with the qadi, the leading actors in these socio-legal episodes are undoubtedly the legal representatives of the parties. While the litigants may be marginalized and patronized in court,[10] the councilors maintain close relations with the qadi. In fact, both the qadi and the councilors take on the role of "actors-directors"—people who do not only play an active part in the scene, but are also in charge of directing it (see Griffiths 1986b, Erlanger, Chambliss, and Melli 1987). Thus, I was often notified in advance by a proud councilor, that I should observe carefully in the next hearing how he is about to "nail" his colleague, or how he is going to embarrass the qadi.[11]

10 On the process of marginalization of litigants during legal litigation, see Sarat and Felstiner (1995).

11 The close relations between the qadi and most of the councilors cannot conceal the constant power struggle that unfolds between them. Rarely, however, are there any open confrontations which go beyond cordial teasing.

As directors of the unfolding socio-legal interaction, councilors may come up with surprising scenarios. In one case, for example, in the middle of a hearing concerning a maintenance suit, the husband suddenly stood up and informed the qadi that he has something to say. He then announced, turning to his wife, that "in front of all the witnesses here, in front of the qadi of the shari'a court, I hereby declare that you, my wife, are divorced in an irrevocable divorce (*talaq bayyin*)." His announcement took everybody present by surprise. The wife continued to sit quietly, and everybody seemed puzzled. The qadi was the first to come to his senses, and addressing the husband in a low, grave voice, he asked him whether he understands that what he has just done is a felony.[12] He also asked him if someone was pressuring him to divorce his wife, and if he is in his right mind presently. The man answered that it is his right to divorce his wife, and that he is fully conscious. Hearing this answer, the qadi asked the scribe to write down that the husband had just committed an arbitrary repudiation (*talaq ta'assufi*), and that his wife is entitled to maintenance during the three months of the waiting period (*'idda*).

After the hearing had ended, I spoke with the repudiating husband in the waiting room, and asked him if he is not afraid that his (ex)wife will file a suit against him in a civil court, claiming compensatory damages. He told me that his *shar'i* advocate assured him that this will never happen.[13] I was surprised by this answer, so I asked whether he spoke with his advocate in advance about his announcement in court. His response was that it was the advocate's idea in the first place. "He told me," the husband said, "that if I want a divorce, why wait? Why do I need all this headache? It is my *shar'i* right to divorce my wife, according to Islam and God, and so I did."[14] We can see, therefore, that even when a litigant performs a seemingly spontaneous and unexpected move in court, this move may very well be meticulously planned and orchestrated by the councilor.[15]

12 The Israeli legislature sought to protect Muslim wives from arbitrary, unilateral divorces. Thus, Article 8 of the Women's Equal Rights Law (5711–1951), and later Article 181 of the Penal Law (5737–1977), state that: "Where the husband dissolves the marriage against the will of the wife, and there is, at the time of the dissolution, no final judgment of the [civil] court or of the competent religious court making the dissolution binding on the wife, the husband shall be liable to imprisonment for five years."

13 It appears that this might have been rather imprudent advice, since in the recent years several Muslim wives have won considerable sums of money as compensation from their husbands, who were found guilty—by civil courts—in committing unilateral divorces. Compensations were ruled according to Article 63 of the Civil Wrongs Ordinance (new version), which facilitated the filing of such suits (see Meron 2001: 212–13, and the court judgments mentioned in note 12 there).

14 The file number and date of this hearing will not be mentioned here for obvious reasons.

15 This case also demonstrates the "normative" or value legal pluralism (Bowen 2003) characterizing the legal interaction in the Israeli shari'a court in West Jerusalem: whereas the husband's move is perfectly legitimate within the framework of Islamic law, it constitutes a felony within the framework of Israeli legislation.

In the vast majority of hearings, however, such unexpected events do not occur. Most hearings proceed in a rather technical and expected trajectory, according to the category of lawsuit under consideration. Generally speaking, the first hearing characteristically begins with a short speech by the plaintiff's legal representative, who presents his/her client's claims. Afterwards, the defendant's legal representative typically rejects these claims, and the qadi lays the burden of proof on the plaintiff. A date for another hearing is then agreed upon (usually three to four weeks ahead), and everybody (the qadi, the legal representatives, and the parties) sign the protocol. By this, the hearing ends, and the parties with their companions leave the room.

The next hearing begins where the previous one ended: the plaintiff has to present his/her evidence. The defendant's legal representative probably tries to undermine the significance and the validity of this evidence. However, if the defendant does not confine him/herself to a denial of the plaintiff's claims, and sets an alternative claim, than he/she might also be asked to substantiate his/her claims by evidence. Most substantive cases unfold in this manner for several hearings and several months. Eventually, the qadi gathers enough information to come to a decision, and he therefore terminates the hearings, informing the parties and their representatives that a ruling will be issued according to the law (that is, within ten days).

The ruling usually contains a summary of the claims raised by the parties, and a summary of the procedural actions taken by the court in dealing with this case. These summaries are usually written down by Salih, based on the court protocol. The qadi then goes over the draft prepared by Salih, adds corrections and references (in handwriting), and formulates his decision. This corrected draft is then handed to Siham, who is in charge of typing the court rulings. When it is ready, the qadi signs three original copies—two of which are sent by mail, or delivered by hand, to the parties. One copy is kept in the file dossier and archived for three years in the court's small archive. Afterwards, it is transferred to the central archive of the Israeli shari'a courts near Petah-Tiqva (a city in central Israel).

All in all it may be argued that hearings in the Israeli shari'a court in West Jerusalem constitute a peculiar combination of highly formalistic, procedural altercations (between the legal representatives of the parties), and tense, emotionally loaded verbal disputes between the litigants. The qadi manipulates the social interaction between these two poles—sometimes letting the advocates altercate for long minutes, and sometimes addressing the parties above the heads of their representatives—seeking to understand the "real reasons" for the dispute, which are supposedly hiding behind the legal phrases. Often the qadi offers the parties to halt the legal confrontation, and to try and resolve the dispute by way of mediation.[16] In other times, he may invite the parties to speak with him tête-à-tête in his chambers, without their representatives and relatives. His intention in such cases is to find out personally whether there is a chance for reconciliation between the disputing parties.

16 According to Article 210 of Qadri Basha's codex. The mediators may come from the court's "pool" of mediators, described above.

Chapter 8

Doing Ethnography in the Shari'a Court in West Jerusalem: Some Reflexive Notes

Throughout my fieldwork, gaining access to the research sites was a challenging task. As mentioned, I initially intended to conduct fieldwork in the Jordanian shari'a court in East Jerusalem. Although Israeli scholars were allowed in the past to study the archive of the East Jerusalem shari'a court,[1] I discovered that getting permission to conduct participant observations is much more difficult. I made numerous attempts to contact the court's "gatekeepers" (the *qadi al-quda*, and the chief scribe), but I was rejected again and again by dodging and evasion. Even appeals made on my behalf by Prof. Layish and Dr Reiter of the Hebrew University did not yield results.[2] I therefore settled, eventually, for the Israeli

1 The first Israeli scholar who was granted permission to study *sijillat* in the archive of the East Jerusalem shari'a court was historian Amnon Cohen of the Hebrew University (see Cohen 1984). Following Professor Cohen, several other scholars—namely, Haim Gerber, Dror Ze'evi, Amy Singer, and Itzhak Reiter—were also permitted to conduct research in this archive (see Gerber 1985, Singer 1994, Ze'evi 1996, Reiter 1997b).

2 I can think of two main reasons for Jordanian court officials' reluctance to grant me access to the court. First, there is the obvious sensitivity of letting a Jewish Israeli student enter the court on a regular basis. Jordanian court functionaries have refused repeatedly to recognize the legitimacy of Israeli rule in East Jerusalem, and under these circumstances, granting me access would have been problematic. Second, there was also a problem of bad timing. When I made my request for access, the Jordanian courts system had been undergoing some radical changes. The Palestinian National Authority (PNA) established its own legal system, including a Palestinian shari'a court system (see Brown 2003: 22–4). Consequently, the Jordanian shari'a court of appeal in East Jerusalem lost its authority as the *shar'i* appellate court of the West Bank. The Jordanian courts remained, therefore, in a rather obscure position—with questionable and contested authority (and this time by both Israel and the PNA), limited to East Jerusalem. Furthermore, power struggles between Israel and the PNA over real and/or symbolic bastions in the city of Jerusalem did not skip the Muslim religious establishment of the *waqf* administration and the shari'a courts. Since 1948 this establishment was controlled by the Hashemite Kingdom of Jordan, but since the late 1990s, it was being seriously challenged by the PNA (see Amirav 2003: 29–34). The PNA managed, for example, to replace the deceased Mufti of Jerusalem, who had been appointed by Jordan, with a Palestinian appointee (Klein 2001: 128). Moreover, as reported in an Israeli newspaper, guards belonging to one of the PNA's security forces were posted in the Jordanian shari'a court (Sharga'i 1999). All in all, the Jordanian courts in East Jerusalem were at the time of this research in a state of political and institutional uncertainty, and it was therefore rather bad timing for uninvited requests for access.

shari'a court in West Jerusalem. In retrospect, however, this proved to be for the best, since it appears that the Israeli court is currently of much more importance in the lives of Jerusalemite Palestinians than the Jordanian court.

And yet, I did not know this at the time. In January 1998 I set out to conduct my first participant observation in the West Jerusalem shari'a court. Over the next two years I visited the court two or three days a week and tried to stay there throughout the opening hours. I observed hearings, followed administrative routines, and spoke with litigants, legal councilors, and court personnel. I carried my field diary with me, and meticulously recorded occurrences that I witnessed and conversations that I engaged in. My intention was to carry out a full-fledged legal ethnography, in the tradition of legal ethnographers such as Sally Falk Moore (1978), Laura Nader (1990, 2002), and Sally Merry (1990). In line with this tradition, I planned to make excursions out of the court and conduct a "community ethnography" (Vidich and Lyman 2003: 80) by tracing "extended case studies" and by performing "situational analysis" (see Gluckman 1961, Burawoy 1998). During the first two years of fieldwork, I thus tried to conduct a "multi-sited research" (Marcus 1995, Goodale 2002) and to extend my observations to other sites and situations related to the shari'a court. For example, I joined the court courier in his mail-delivery journeys; I visited several attorneys—members of the court's "repeat players" group—in their offices in town; and I accompanied the court clerk on "*shar'i* inspections" (*kashf shar'i*) of marital homes.[3]

In February 2000 I discontinued my fieldwork in the court and turned to writing my MA thesis. I resumed fieldwork one year later, in April 2001, this time as a PhD student at Ben Gurion University. My return to the court was accompanied, however, by some troubling question marks: on October 1, 2000—six months before I resumed my fieldwork—the second intifada (or *al-Aqsa Intifada*, as it is dubbed by Palestinians) erupted. This Palestinian uprising began following a heavily guarded visit of Ariel Sharon to the Temple Mount in Jerusalem, and it soon deteriorated into severe violence. Both sides—Israelis and Palestinians—resorted to violent actions, unprecedented even in the context of the continuous Israeli–Palestinian conflict (see Hammami and Tamari 2001). Moreover, while Jerusalem was generally excluded from the violent confrontations during the first intifada (1987–93), violence ran wild in the city during the first months of the second intifada (see Sarsar 2000). Consequently, hostility, fears, and suspicion between the Jewish and the Palestinian communities in the city grew deeper, and

3 According to the OLFR (Article 70), the husband must accommodate his wife in a "*shar'i* house" (*maskan shar'i*)—a house that contains all the necessary household accessories. Since the issue of the marital home's compliance to Islamic law is raised regularly in court hearings (and in particular in maintenance suits and obedience suits), the common procedure in such cases is to appoint the court clerk to perform an inspection of the house (*kashf shar'i*). Some forty such inspections are conducted each year (after the court's working hours), and I accompanied the court clerk on eight of them (see Shahar 2000: 109–11).

the invisible walls separating the communities became almost insurmountable. Jews, in particular, fearing abductions and assassinations, abstained almost completely from visiting the Eastern, Arab parts of Jerusalem.

Returning to the court after more than one year of absence, I was thus rather apprehensive about the impact of the grave developments at the national level on my relations with my old acquaintances in the court (that I describe in more detail below). I was grateful to be greeted with the same hospitality and friendliness as before. However, when I set out to resume my travels outside the court, I found that the circumstances had changed radically. I was warned by one of the legal councilors that for my own safety, I better minimize my visits to Palestinian neighborhoods. Even Abu Zayd (then aide to the chief clerk) advised me not to accompany him any more on his *kashf* inspections. He noted that given the grave state of affairs, he can no longer guarantee my personal safety, and I should therefore avoid traveling with him.

Under these circumstances, I found myself limiting my fieldwork to the court itself. In fact, except for several personal visits to the homes of Abu Zayd and Abu 'Uday, my fieldwork during the last four years (2001–04) never took me beyond the court's walls. Even when I realized the profound effects of legal pluralism and of other courts on the operation of the shari'a court I was studying, I could not expand my fieldwork beyond that particular site. Surely, in a study that traces the interrelations between four legal institutions, it makes more sense to conduct a multi-sited research and to observe hearings in all four institutions. Nevertheless, I was still unable to gain access to the Jordanian and the Palestinian courts in East Jerusalem, and as I was soon to find out, judges and bureaucrats in the Israeli family courts were also not very enthusiastic about letting an anthropologist inside their courtrooms.[4] Facing these difficulties, I continued my "one-sited" fieldwork at the Israeli shari'a court. Yet, while I was obviously studying this "focal organization," my perspective gradually became more relational in nature. In other words, I became more interested in the complex relations that the Israeli shari'a court maintains with other organizations in its environment.

Since my fieldwork was now restricted to the site of the Israeli shari'a court, I spent countless hours in this location. Between April 2001 and July 2004 I visited the court recurrently, although not very regularly: during university vacations (in the summers and between semesters) I was present in the court almost every day, while during the academic year my visits were restricted to one or two days a week. There were also some periods of detachment from the court, each of which lasted several weeks, but I remained in contact with the court's staff and with several *shar'i* advocates throughout the entire period.

4 In April 2002 I sent letters to the president of the family courts in Jerusalem and to the director of the court administration, asking for permission to conduct participant observations in hearings concerning Muslim litigants. Although I emphasized that my entrance would be conditional on the parties' consent, both of them answered that they have no authority to grant such permission.

Attending this social arena for such a long time and for so many days, I became a familiar figure for the regular visitors in the court—their "own" anthropologist. Yet, being an Israeli Jew, my sojourn in the court was anything but unproblematic. Generally speaking, Palestinians living in East Jerusalem and the West Bank are accustomed to humiliating and degrading interactions with Israeli officials. Furthermore, they tend to view the presence of Israelis in Palestinian public arenas as a manifestation of control and supervision. It is no wonder, therefore, that—recognizing me immediately as an Israeli Jew—people's reactions to my awkward presence in the court (carrying a notebook and filling it with mysterious notes) were suspicion, antagonism, and resentment.

Occasionally, especially during my first months in the field, I was approached by litigants who inquired (either in Arabic or in Hebrew) who I am and what I am doing there. I usually responded by saying that I am a student in the Department of Islamic and Middle Eastern Studies, and that I am interested in seeing how Islamic law is actually practiced. Hearing this answer, they sometimes initiated a political debate. In such cases, I was soon encircled by several people, who would usually pronounce harsh condemnations of Israeli policy in the occupied territories.[5] As I see it now, such occurrences were meant, first and foremost, to test me and to test the boundaries of the social situation: they needed to know that the shari'a court was still a Muslim-Palestinian arena.[6]

In response to such "provocations," I often tended to agree with my interlocutors and to express my own dissatisfaction with Israeli occupation measures. Such responses certainly caught most people by surprise, and soon my pro-Palestinian views became common knowledge among the "repeat players" in the court.[7] In fact, I believe that one of the things that facilitated my initial acceptance by these people was the fact that in one of my first visits to the court, I was recognized by two legal councilors who had seen me in a joint Palestinian–Israeli demonstration that was held several weeks earlier, protesting against the demolition of houses in East Jerusalem.

---

5 Such events were not pleasant, to say the least, not only because of the political views that my interlocutors expressed, but also because of the need to converse at once with more than one person. Since my proficiency in Arabic was far from being fully developed at the time, I can attest that this was not a joyful experience.

6 Perhaps such tests were especially needed because of the hybrid, liminal, ambiguous nature of the Israeli shari'a court, which makes it particularly difficult to determine the symbolic location of this court on Israeli or Palestinian "grounds."

7 Never was this phenomenon more salient, however, than after I returned from a month of imprisonment in a military prison for refusing to serve in the occupied territories (I was imprisoned during November 2003). Abu Zayd greeted me with hugs and kisses, took me by the hand, and led me from one person to another—telling them that I have just returned from prison. We even entered the adjacent shari'a court of appeal and the administration of the shari'a courts, so that I could be proudly presented before the employees there.

"Tactical leftism"—to paraphrase Lila Abu Lughod's "tactical humanism" (Abu Lughod 1991: 138)—definitely served, therefore, to legitimize my presence in court.[8] In addition, on several occasions I attempted to help people who were having trouble with the Israeli authorities. Thus, for example, I tried to help some litigants who sought to obtain the approval of the Ministry of the Interior for family unification.[9] I wrote letters, made some phone calls, and even enlisted to this task some acquaintances of mine, as well as a relative who had been in the past of some political stature. These attempts proved completely futile, but there is reason to assume that they nevertheless made the impression that I am an Israeli Jew who identifies with the Palestinian cause.[10]

And yet, even though I became a "member of the court family"—as Abu 'Uday once told me—some tensions between me as a Jew, member of the dominant community, and court users still surfaced from time to time. First of all, although I was familiar to all the "repeat players" in the court, "one-shotters" usually did not know me. Hence, it was not a rare occasion that a litigant questioned my presence in the court, or even pronounced his/her objection to my being there. In such cases my "sponsors" in the court—the qadi, the staff, and some councilors with whom I maintained friendly relations—usually spoke in my favor and explained that I am a student who conducts research in the court. On most occasions such explanations were sufficient and litigants agreed to my presence in their hearings.[11]

8 Surely, I was not untrue to myself when I expressed leftist views, but in retrospect I can admit that sometimes—especially during the initial period of my fieldwork—it was more convenient to agree with my interlocutors than to engage in a political argument with them. On tactical uses of humanism in anthropological research, see also Knauft (1994).

9 Family unifications are a sour issue in the tense relations between the State of Israel and its Arab-Palestinian citizens. Article 7 of the Nationality Law (5712–1952) determines that "the spouse of a person who is an Israeli national or who has applied for Israeli nationality […] may obtain Israeli nationality by naturalization … ." However, haunted by the "demographic demon," Israeli authorities adopted in the 1990s a policy that aims to prevent the naturalization of Palestinian residents of the West Bank and the Gaza Strip who are married to Israeli citizens (or to permanent residents). The Ministry of Interior Affairs has refused many times, and for various reasons, to permit "family unifications" and to grant Palestinian non-Israeli spouses with anything more than temporary visas to stay in Israel. In July 2003 the Knesset passed a law determining that new appeals by Israeli citizens asking for the nationalization of their spouses from the West Bank or the Gaza Strip will not be accepted. A petition challenging the constitutionality of this law was rejected by the High Court of Justice in May 2006 (HCJ 7052/03). For a critical discussion of this law and of the High Court of Justice decision, see Adalah: The Legal Center for Arab Minority Rights in Israel, http://adalah.org/eng/Articles/1556/Family-Unification [accessed: 10/11/2014].

10 Since my efforts to intervene on behalf of Palestinians in the hostile Israeli bureaucratic maze were a complete failure, I abandoned such attempts altogether. In this sense, my ethnography was perhaps less "engaged" than it may or should have been (on "engaged anthropology," see Bornstein 2001, Clarke 2010).

11 In principle, hearings dealing with matters of personal status are supposed to be held in chambers. But in effect, hearings are usually open to the public, and only when the

Second, every now and then a particular occurrence would reactivate the cultural and political differences between me and other court attendees. Thus, for example, during the first weeks of the Second Gulf War, I had numerous arguments with various people concerning fantastic rumors that were widespread and well-accepted among the Palestinian public. My interlocutors all shared the firm belief that Saddam Hussein and his forces had inflicted terrible losses upon the Americans, and that this crucial information was being concealed from the public eye. I was in "splendid isolation" in my refusal to believe such rumors—a position that emphasized the cultural and political differences between me and my interlocutors.

Such feelings of cultural and political alienation have been quite common during my fieldwork. To give just one more example: in Israel it is customary to sound sirens for a minute or two on every official commemoration day (there are two such days: the Holocaust Day and the Remembrance Day for Fallen Soldiers). As a token of respect for the dead, people are expected to stand in silence during these siren sounds. During the Holocaust Day of 1999 I happened to be present in the court. The place was particularly crowded with visitors that day, and there was no sign of awareness by the staff or the litigants as to the impending event. I knew that there would be a siren sound at 11:00, and I began to feel discomfort about it. I was preoccupied with the question: what will the qadi and the other people sitting in the courtroom do when the siren sounds? Will they stand up, as Israeli Jews do? Or perhaps they will simply ignore the siren and continue with their business, despite the fact that this is a court of the Israeli state? More important, is it possible that my presence in the court—which has only recently become more natural and self-evident—will influence their behavior? I was increasingly stressed by this awkward situation, and eventually I decided to leave the court early that day, half an hour before the siren sound. I have never asked my friends in the court what they do on such occasions, and I strictly avoided the court, ever since this experience, on commemoration days of all kinds.

Another event that vividly brought to my awareness the different positions occupied by myself and by my Palestinian interlocutors, within the power structure of present-day Jerusalem, involved a Palestinian social worker—an employee of the Jerusalem municipality—whom I met in court several times. I set up a meeting with this man, who was in charge of social services in one of the neighborhoods of East Jerusalem. We agreed to meet near the gate of the Israeli Ministry of Justice in East Jerusalem, and at the scheduled time I arrived there and sat on the staircase at the entrance to the building. Since I had waited for him for more than 15 minutes, I called his cellular phone and was surprised to learn that he, too, was already

---

parties request a closed hearing is the door shut. Since my presence in the court was secured and sponsored by powerful figures (the qadi, the chief clerk, and prominent councilors), I was usually allowed to stay inside even in closed hearings. Admittedly, it was, perhaps, difficult for litigants to defy the qadi and to ask me to leave the courtroom. Nevertheless, litigants did ask me to leave two or three times.

waiting for me for 15 minutes. At first I thought that there was some confusion with regard to the meeting place, but we soon discovered that we were actually standing 20 meters from each other: I felt comfortable and secure to stand near the Ministry's entrance, next to the armed Jewish guard, while he, a Palestinian (again, a senior employee of the Jerusalem municipality and a graduate of the Hebrew University), preferred to wait near a side gate, away from the armed Jewish guard who might suspect him.

Beyond such reflexive moments of strong experiences of difference, my position and my role in the court underwent some significant changes during the six years of fieldwork. Over this time period, the balance between the "observation function" and the "participation function" (the two functions which constitute together the oxymoronic position of anthropologists with regard to their subjects of study) has shifted and fluctuated. As time elapsed, I gradually became a more active participant in the court's routines, and perhaps less of an external observer. Thus, during some periods I was in charge of filling in habeas corpus demands (in Hebrew) for prisoners in Israeli prisons; during other periods, I was helping litigants who were not represented by councilors in filing petitions (*istid'a't* or *hujaj*): I helped them to complete the details, I explained to them the procedure; and I even accompanied them to the post office to pay court fees (see Appendix no. 2 for an istid'a' form). Sometimes I answered the secretariat phone, although this was more of a practical joke by Abu Zayd, who enjoyed listening—by turning the phone loudspeaker on—to the bafflement of people who suddenly heard "stammering Jewish-Arabic" (as Abu Zayd referred to my linguistic skills) on the other side of the line.

Undoubtedly, the natural, cordial, unproblematic manner in which the court staff accepted my presence in their workplace made my fieldwork not only possible (to begin with), but also pleasant. Presumably, the court staff—and in particular the senior staff of the shari'a court system (Qadi Natur, the manager of the shari'a courts administration, and the presiding qadis in the shari'a court in West Jerusalem)—had an interest in letting me conduct fieldwork in the court. They were probably striving to present the shari'a court system as an open, well-administered, progressive legal institution—and granting an anthropologist free access to observe court hearings served that purpose very well. Yet, the generosity and warm-heartedness with which I was accepted in the court go far beyond such PR interest. I consider myself lucky, therefore, to have met these generous people.

My status in the court gave me almost complete access to all of the court's activities. I was allowed free entrance to the secretariat, to the small court archive, to the kitchen and to the typists' room. I had all the court files (*milaffat*) at my disposal, and as noted above, I was usually allowed to be present in closed hearings, which took place either in the courtroom or in the qadi's chambers. I was often invited by Qadi Zibdi to sit with him in his chambers while he tried to conciliate disputing spouses. I even had the good fortune of observing clients' consultations with their legal councilors, when some of my lawyer friends allowed me to witness these conversations. And yet, my fieldwork also suffered from several drawbacks: I could not tape-record court hearings[12]; and, as described above, I could certainly not extend my research beyond the court, and therefore could not observe the operation of other dispute-resolution mechanisms employed in many of the disputes. Especially frustrating was the fact that I could not observe informal (or semi-formal) interventions in disputes, which as a rule occur outside the court.

All in all, my presence and my status in the court may be described as "ambiguous:" I became an acceptable "repeat player," who takes an active part in court routines, but I also remained an outsider, whose presence in the court might jeopardize the institution; I enjoyed the privileges of being a member of the dominant Jewish community, but my ability to conduct "community ethnography" was limited for the exact same reason; I was totally dependent on the goodwill of my patrons in the court, but I also maintained a patronizing position towards most of the people that I met there[13]; I was recognized and regarded, most of the time, as a sympathizer of the Palestinian cause, but occasionally cultural and political differences surfaced and created tensions between other court-users and myself.

Ethnographic fieldwork, almost by definition, is characterized by ambiguity, ambivalence, and inherent tensions. Yet each and every research site, each and every researcher, produces a different set of ambivalences, different kinds of research problems, and different types of research solutions. The unique set of ambiguities and tensions presented here, which accompanied my fieldwork in the Israeli shari'a court in West Jerusalem, framed this research and affected the form it eventually assumed.

12 This was explicitly forbidden by Qadi Natur as early as our first meeting, in January 1998.

13 For example, trying to intervene in favor of a litigant who faces difficulties in the National Insurance Institution can certainly be perceived as a patronizing act. Likewise, accompanying Abu Zayd to his bank branch and translating/mediating between him and the bank teller is also a patronizing act.

PART III
The West Jerusalem Shari‘a Court and the Family Court

Chapter 9
Breaking Shari'a Courts' Monopoly in Jurisdiction

My long years of acquaintance and involvement with the shari'a court in West Jerusalem were marked with some significant shifts in focus. During my first years in court (1998–2000), I was preoccupied with the political context within which the court operates (see Shahar 2000). Later on, while I was writing my PhD proposal and during the first year of PhD research (2001–02), I shifted my focus to the processes of text production in court, and to the "dialectics of entextualization and contextualization" that take place in court procedures (see Shahar 2001).[1] Only in my final years of field research was I drawn to focus upon organizational aspects of the court's operation, and in particular, on its interrelations with other courts that operate parallel to it in Jerusalem. This issue came to constitute the major theme in my research, and the rest of the chapters in this book all dwell upon it.

Undoubtedly, the conspicuous legal-pluralist environment in Jerusalem has to do with its unique political situation, and with the fact that despite the Israeli annexation of the Eastern part and the unification of the city, it is still very much contested. Indeed, it is precisely this political contestation that brought about a situation in which three different shari'a courts (Israeli, Jordanian, and Palestinian) operate parallel to each other in the city. The interrelations between the Israeli shari'a court and the Jordanian and Palestinian shari'a courts are therefore particularly interesting and meaningful.

Yet, I begin the systematic review of the interrelations between the shari'a court in West Jerusalem and other courts operating parallel to it in the city with a more trivial and seemingly less unique counterpart: the Israeli family court. The shari'a court in West Jerusalem and the family court in the city are both tribunals of the Israeli state: both are bound by Knesset legislation and by rulings of the High Court of Justice, and both are part and parcel of the Israeli legal system. The subjection of the Muslim population in Jerusalem, in certain matters of personal status, to both tribunals is therefore a clear case of "state legal pluralism" (Woodman 1998, 1999). Nevertheless, despite the fact that these two tribunals operate under the aegis of one overarching system, they are also radically different in almost every respect: they employ different bodies of law and different rules of procedure; they speak different languages (Arabic is spoken in the shari'a court,

1 The analysis of text production in terms of "entextualization and contextualization" is based on the work of Bauman and Briggs (1990).

Hebrew in the family court); and they are characterized by different legal and organizational cultures.

According to John Griffiths (1986a), this type of legal pluralism, which occurs within the framework of the state legal system, should be regarded as "weak" legal pluralism—that is, legal pluralism that bears no social significance. In his view, real, "empirical," "strong" legal pluralism cannot exist within the framework of the state legal system, for after the state grants recognition to a body of law, this law may no longer be considered a separate legal system. Thus, if scholars refer to such a situation in terms of legal pluralism, their point of view is normative or doctrinal (hence "juristic"), but not empirical or "social-scientific." And yet, contrary to Griffiths's view—that has become prevalent among scholars of legal pluralism—I contend that this type of "state legal pluralism" is in fact very significant and very consequential (see Shahar 2008a). I argue that if we replace Griffiths's state-centered perspective with an agent-centered perspective, and focus our attention on the litigants' point of view, it becomes clear that appealing to one tribunal rather than the other may have crucial implications even though both tribunals belong to the same state apparatus. State legal pluralism cannot be perceived, therefore, as "weak" or socially insignificant.

As I will try to show, the choice whether to appeal to the shari'a court or to the family court in certain matters (e.g. maintenance suits) is indeed a significant choice: it is consequential not only with regard to the legal outcomes of the suit, but also with regard to the very future of the family unit (see Chapter 11). No wonder, therefore, that Muslim litigants in Jerusalem are engaged in active "forum shopping," striving to have their dispute adjudicated in a particular court, where they feel they will attain the most favorable ruling.[2] The staff members of the Israeli shari'a court in West Jerusalem are not indifferent to the implicit (and sometimes explicit) competition posed by the family court, and they respond to this competition in various manners (see Chapter 10).

The following three chapters therefore examine the far-reaching consequences—from the litigants' point of view, as well as from the institutional point of view—of the parallel operation of the shari'a court and the family court. Since the relations between these two court systems and their respective jurisdictions have changed over the years, the current chapter traces the historical development of these relations. The most significant landmark in the history of the relations between the two systems was an amendment to the Family Courts Law (5755–1995) that was passed by the Knesset in November 2001. The amendment accorded family courts with jurisdiction in several matters pertaining to the personal status of Muslims that were previously under the exclusive jurisdiction of shari'a courts. The direct result of this legislation was that Muslim litigants gained greater freedom of choice between the shari'a and the civil courts, and that legal pluralism became even more pronounced. The chapter opens, therefore, with a discussion of the state of legal pluralism that had prevailed before the amendment

2 For a simple definition of legal forum shopping, see Garner (2001: 590).

of 2001. Afterward, the second section reviews the conflictual process that led to the amendment, focusing on the fierce struggle between various groups and interests that pushed for and against the legislation.

Shari'a Courts in the Israeli Legal System until 2001

As mentioned, my conceptualization of "weak" and "strong" legal pluralism diverges from Griffiths's (1986a) conceptualization. Griffiths's criterion for distinguishing "strong" from "weak" legal pluralism is the recognition or non-recognition of the state: according to his terminology, "weak" legal pluralism occurs when the legal systems under consideration are recognized by the (same) state, while "strong" legal pluralism occurs between the state legal system and other systems external to it. My own suggestion, following Vanderlinden (1989, 1993), is to distinguish between these two types of legal pluralism on the basis of the actors'—or in this case, the litigants'—point of view. "Strong" legal pluralism, according to my approach, exists when an active individual, an agent, may choose to appeal—in a particular situation and for particular purposes—to more than one tribunal of law. In contrast, when a legal system designates specific tribunals (or "legal mechanisms," to use Vanderlinden's term) to specific categories of population (e.g. Muslims, Chagas, Navahos, soldiers, tradesmen, minors, etc.), and any one individual may only appeal to one of the tribunals, then this is a case of "weak" legal pluralism.

Bearing this conceptualization in mind, we may claim that from the point of view of Muslim litigants in Israel, legal pluralism was relatively weak until 2001. As described in Chapter 3, due to historical contingencies, shari'a courts in Israel maintained broader jurisdiction than any other religious courts. In fact, unlike the rabbinical, the ecclesiastical, and the Druze courts, the shari'a courts were awarded exclusive jurisdiction in almost all personal status matters of Muslims. As a result, unlike their Jewish or Druze counterparts, Muslim women were unable to file maintenance suits in civil courts, for example. Furthermore, while the Israeli legislator granted the civil courts jurisdiction in matters of child custody and child support among Jews, Druze, and all Christian denominations, for Muslims the exclusive jurisdiction of the shari'a courts in these matters was retained.

Thus, from Muslim litigants' point of view, legal pluralism was relatively weak until 2001. Still, civil and penal legislation passed by the Knesset resulted in the strengthening of legal pluralism for Muslims as well. Several laws (e.g. the Age of Marriage Law, the Succession Law) granted the civil courts jurisdiction in some matters of personal status of Muslims (see Chapter 3). Moreover, the strategy adopted by the Israeli legislator, of criminalizing certain "traditional" mores sanctioned by Islamic law (such as polygamy, minor marriage, unilateral repudiation of a wife), also enhanced legal pluralism.

Thus, for example, the ban on unilateral repudiation, i.e. without the wife's consent, (Article 8(b) Women's Equal Rights Law, 5711–1951) created a situation in which a matrimonial dispute between Muslim spouses could be dealt with in three separate legal procedures: a *shar'i* procedure, a civil one, and a penal procedure (each in a separate court). Even if these parallel procedures are not held simultaneously, the mere option of resorting to more than one court of law has implications for both the management of the dispute and the legal litigation in each of these courts (Shahar 2004). In addition, since matrimonial disputes often constitute complex, multi-dimensional conflicts, spouses may resort to different legal mechanisms or different legal tactics in their struggle with the opponent party.

This is illustrated by a case I witnessed back in 1998, where an obedience suit (*ta'a*) was filed by a wealthy husband against his wife, who allegedly left the marital home without a proper *shar'i* justification (on *ta'a* suits, see Chapter 5, note 7). The husband therefore demanded the immediate return of his wife to the marital home. During the hearings in the shari'a court it became clear, however, that the *ta'a* suit was filed in response to a civil suit for the "division of property between spouses," filed by the wife in the family court (on the establishment of family courts see below). Although the procedures for handling these parallel suits were very different, and although the legal confrontation between the spouses was conceptualized in a totally different manner in the two tribunals, the matrimonial dispute behind these two suits was one: the wife, who had been separated from her husband for more than two years, was afraid—as I was later told by her lawyer—that the sewing workshop that her husband owned was about to go into liquidation. Seeking a way to ensure her share in this family asset, she filed a suit for the division of property between spouses in the family court (for a detailed description of this case, see Shahar 2000: 68–71).[3]

Eventually, this dispute was apparently resolved outside the courts that dealt with it,[4] but it clearly demonstrates litigants' ability to manipulate the legal system for their advantage. It appears that although Muslim women were unable to file maintenance suits in civil courts until 2001, they could circumvent this restriction by filing a civil suit for the division of property. Conversely, husbands who felt that the litigation in the family courts would work against them, could always file an obedience suit in the shari'a court, striving—if not to compel their wives

3 I could not follow the hearings in this case closely, in 1998. Nevertheless, since it was an interesting case, I returned to the file several years later. It appears that the hearings were postponed several times, and that eventually the case was deleted from the court schedule, after the parties did not return for more than six months. I asked the wife's lawyer—a prominent "repeat player" in the shari'a court—why this suit was abandoned by the husband. He told me that the wife's family—some of them high ranking officers in one of the Palestinian Authority's security apparatuses—has exerted some not-very-delicate pressure on the husband, who consequently agreed to pay the wife 100,000 NIS. Following that, all the cases were dropped in all the tribunals (conversation with M.R., June 16, 2002; file number not disclosed).

4 It is noteworthy that the husband, who was not satisfied with the obedience suit he filed in the Israeli shari'a court, has also filed a similar suit in the Jordanian shari'a court (see Shahar 2000: 70).

to return to the marital home—at least to complicate things and to forestall the legal proceedings.

We may conclude, therefore, that although prior to 2001 the shari'a and the civil courts did not have parallel jurisdiction in most matters of personal status (except for succession), the same matrimonial dispute could yield several suits, which were adjudicated simultaneously in both these courts (and in other courts as well).[5] In such cases, the actions taken by one of the courts and its rulings affected the actions and rulings of the other court(s) dealing with the same dispute. Thus, from Muslim litigants' point of view, legal pluralism was quite significant even before November 2001. However, the 2001 legislation created an even stronger situation of legal pluralism, as will be described in the next section.

The Struggle over Exclusive Jurisdiction, 1995–2001

The Family Courts Law (5755–1995) that ordered the establishment of family courts in Israel, was enacted by the Knesset on July 31, 1995. A persistent debate concerning the need for family courts in Israel, their possible jurisdiction, and their place within the Israeli legal system preceded the enactment of this law (Arbel and Geifman 1997, Zamir 2002: 463–4). The main purpose of the Family Courts Law was to concentrate all the judicial jurisdictions of the various civil courts in matters relating to family matters within the jurisdiction of one civil tribunal—the family court. Furthermore, the law was meant to concentrate all legal litigation relating to a single family dispute in the hands of a single judge, presiding in the family court (Shava 1998a: 49). The Family Courts Law was therefore a centralizing law, designed to solve the problem of "split hearings" in matters relating to the same matrimonial dispute (Arbel and Geifman 1997: 432).[6]

Undoubtedly, the establishment of integrative family courts constituted a major reform in the field of family law in Israel that affected not only the institutional structure of the judicial system, but also procedural and material laws (ibid.; see also Geifman 1998: iii). However, this reform was not intended—as specifically

5 For a detailed discussion of the powers of Israeli civil courts—before the amendment of 2001—to deal with the "civil aspects" of family disputes of Muslim litigants, see Shava (1998b: 361–4).

6 According to Arbel and Geifman (1997: 432), the previous arrangements "opened room for manipulations employed by litigants, and invited multiplicity of pleas and suits, which were only meant to thwart the legal procedure, or at least meant to serve as a tactical move, aimed to put pressure [on the other party], in order to achieve a better result." Thus, it may be argued that the purpose of the law was to reduce the legal pluralism that prevailed in the legal system. This pluralism is often viewed by lawyers and legal scholars in negative terms, for not only does it reduce the "efficiency" of the legal system, it also impairs the principle of the unity of law (see e.g., Steinberg 1990, Norwood 1996). For a succinct criticism of the plurality of legal procedures in the field of family law in Israel, see Rosen-Zvi (1989: 203–9).

noted in Article 25 of the Family Courts Law—to reduce the jurisdictions of the religious courts. Thus, as revolutionary as it was, the establishment of family courts should be viewed as an internal reform within the civil legal system, and not as an attempt to change the "status quo" between religious and civil domains. Indeed, the enactment of the Family Courts Law in July 1995 was not meant to change the basic *millet*-like features of the personal-status regime employed in Israel.[7]

Nevertheless, during the early 1990s, concurrent with the debate concerning the establishment of family courts, voices—originating primarily from liberal and feminist circles among the Palestinian Israeli community—began to demand a change in the respective jurisdictions of the civil and the shari'a courts. Specifically, they called for the equalization of the status of Muslim and Christian women to that of Druze and Jewish women. These Palestinian-Israeli activists argued that Muslim and Christian women are discriminated against since, unlike Jewish and Druze women, they are not allowed to file maintenance suits against their husbands in civil courts and have no choice but appealing to religious courts. Muslim women in particular, more than the women of any other religious community, were denied access to the civil courts in family disputes,[8] which according to those feminist activists, prevented them from improving their position within the traditional patriarchal family (see e.g., Ibrahim 1993: 26–7).

Blaming the qadis presiding in the shari'a courts for being "conservative," and viewing the procedural and material laws employed by shari'a courts as inherently discriminating against women (Bishara and Toma-Suliman 1997), Palestinian feminists demanded that jurisdiction in matters of personal status of Muslim litigants be conferred upon civil courts. Several women's organizations and civil rights organizations, both Palestinian and non-Palestinian, joined hands in this struggle, and by 1995, a "Working Group for Equality in Personal Status Issues"

7 Nevertheless, some judges presiding in the recently established family courts seized the opportunity to reshuffle the "division of labor" between the civil and the religious courts. Their attempts further to broaden the jurisdictions of family courts, at the expense of the rabbinical courts, were promptly blocked by appellate court decisions and by legislation amendments (see Shava 1998a, 2003).

8 While Christian women were allowed to resort to civil courts in order to obtain maintenance for themselves or for their minor children, Muslim women were denied this option. Due to historical circumstances (discussed in Chapter 3) shari'a courts had exclusive jurisdiction in all types of maintenance suits, while ecclesiastical courts held exclusive jurisdiction in alimony suits, and only concurrent jurisdiction in other types of maintenance suits. The difference between alimony and maintenance suits is as follows: "alimony" denotes the allowance that a husband who deserted his wife is ordered to pay to her; "maintenance" denotes the payments by parents for the support of their children, by children for the support of their parents, or by other relatives. "Maintenance" also denotes the allowance secured to a wife when the parties are separated by mutual consent, as well as the payment that a court orders following a divorce or a judicial dissolution of the marriage (see Goadby 1926: 160–62, Shava 1998a: 283, n. 18; see also HCJ 106/79). Notably, in Islamic law, a divorcee is not entitled to maintenance beyond the period of the *'idda.*

had been established.[9] The group's proclaimed goal was to "combat discrimination against Arab women in the area of personal status, and change social norms by promoting significant changes in attitudes and behavior toward Arab women and their personal status issues."[10]

The Working Group waged a public and political campaign for equalizing the legal status of Muslim and Christian women to the status of Jewish and Druze women. In 1995, shortly after the Family Courts Law passed in the Knesset, the group initiated a bill for the amendment of this law.[11] The main purpose of the proposed amendment was to grant Muslim and Christian women the option of recourse in maintenance suits—as well as in all other matters of personal status, except for marriage and divorce—to the new family courts.

In a clarification appended to the legislative bill, the drafters presented statistical data from the database of the National Insurance Institute, indicating that the amounts of maintenance payments for wives and children adjudicated by shari'a courts are significantly lower than those adjudicated by family courts. They therefore concluded that in order to improve the status of Muslim and Christian women, it is mandatory to grant these women better access to family courts. The implicit underlying assumption was that substantial and comprehensive legal equality between men and women can only be achieved in the civil courts, and not in the patriarchal shari'a courts.[12]

The relatively meager maintenance payments that shari'a courts allocated to Muslim women not only attracted criticism toward these courts, but also motivated women's organizations to demand a restriction of their jurisdiction. This enterprise met with fierce opposition from qadis presiding in shari'a courts. Realizing the danger for shari'a rule and aiming to prevent any detraction from their status and authority, the qadis—led by the charismatic, newly appointed president of the shari'a court of appeal, Ahmad Natur—initiated a reform of their own.

---

9 The following organizations participated in the working group: Women Against Violence; The Association for Civil Rights in Israel; The Arab Association for Human Rights; Altufula: Pedagogical and Multipurpose Women's Center; Israel's Women Network; Shatil: Equal Access Project; Al-Siwar: Arab Feminist Movement in Support of Victims of Sexual Violence; Haifa Women's Shelter; The Association for Nurturing Family Relations; The Social Workers Association.

10 Most of the information I managed to gather on the activities of the Working Group for Equality in Personal Status Issues regarding the matter of jurisdiction, was drawn from other civil society organizations that cooperated with the organization. See e.g., the websites of the Association for Civil Rights in Israel (http://www.acri.org.il/); and the New Israeli Fund (http://www.nif.org/). The website of the Working Group (http://www.pstatus.org/) was inaugurated at a later date and therefore contains only little information about this episode.

11 See report in the website of the Association for Civil Rights in Israel (http://www.acri.org.il/he/5593) [accessed: 10/02/2014].

12 Draft bill prepared by the Working Group for Equality in Personal Status Issues, no individual author, no date mentioned.

Striving to take the sting out of the feminist-liberal initiative, Qadi Natur sought a way to increase systematically the amounts of maintenance payments adjudicated in shari'a courts. The solution he found was to initiate a reform that transfers the authority to determine the amounts of such payments, from appointed informants (*mukhbirun*) to the qadis themselves. Instead of relying on informants for the purpose of gathering information concerning the husband's financial situation, Natur suggested that the qadis themselves would determine the sums of maintenance payments, relying, for that purpose, on official state documents such as income tax and national insurance statements.

Interestingly, the qadis made creative use of a unique judicial mechanism in order to achieve this reform: the judicial circular (*marsum qada'i*). This is a highly unusual legal instrument, both within the framework of the Israeli legal system and in the context of Islamic law. Prof. Aharon Layish, in a lecture at the Van Leer Jerusalem Institute on May 14, 1997, described the circumstances under which the idea of issuing a "judicial circular" was conceived. He recounted that Qadi Ahmad Natur—who is a former graduate student of his—had been searching for a mechanism that would allow the introduction of legal reform without resorting to the statutory legislation of the Knesset.[13] Having studied legal documents from the period of the Sudanese Mahdi (Layish 1996, 1997), Layish suggested the mechanism of the "judicial circular" (*Manshur qada'i*), which the British applied in the Sudan after the Mahdi's defeat. Qadi Natur embraced the idea, and the Israeli "judicial circulars" (*marsumat qada'iyya*, as they were called in the Israeli context) came into being. Yet, while the Sudanese circulars were ratified by the British colonial administration and thus became legally binding, the circulars issued by the president of the Israeli shari'a court of appeal have no legal standing whatsoever.[14]

Nevertheless, all the qadis in Israeli shari'a courts signed the circular, thereby committing themselves to apply the procedural reform suggested by it.[15] It seems

13 From the point of view of the qadis presiding in Israeli shari'a courts, any interference of the Israeli parliament in procedural and material laws applied in the shari'a courts is highly problematic, for it might undermine the Islamic legitimacy of these courts. See Chapter 14 for further discussion of the legitimacy problems encountered by Israeli shari'a courts.

14 Indeed, Abou Ramadan (2003b: 287, n. 153) claims that the *marsum*, being an act of legislation, violates the principle of separation of powers. Prof. Layish also wondered in his lecture what would happen "if someone were to appeal to the High Court of Justice against a ruling based on these circulars." And yet he also quoted Qadi Natur, who claimed that the *marsumat* may be defended in the High Court on the grounds that they fall within the interpretive authority of the qadi (Layish, lecture at the Van Leer Jerusalem Institute, May 14, 1997, and personal communication; see also Layish 2006). For a detailed discussion of this circular, see Shahar (2007).

15 The qadis gathered for a three-day seminar, in which they discussed the implications of the reform (personal communication with Qadi Ziyad 'Asaliyya, former qadi in Jerusalem and Haifa).

that the qadis adopted not only to the procedural reform, but also the notion of allotting more generous sums as maintenance payments. In the months following the issuance of the circular, a fifty percent rise in the sums of maintenance payments was noted in the shari'a court in West Jerusalem.[16]

This procedural reform, initiated and realized by the qadis independently of Knesset legislation and of any other governmental ministry/agency, was explained and legitimized by way of adopting a liberal "Islamicized" discourse, combined with a Palestinian nationalistic one. Thus, the author of the "judicial circular," Qadi Natur, acknowledges that the previous procedure of determining the sums of maintenance payments in shari'a courts was deficient, and that it is only natural that "certain—justifiable—voices were heard, calling for a rectification of the harm caused to Muslim women." Yet Qadi Natur also severely criticizes "those voices" that are:

> vague, unable to offer a remedy, [because they tend to] generalize, rather than to scrutinize [the problem] in detail. A few [of these voices] even went so far as to accuse the shari'a courts and the shari'a itself of iniquity, suggesting therefore to transfer the jurisdiction over maintenance cases [of Muslims] from the shari'a courts to the regional [civil] courts. Surely, from the start we have understood that such calls emanate from a grave distortion of sight, and from incredible shallowness and myopia. Instead of calling for the destruction of the shari'a courts, and for throwing Muslims' affairs into the grip of worldly laws, it is proper to call—and moreover, to struggle—for a reform in the shari'a courts, which are the most just and most truthful among all [courts]. We firmly believe that the shari'a court is the only official Muslim institution left for the Muslims in this country, [and therefore it is] our duty to strengthen it, in order to apply the shari'a and to foster the adherence to the principles of creed in God's land. The preservation of the shari'a courts is, thence, a basic Islamic demand, providing that they will implement justice and equity.
>
> (Natur 1995: 2)

Nevertheless, despite the pungent rhetoric, and despite the reform and the substantial increase in maintenance sums adjudicated by shari'a courts, the initiative to confer jurisdiction to the family courts in personal status matters of Muslims refused to fade away.

16 My data is based on a sample of maintenance files adjudicated by the shari'a court in West Jerusalem between 1994 and 1998. I have no systematic estimations of the maintenance sums in other shari'a courts in Israel, but I was told (proudly) by Qadi Natur, who is actually the author of the "judicial circular," that the sums of maintenance payments have significantly increased following the issuance of the circular (interview with Qadi Natur, January 1998). It is therefore reasonable to assume that a similar rise in maintenance payments also occurred in other courts (see also Reiter 1997a: 226).

In their struggle against this draft bill, the qadis found a strong, influential ally: the Islamic Movement. Although the leaders of this Movement (and in particular, the leaders of the more "radical" northern faction) were usually critical toward the Israeli shari'a courts system,[17] they were willing, under these circumstances, to cooperate with the qadis in order to thwart the initiative. The following years witnessed a heated debate within the Palestinian community in Israel, between feminist and liberal circles that called for conferring jurisdiction on the family courts, and Islamist circles insisting that the shari'a courts must retain exclusive jurisdiction. On May 2, 1997, for example, a fatwa, signed by two qadis presiding in the shari'a court of appeal, and by three prominent leaders of the Islamic Movement, was published in the Movement's official journal, *Sawt al-Haqq wa'l-Hurriyya.*[18] The fatwa declared bluntly that the draft bill is a damaging, erroneous endeavor, that it is detrimental to Islam in Israel, and that it contradicts the holy Qur'an and the benevolent shari'a, for it will result in the application of non-*shar'i* rules in personal status matters of Muslims (*Sawt al-Haqq wa'l-Hurriyya*, May 2, 1997: 8).

Several weeks after the fatwa was published, another one was issued—this time by the highest religious authority in Palestine, the Mufti of Jerusalem, Sheikh 'Akrama Sabri.[19] Sheikh Sabri was an appointee of the Palestinian National Authority,[20] and his rulings have no legal standing in Israel. Nevertheless, he was considered a highly respectable 'alim, and the opponents of the legislation amendment sought to recruit his voice in support of their struggle. Zahi al-Majidat—secretary of the *Mizan* Association[21] affiliated with the Islamic Movement—addressed a query (*istifta'*) to Mufti Sabri, asking for his opinion with regard to the proposed legislation amendment.[22] Sheikh Sabri responded with an unequivocal fatwa:

17 See for example the harsh criticism voiced by the speaker of the Islamic movement, Shaykh Hashim 'Abd al-Rahman, concerning the lack of Islamic education of presiding qadis in Israeli shari'a courts (*Sawt al-Haqq wa'l-Hurriyya*, July 1, 1994: 28; see also Landau 1969: 10, Dumper 1994, Peled 2001: 121, Abou Ramadan 2008).

18 The fatwa was signed by Qadi Natur and Qadi Da'ud Zini, and by Shaykh Ra'id Salah, Shaykh Kamil Rayan, and MK Taufiq Khatib of the Islamic Movement. As noted by Abou Ramadan, although this document was titled "fatwa," it cannot be viewed as a proper fatwa, for it was not given in response to a petition or query.

19 I thank Dr Moussa Abou Ramadan for bringing this fatwa to my attention, and for providing me with a facsimile copy of it. See the fatwa in Appendix 3.

20 Sheikh Sabri served as the Mufti of Jerusalem from 1994 to 2006.

21 The *Mizan* Association deals with issues of human rights and with the status of the Palestinian minority in Israel. It is affiliated with the southern faction of the Islamic Movement in Israel.

22 The *istifta'* was posed on July 21, 2001, and the fatwa was issued ten days later, on July 31. Undoubtedly, the issuance of this fatwa illustrates the close cooperation of the Israeli and the Palestinian Muslim establishments. For a discussion of the interrelations between the Israeli shari'a court system and its Palestinian and Jordanian counterparts, see Chapter 14.

> Matters of personal status—which include in addition to the issue of *waqf* such issues as marriage and divorce, maintenance, guardianship, bequests and so forth—belong to the domain of acts of worship (*'ibadat*). Therefore Muslims are forbidden to act in discordance [with shari'a rules] in these matters. A Muslim must perform God's directives with regard to maintenance or bequests, just as he must perform God's directives with regard to the duties of prayer, alms giving and the Hajj, even if he lives in a non-Muslim state.
> [… .] The implementation of non-Islamic laws in matters of personal status is hence considered a direct assault on the realm of worship […] and therefore it is forbidden for Muslims to resort to courts which adjudicate in these matters in a non-Islamic manner. What we need is to safeguard the shari'a courts, and to invest effort in broadening their jurisdiction so that it will include all aspects of life, and not in reducing it.
> (Sheikh 'Akrama Sabri, July 31, 2001; see Appendix 3)

Despite this "heavy artillery," and despite all the qadis' efforts,[23] the legislation bill was laid before the Knesset in July 1997.[24] It was presented by Nawaf Masalha, a Muslim MK representing the (Zionist) Labor Party, but 53 other MKs (including four Muslims and all women MKs) added their signatures to the bill. At this phase, the confrontation between the opposing parties shifted primarily to the parliamentary arena, where MKs affiliated with the Islamic Movement did their best to forestall and thwart the legislative process. Consequently, the process lasted more than four years, and raised impassioned debates whenever the bill was discussed—both in the Constitution, Justice and Law Committee, and in the Knesset plenum.[25]

Unexpected support for the opponents of the legislation bill came from an academic scholar—Prof. Menashe Shava, a well-known expert in Israeli family law, who published an article, harshly criticizing the legislation bill (Shava 1998a). He argued that the aspiration of the bill institutors to equalize the jurisdiction of the shari'a and the ecclesiastical courts with the jurisdiction of the rabbinical courts may cause more damage than benefit to Muslim and Christian women. Such

---

23 Qadi Ahmad Natur was particularly active in this struggle. Not only did he personally participate in meetings of Knesset committees that dealt with the bill, he also wrote and spoke extensively against this legislative reform on various occasions (see e.g., Natur 1998).

24 Legislation Bill No. p/1421, presented on July, 16, 1997 (see *Official Acta* 5758, Legislation Bills, 2749, 570).

25 See for example: Legislation Bill: The Family Courts (Amendment—equalization of jurisdiction), 1997, Knesset minutes, July 16, 1997; Legislation Bill: The Family Courts (Amendment No. 5), 2001, Knesset plenum minutes, October 23, 2001 (the files may be downloaded from the Knesset website: www.knesset.gov.il); see also Minutes No. 208, The Constitution, Justice and Law Committee, June 28, 1998; Minute No. 91, The Constitution, Justice and Law Committee, February 22, 2000 (http://www.knesset.gov.il/protocols/data/html/huka/2000–02–22.html [accessed: 10/15/2014]).

an unwanted outcome, according to Shava, may be the result of the application of the "connection principle" (*iqaron ha-krikhah*) in the shari'a and the ecclesiastical courts, in a similar way to its application in the rabbinical courts. This principle restricts the ability of Jewish wives to file civil suits in family courts (e.g. maintenance suits), since it maintains that the rabbinical courts have exclusive jurisdiction in any matter that is connected to a divorce suit.[26] Shava argued that the application of this principle in other religious courts may actually decrease, rather than increase, the ability of Muslim and Christian women to file suits in family courts.

Following Shava's criticism, some changes were introduced into the bill, to ensure that the "connection principle" will not apply to shari'a and ecclesiastical courts. Nevertheless, the main subject of the legislation amendment—granting family courts jurisdiction in matters pertaining to the personal status of Muslims and Christians—remained intact. The legislation bill passed in the Knesset on November 5, 2001, and thus a new era of interrelations between the family courts and the shari'a courts commenced.

We will return to the struggle over the legislation amendment in Chapter 14, which elaborates a New Institutional perspective on this episode. At this stage we shall move, however, to a detailed discussion of the implications and consequences of the legislation amendment.

26 Article 3 of the Rabbinical Courts Jurisdiction (Marriage and Divorce) Law (5713–1953) states that "[w]here a suit for divorce between Jews has been filed in a rabbinical court, whether by the wife or by the husband, a rabbinical court shall have exclusive jurisdiction in any matter connected with such suit, including maintenance for the wife and for the children of the couple." This seemingly harmless article created an incessant "jurisdiction race" between the rabbinical and the civil courts (now the family courts). The "connection principle" determines that if a divorce suit was filed in the rabbinical court, and if maintenance and other issues (such as child custody, for example) were connected to this suit, then the other party was forbidden from filing legal suits in these matters in the civil court. Thus, the question of who files the suit first, and in which tribunal, became of utmost importance, and husbands and wives were racing each other to the courts (for a critical discussion of this "connection principle," see Rosen-Zvi 1989, Maoz 1989, Shava 2003).

Chapter 10

Shari'a Courts' Response to Competition

During the years of parliamentary struggles over the issue of according family courts jurisdiction in personal status matters of Muslims and Christians, opponents of the legislation amendment voiced their grave concern regarding the consequences. They anticipated that the religious courts will be left with no litigants, and that the family courts will not be able to deal with Muslim and Christian litigants in a proper manner. Their main concern was that the civil judges (who are almost exclusively Jewish) will not be able—for lack of knowledge—to apply the material Islamic and Christian laws,[1] and that religious values and norms will therefore not be sustained.[2] Supporters of the amendment argued in response that the entrance of family courts to this field will only benefit the religious courts, which will have to become more efficient. State officials from the Ministry of Justice (that supported the legislation amendment) have also sought to appease the opponents by pledging that Muslim and Christian judges—versed in religious law—will be appointed to family courts, and that the presiding judges in these courts will be trained in religious law.[3]

More than a decade after the legislation amendment passed, we still lack a systematic study of its effects.[4] Nevertheless, it is to my mind arguable that both its opponents and its supporters were partly right. Supporters of the amendment were right in estimating that the new competition posed by the family courts will drive the religious courts to implement some duly needed reforms. Indeed, as will be shown in this chapter, the fact that the shari'a courts have no longer a monopoly in the legal "niche" of personal status matters of Muslims has driven qadis to turn their courts into a more "user-friendly" arena.

While the opponents' fear that the religious courts will be drained of litigants has not materialized to date, their skeptic attitude toward the promises that

1 As explained, the legislative "status quo" was not changed by the establishment of the family courts. As a result, the material laws in matters of personal status remain religious, and the family courts are obliged to employ different laws for litigants of different religious affiliations (see Arbel and Geifman 1997, Shava 1998b).

2 See e.g., Legislation Bill: The Family Courts (Amendment No. 5), 2001; Knesset plenum minutes, October 23, 2001.

3 See for example the comments of the Ministry of Justice's delegates to the Constitution, Justice and Law Committee, Minutes No. 91, February 22, 2000.

4 See a discussion of this issue by Adv. Hiba Yazbak at the website of the Working Group for Equality in Personal Status Issues (http://www.pstatus.org/index.php?todo=articles&aid=00000043 [accessed: 10/1/2014]).

accompanied the legislation seem rather accurate. Despite the fact that the family courts have become accessible to a large constituency of Muslim and Christian Israeli citizens (and permanent residents), no re-organization has taken place in these courts: no training workshops for judges were held; no additional translators to and from Arabic were enlisted; and the number of appointments of Muslim and Christian judges is insignificant.[5] As a matter of fact, it appears that the broadening of the family courts' jurisdiction had no significant impact on their operation, and that they continue to function pretty much as they did before.

The family courts' reaction—or rather, lack of reaction—to the changing situation is of course symptomatic of the indifference that often characterizes Israeli authorities' treatment of non-Jewish populations. This indifference may provide us, nonetheless, with another clue for understanding Muslim and Christian women litigants' less than enthusiastic attitudes toward family courts. As mentioned, these courts are seen as rather hostile toward non-Jewish, non-Hebrew-speaking litigants, and their lack of preparedness to cater for the legal needs of that population may indeed drive those litigants away from the family courts.

Outlining Reform Strategies

Whereas the family courts did not react in any significant way to the 2001 legislation, the shari'a courts took quite considerable measures. After investing extensive efforts in thwarting and forestalling the legislation initiative, the qadis must have felt a sense of defeat when the amendment finally passed in the Knesset. Facing a concrete and palpable danger of a personal and institutional "fall from grace," the qadis had two options: they could decide to compete or not to compete with the family courts which encroached on their jurisdiction.

It would have been perfectly understandable if the qadis had decided that they no longer wished to participate in the game after the Knesset passed the legislation amendment. Frustrated with a civil legislation policy that completely ignored their opinion, the qadis could have resigned from their offices in protest,[6] or they could have decided completely to ignore the new legislation and to continue doing exactly

5 For harsh criticism of this state of affairs, see Adalah's newsletter (http://adalah.org/features/misc/Inequality_Report.pdf [accessed: 10/1/2014]); see also a report (in Hebrew) on the representation of Arabs in the Israeli civil service, governmental companies, and the judicial system, by Sikkuy Association (http://www.sikkuy.org.il/wp-content/uploads/2013/11/equalitygov2007.pdf [accessed: 10/1/2014]).

6 In fact, Sheikh Ra'id Salah, the leader of the northern faction of the Islamic Movement in Israel, had threatened at some point that if the legislation amendment passes, Muslims in Israel will boycott the Israeli legal system altogether and establish their own private shari'a courts. Sheikh Ra'id also advised the qadis presiding in Israeli shari'a courts to resign from their offices if the legislation passes (see Salah 2001).

what they did before. In effect, the qadis' response was nothing of the sort. Instead of falling into acrimony and resentfulness toward the state, the qadis reacted by taking a wide range of initiatives aimed at internal reform and improvement of the services provided by the shari'a courts. Irrespective of whether they were motivated by direct personal interest or by a genuine sense of Islamic, nationalist-Palestinian, or communal commitment (or all of these together, of course), the qadis have waged a determined struggle over potential litigants—striving to convince as many litigants as possible that their courts constitute the best place to deal with matrimonial problems. Thus, unlike the family courts, which displayed no interest whatsoever in attracting Muslim litigants into their courtrooms, the qadis went out of their way in order to preserve—and even to increase—the number of files adjudicated in their courts.

Why did the qadis react in a competitive manner? Why do they care at all about attracting more litigants—after all, courts are not business firms, and litigants are not customers? Indeed, the motivation behind the qadis' efforts is probably not economic: their salaries remain the same regardless of the number of cases they handle, and they are not compensated in any way for a greater workload. I argue that the answer to their competitive attitude lies in the realm of legitimacy: from the qadis' point of view, the more litigants appeal to the shari'a courts, the more legitimacy the courts—and the qadis presiding in them—have. In contrast, a decrease in the number of appeals might constitute a serious blow to the legitimacy and prestige of the courts and their qadis.

As observed by organizational theorists, nonprofit organizations (such as courts of law), much more than business organizations, tend to compete over legitimacy and prestige (see e.g., DiMaggio and Powell 1983, Scott and Meyer 1991: 123, 125). All the more so when an organization suffers from a chronic problem of legitimacy. Bearing in mind the problematic status of Israeli qadis—who are appointed by a non-Islamic regime, to serve in "contaminated courts" (see Chapter 2)—it is easy to understand why it was so important for them not to lose litigants to the family courts.[7] This need is even more obvious in Jerusalem, where the Israeli shari'a court suffers not only from dubious religious prestige (like other Israeli shari'a courts), but also from a nationalist resentment.

In response to the 2001 legislation, the qadis of the Israeli shari'a courts have preferred, therefore, the active, competitive way of action. Even before November 2001, and surely afterwards, they have gathered for several times, trying to figure out how they can make their courts more appealing to litigants. Three years later, in June 2004, the qadis convened in an emergency meeting in order to discuss a slight decrease in the number of files in Israeli shari'a courts during 2003 (see Table 10.1). Their main concern was that despite the demographic growth of

7 Indeed, the qadis could have chosen another parameter as a measure of legitimacy, such as legal equity or religious prestige that is based on the level of expertise in *shar'i* jurisprudence. In a way, their choice to earn legitimacy by concentrating on quantity (of files) rather than on quality (of rulings) expresses their lack of confidence and their shaky positioning.

the Muslim population in Israel, the number of files adjudicated in the shari'a courts had fallen. In the meeting they also discussed what they called "the bad reputation of the shari'a courts," and tried to suggest possible measures that might help to improve the courts' image.[8] Thus, for example, they decided to ease court procedures for issuing declarative judgments and registered deeds (such as marriage and divorce ratifications); they decided that legal councilors and litigants will be allowed to ask for postponements of hearings by fax, instead of having to come to court in person in order to file such a request; and they decided to enforce a stricter dressing code on lawyers and *shar'i* advocates (dark trousers, white shirt, dark jacket).[9]

Table 10.1 Number of Files Opened in Israeli Shari'a Courts, 2001–2004

Courts	2001	2002	2003	2004
Jerusalem	2,547	3,144	3,021	3,164
Beer-Sheva	1,580	1,566	1,524	1,668
Jaffa	515	679	499	569
Tayyibe	1,533	1,435	1,498	1,595
Haifa	667	669	629	582
Acre	1,279	1,298	1,191	1,281
Nazareth	722	699	653	760
Sum Total	8,843	9,490	9,015	9,619
Appellate Court	271	369	343	383

Source: based on data from The Shari'a Courts Administration (http://index.justice.gov.il/Units/BatiDinHashreim/Pages/Report.aspx?WPID=WPQ7&PN=1 [accessed: 10/16/2014])

The institutional responses of the shari'a courts to the competition posed by the family courts may be divided into two categories:

1. Minor adjustments were introduced into the courts' administrative procedures and daily routines, with the aim of making the court bureaucracy less burdensome for litigants and councilors. Indeed, in recent years, following the 2001 legislation amendment, the principle of being "user-

8 This description is based on a conversation with one of the qadis on June 22, 2004.

9 On the dress code, see also Administrative Directive No. 18 (*zii al-murafa'in al-shar'yyin*), issued by the administration of the shari'a courts in February 2005. For whatever reason, the document was recently removed from the shari'a courts website.

friendly" has become a major organizing principle in the Israeli shari'a court in West Jerusalem.

2. Minor legal reforms have been initiated and enacted by the qadis, who made, for this purpose, creative use of their relatively broad judicial agency. As could be expected, most of these legal reforms were designed to improve the status of women litigants in court. There are three possible reasons for the fact that the legal reforms were meant to improve women's status (and attract women litigants), rather than cater to men's interests (and attract men). First, we have seen that women, unlike men, have much to gain from appealing to the family court, and it is therefore they who are targeted for persuasion. From a marketing perspective, men may be viewed as "captive clients" of the shari'a courts, simply because they have no better alternative; women, on the other hand, constitute a much more difficult clientele, since they have an alternative, and presumably, a good one. Thus, in order to prevent the desertion of women in favor of the rival family courts, they are being offered "better bargains," to convince them to remain loyal to the shari'a courts.

   Second, since women are undoubtedly the largest constituency of the court,[10] it makes perfect sense to give precedence to their interests, even at the expense of smaller constituencies (that is, men). Third, the current generation of qadis presiding in Israeli shari'a courts are all graduates of Israeli universities—either of law schools or of social sciences and humanities departments (see Reiter 1997a). Such an educational background may enhance their inclination toward liberal and feminist conceptions of gender equality and drive them to implementing such ideas in their judicial practice (see also Shahar 2004).

Let us now explore the procedural and judicial reforms introduced in the Israeli shari'a courts, and especially in the shari'a court in West Jerusalem, since 2001.

Identification of Litigants and Witnesses

Two of the most burdensome procedures in shari'a courts have been the practices of identifying the litigants and the witnesses (*ta'rif*) and of establishing their personal credibility (*ta'dil*; *tazkiyya*). As a rule, any person appearing before the court must first be identified by two other persons who personally know him/her. In addition, if a person is required to testify, the court must first establish the "good moral standing" (*'adala*) of this person,[11] by performing a rather complicated procedure (see Tyan 1964: 209a). As one can imagine, such procedures, if strictly

10 Women initiate more than 70 percent of the cases handled by the shari'a court.

11 Article 1705 of the *Majalla* determines that: "The *'adl* person is one in whom good impulses prevail over bad ones."

enforced, may become truly costly in terms of court time, and it may also put some extra burden on the litigants and their legal representatives, who need to bring such "accrediting agents" to court.[12] Thus, being loyal to the principle of "user-friendliness," the qadi presiding in the Israeli shari'a court in West Jerusalem decided to nullify these procedures altogether. Instead of identifying litigants and witnesses by the testimony of two acquaintances, identification is presently performed by way of reviewing their ID cards. When opening a case file, the court secretary will usually add a photocopy of the plaintiff's ID card to the file. Photocopies of the defendant's ID card and those of witnesses who were summoned to give testimony are added to the file on the day of the hearing. Witnesses are also asked to present their ID cards to the qadi just before they are put under oath,[13] but no *ta'dil* procedure is enacted.

Facilitative Measures for Registering Deeds

As mentioned in Chapter 7 (see Figures 7.1 and 7.2), about half of the decisions issued by the Israeli shari'a court in West Jerusalem may be categorized as "declarative judgments" or as registered deeds (*mu'amalat*; *musadaqat*; *hujaj*). The court staff makes a particular effort to provide such decisions in minimum time (that is, within a single day), but beyond that, the court staff goes out of its way in order to assist litigants in filing these lawsuits. Generally speaking, filing such a petition does not require significant expertise in legal language, nor in court procedures: all it takes is to provide the necessary documents and to testify in front of the qadi to the truthfulness of these documents.[14] Nevertheless, many litigants are so insecure that they tend to hire a legal representative even for this evidently simple task. In fact, some lawyers or *shar'i* advocates have specialized in "hunting" such litigants just before they enter the court. The lawyers wait in the corridor leading to the court or at the entrance to the building, and approach people who come to court unattended by lawyers. They offer to assist them in filing their petitions, and charge for their services a "modest" fee (usually several hundred NIS).[15]

---

12 See a description of these procedures as they were performed in a Cairene shari'a court some 150 years ago (Lane 1954 [1908]: 117).

13 After examining their ID cards, the qadi hands them to the court scribe, who writes down the ID numbers of the witnesses in the court minutes. The ID cards are then handed back to the witnesses.

14 For example, in cases of marriage ratification, the couple is required to provide the following documents: an original marriage certificate, two photocopies of their ID cards, and a signed deposition by the two spouses that the marriage is still intact, and that there are no legal or religious grounds to nullify the marriage.

15 Abu Zayd, the court's acting chief secretary, often expresses his resentment of these lawyers' conduct. He may even refer to them as "vultures" (*'uqban*).

In recent years, the court staff has begun to assist litigants in filing such petitions—first by providing them with a detailed list of required documents that they need to supply; and second, by preparing detailed, printed forms for each and every type of petition, to be filled by the litigants.[16] When some people still found it difficult to get by, Abu Zayd either directed them to me for assistance, or provided them with a photocopied example of a relevant petition, that they may use as a model for their own deposition. All this, of course, is done in order to assist litigants and to "rescue" them, as Abu Zayd says, from the "vultures' talons" (that is, from exploitative legal councilors).

Judicial Pliability

In recent years, it appears that the ideology of "user-friendliness" has become salient not only in the court's daily routines, but also in the judicial practices of the qadis.[17] The qadis often display a particularly lenient approach in regard to both procedural and material "formalities." For example, the qadis usually abstain from imposing extra fees on litigants, beyond the fee that they have already paid. Thus, they sometimes insert seemingly irrelevant statements into court rulings, which are meant to exempt litigants from the need to file additional lawsuits. They may add, for instance, to a declarative judgment of divorce (*ithbat talaq*) a sentence stating that the children are under the custody of the mother/father, or a sentence establishing the financial arrangements agreed upon by the couple (e.g. maintenance payments for the waiting period, payment of the deferred dower, etc.).

Qadi Zibdi in particular goes even further than that, and actively corrects statements of claim during hearings, in a manner that better serves the interests of the litigants. For example, he may advise a woman litigant to change the formulation of a lawsuit from "request for approval to rent an apartment" (*idhn bi-'isti'jar maskan*) to "lodging maintenance" (*nafaqat sukna*).[18]

---

16 See, for example, such a form in Appendix 2.

17 I refer here to the judicial practices of the two qadis that presided in the Israeli shari'a court in West Jerusalem during my fieldwork: Qadi Ziyad 'Asaliyya and Qadi Muhammad Rashid Zibdi.

18 The second type of request is much easier to attain. Assuming that the court already established that a separated woman (and her children) are entitled to maintenance, a lawsuit for additional lodging maintenance becomes only a matter of formality (a woman is automatically entitled to this kind of maintenance. See discussion of this issue below). An approval to rent an apartment is much more difficult to attain, for the husband may raise all sorts of objections: the rental price may be too high in his view, the neighborhood not fit for his children, etc. In addition, the husband may offer to accommodate his wife and children in an apartment that he himself provides (the marital home or any other apartment for that matter), and the wife may be forced to agree to this settlement, or otherwise begin a long legal confrontation as to the lawfulness of this accommodation (*shar'iyyat al-maskan*).

The following case may serve as an illustration of the qadi's pliable approach. A woman, aided by a *shar'i* advocate, filed a lawsuit, claiming custody over her two minor children. The woman and her husband were familiar to the qadi, since they have been confronting each other—in various lawsuits—for several months. This time, the husband did not attend the hearing, nor did he send a legal representative, and it appeared that he had not been notified of the lawsuit in a proper manner (*hasab al-'usul*).[19] The qadi told the woman that the hearing must therefore be postponed. In response, the woman burst into tears. Qadi Zibdi tried to calm her and asked what the problem was. She told him that even now, when she was finally granted child maintenance payments, she cannot obtain the payments, since the NII demands that she first present a court ruling giving her custody over the children.[20] Hearing the woman's story, the qadi reproached her legal representative, telling him that he filed the wrong suit: the children already live with their mother, under her custody, so what was needed was "a request for a declarative custody judgment" (*qarar tasrihi bi'l-hadana*), and not a "custody lawsuit" (*da'wat hadana*). The qadi explained to the *shar'i* advocate and to the woman that in cases of "requests for declarative custody judgment" there is no need to inform the other party at all, so no harm was done if the husband was not notified of the hearing. He therefore suggested that the *shar'i* advocate would reformulate the statement of claim, and change it into "a request for a declarative custody judgment." Moreover, Qadi Zibdi himself dictated the request for a reformulation of the claim (on behalf of the advocate), and immediately accepted this request.

The woman left court that day with a declarative custody judgment in her pocket.[21] Not only was she not obliged to file a new suit and to pay an additional fee, she also obtained the court ruling that she needed in minimum time. Such instances of active correction or rephrasing of statements of claim by the qadi are not rare occasions. Yet, it is noteworthy that Qadi Zibdi usually intervenes in this manner only when the litigants are not represented by professional lawyers. If lawyers are involved in a case, his attitude is usually much more formalistic and reserved.[22]

19 There was no delivery confirmation in the dossier, so there was no indication that the defendant or his representative had been properly notified of the hearing.

20 In recent years, the NII has begun to demand that women who had been granted child maintenance payments must first present a court ruling confirming that they have custody over their children. Without such a document, no maintenance benefits are provided by the NII. As a result of this new requirement the number of declarative custody judgments has risen dramatically in the Israeli shari'a court in West Jerusalem (see Tables 7.1 and 7.2).

21 ISC 2295/2001. The described event took place on March 3, 2002.

22 In this sense, the event described above was unique. My guess is that the qadi really felt sorry for the woman, and for that reason he went out of his way and corrected the statement of claim, despite the presence of the *shar'i* advocate. We may also speculate that if the other party was properly notified of the hearing, and if the husband or his legal representative were present in court, such intervention on the part of the qadi would not have occurred.

Another example illustrates Qadi Zibdi's permissive approach in a somewhat different context. A young couple—a Jerusalemite man and his Brazilian (Muslim) wife—accompanied by their two and a half year old daughter, came to court and filed a request for formal recognition of their marriage. It turned out that the couple had married several years earlier in Las Vegas. The marriage ceremony was conducted by a civil judge, but it was also confirmed by a dubious document that was issued by the Center for Islamic Culture in Las Vegas. As the couple stood in the courtroom (the man translating what was being said to English, so that his Brazilian wife could follow), the qadi inquired whether this union could be regarded as a proper Islamic marriage. Were two Muslim witnesses present when the judge conducted the marriage? Were there unequivocal declarations of offer and acceptance (*ijab waqabul*)? And did they agree on the amount of the dower (*mahr*)?[23]

The husband answered the qadi's questions reluctantly, admitting that he is not sure whether all these conditions were fulfilled in their marriage ceremony. The qadi then replied that in case of doubt, it will be better perhaps to perform another marriage ceremony, and this time in a proper way. Clearly disappointed with this development, the husband inquired how this would affect the status of their little daughter. Will she not be regarded as a bastard, fruit of an illegitimate liaison (*bint al-haram*)? Qadi Zibdi admitted that this may constitute a problem. After several seconds of hesitation, he instructed the husband to write a new request, and this time to state explicitly that the marriage had been conducted according to Islamic law. He also advised him to add that the marriage was affirmed by the Center of Islamic Culture in Las Vegas. The husband did exactly that—with the aid of Abu Zayd—and the qadi signed a registered deed, recognizing the validity of the couple's marriage.

Later on that day I asked Qadi Zibdi about the case,[24] and he told me:

> This was the best solution. He [the husband] was not sure whether the marriage was conducted according to Islamic law or not, so it was better to say that it was [according to Islamic law]. This way we recognize their marriage, and we avoid the entanglement of a bastard daughter. You think that I should have handled this case differently?
>
> *No. I ...*
>
> You tell me, who would have benefited if I had insisted on the necessity of remarriage? Me? Islam? This couple? Certainly not their daughter, who is completely innocent. Believe me, this was the best solution.
>
> (Conversation with Qadi Zibdi)

As the case clearly illustrates, Qadi Zibdi does not perceive himself as a servant of some rigid, sacred doctrine, but as a servant of the public good—he considers

23 On the mandatory requirements for a proper *shar'i* marriage, see Schacht (1995: 26b).

24 The date of this occurrence and the file number are not disclosed for obvious reasons.

himself obliged to contribute to the well-being of the litigants who appeal to his court.[25] This approach has become increasingly prominent in the West Jerusalem shari'a court in recent years, and it definitely turned it into a more "litigant-friendly" institution. Yet another, even more significant means employed by qadis in their efforts to attract litigants (and again, mainly women litigants) is their ability to introduce minor judicial innovations in material law. Here are some examples.

Substantial Increase in Maintenance Payments

As described in Chapter 9, during the 1990s liberal and feminist circles harshly criticized the shari'a courts for adjudicating relatively meager sums of maintenance payments—especially in comparison to the much more generous sums allotted by the civil courts. In light of this situation, an initiative was launched to confer jurisdiction in personal status matters of Muslims to the civil courts. Aiming to placate some of the criticism, the qadis initiated a procedural reform that accorded them much more discretion in determining the amounts of maintenance payments. This procedural reform, in turn, brought about a significant rise in the maintenance payments adjudicated in shari'a courts. And yet, despite their efforts, and despite the rise in maintenance payments, the qadis were unable to "stop the legislation train."

Nevertheless, as noted, following the 2001 legislation amendment, the qadis have literally doubled their efforts to convince potential litigants that the shari'a courts offer a better "deal" than their "competitors," the family courts. Much of these efforts focused on maintenance payments, which already proved to be a most crucial and sensitive issue for women litigants. Hence, since 2001 the qadis presiding in the shari'a court in West Jerusalem appear to have gradually increased the maintenance payments that they adjudicate for wives and children—far beyond the rise in the cost of living. A comparison of maintenance cases from the years 1998, 2001, and 2004 reveals that the average monthly sum of maintenance adjudicated to a wife and two children has risen from 1,855 NIS (in 1998), to 2,010 (in 2001), to 2,660 (in 2004).[26] This is a rise of more than 40 percent—and

25 This approach may also be viewed as a judicial manifestation of the well-established principles of *istislah* and *istihsan*—namely, of acting for the sake of general welfare (on *istislah* and *istihsan*, see Paret 1978: 255b).

26 The sample included four cases from 1998, eight from 2000, and seven from 2004—each, maintenance cases of a wife and two minor children. It should be noted that it is somewhat complicated to trace general trends in maintenance sums over the years, since the sum allocated to each child depends on the number of children in the family. The more children, the smaller the sum allocated to each child (of course, the total sum of maintenance will probably be larger). For this reason, I chose to compare similar families—wives with two children. These cases are particularly revealing, for the maintenance sums adjudicated by the court may also be compared with the maintenance pensions that were paid during these years by the NII. In 2004 the NII pension for a woman with two minor children stood at 2,716 NIS.

it is far beyond the rise in the consumer price index (see http://www1.cbs.gov.il/shnaton56/diag/13_01.pdf—accessed: 10/1/2014).

This impressive rise in maintenance payments resulted not only from the procedural reform, but also from a new judicial policy that enabled women to ask for much larger sums of maintenance. In May 2003 a precedent ruling of the shari'a court of appeal (SCA 44/2002) defined types of maintenance payments and criteria for eligibility to maintenance, in a much more detailed manner than before.[27] According to this ruling (that relied on both classical *fiqh* texts and modern statutes of neighboring Arab countries), a woman and her children are entitled to maintenance payments that may enable them to live with dignity. This entails, according to the shari'a court of appeal, "that a person (*insan*) will have enough food to eat, proper clothing, and a roof over his head." The general term "maintenance" (*nafaqa*) therefore consists of three subcategories of payments: "provisions maintenance" (*nafaqat ma'kal*); "garment maintenance" (*nafaqat malbas*); and "accommodation maintenance" (*nafaqat sukna*). Only a combination of these different kinds of maintenance payments may enable living with dignity, and therefore a woman is entitled to ask for all of them together. Moreover, the ruling determined that a woman is entitled to accommodation maintenance even if she dwells in her agnatic family's compound.

The ruling may appear trivial and insignificant in its content,[28] but it had actually far-reaching consequences. It meant that a woman "in a state of anger" (*hardane*), who leaves the marital home and stays in her father's house, is entitled to ask for—and hence has a good chance to be granted—"accommodation maintenance." Previously, only a woman who rented an apartment was entitled to ask for reimbursement of her rent expenses from her husband.[29] Following the ruling this option was open also to women staying with their agnatic family, that is, to a much wider group of women litigants. This was indeed a radical change in court policy, and it resulted in an additional rise in the sums of maintenance, beyond the rise that resulted from the procedural reform described above.[30]

Furthermore, as several furious husbands told me, the idea that they will have to finance the accommodation of their wives in their father's house was downright outrageous in their view. While husbands perceived it as their duty to pay children

27 As a matter of fact, treating rulings of the shari'a court of appeal as binding is an innovation, introduced by Qadi Natur, the president of the shari'a court of appeal (see Abou Ramadan 2003a, Layish 2006).

28 It is trivial in the sense that every textbook on Islamic family law uses the same typology regarding the types of maintenance payments (see e.g., Abu Zahra n.d.: 243–73, al-Faqih 1989: 292–6; see also Nasir 2009: 105–6).

29 Of course, she needed first to receive permission from the court to rent the apartment.

30 See e.g., ISC 1198/2003, 1935/2003, 2878/2003, 552/2004—in which separated wives asked for and were indeed granted accommodation maintenance, even though they stayed in their fathers' house.

maintenance, even if the children live in their in-laws' house, they seemed to reject the idea that it was also their duty to support their wives in a similar situation. One man, for example, who sat in the court's waiting room and listened to my conversation with a husband who was sued for "accommodation maintenance," intervened in the conversation and said:

> My wife goes every year to visit her family in Ramallah, and she sojourns there with the children for three weeks. This happens each and every year, since we were married eight years ago. She also stayed there every time a baby was born. Now her father may demand that I will pay for her accommodation in his house! I'm telling you, it doesn't make any sense!
>
> (Conversation in the waiting room, June 11, 2004)

Hearing this man's words, other men who overheard our discussion also nodded their heads with approval. It seems, therefore, that the new policy with regard to "accommodation maintenance" is indeed colliding with some well-established cultural norms. As such, it provides separated wives with an extremely efficient leverage for pressuring their obstinate husbands to either initiate reconciliation or agree to a divorce (see the discussion of this issue in Chapter 11).

Shari'a Courts Broadening their Jurisdiction

If the result of the 2001 legislation amendment was an "encroachment" of the family courts into the jurisdiction of the shari'a courts, the qadis have proved since then that they too are capable of "invading" the jurisdiction of the family courts. Thus, for example, one day in July 2003, I was sitting in the courtroom of the shari'a court in West Jerusalem, watching Qadi Zibdi managing case after case in his calm, tranquil manner. Suddenly it dawned on me that I just witnessed the qadi issuing a "protection order" (*amr himayya*)—an order that forbids a violent party in a dispute (and in the absolute majority of the cases this means men) from entering the marital home or from coming near the victim of the violence. I was so surprised by the seemingly natural and unproblematic way in which this order was issued, since I was accustomed that whenever a woman asks for such an order in the shari'a court, she is told that in order to obtain a protection order, she needs to appeal to the family court.[31] Only these courts, the qadis (both 'Asaliyya and Zibdi) used to explain, have the authority to issue a protection order.

It appears that the qadis were wrong in this point. Later that day I approached Qadi Zibdi and asked how it could be that he suddenly issues protection orders.

31 I must admit that my surprise was mixed with a sense of embarrassment. Just a couple of days before this hearing took place, I told a woman litigant, whom Abu Zayd referred to me for consultation, that she will have to resort to the family court in order to get a protection order. Thus I had a guilty conscience for misleading this woman.

He answered that the shari'a courts always had the authority to issue such orders, but it was simply not exercised by the qadis until now. Indeed, according to the Prevention of Violence in the Family Law (5751–1991), religious courts (shari'a courts included, of course), just like civil courts, have authority to issue protection orders. The qadis were apparently unaware of their jurisdiction in this regard,[32] or perhaps they were reluctant to exercise powers accorded to them by civil legislation. I did not ask Qadi Zibdi that day what brought about the change, but I believe that the answer to this question is straightforward: in light of the increasing competition with the family courts, the shari'a courts could no longer afford to needlessly refer women litigants to the family courts. Thus, since May 2003, the number of protection orders issued by the shari'a court in West Jerusalem has continuously risen (see e.g., ISC 1731, 1744, 1974, 2379, 2438, 2564—all from 2003).

The most salient attempt to "invade" the jurisdiction of the family courts was blocked, surprisingly, by the shari'a court of appeal. In January 2004, Qadis Daoud Zini and Farouq al-Zu'bi, both permanent members of the shari'a appellate court, rejected the appeal of a ruling issued by Qadi Zibdi (SCA 259/2003). The issue that stood at the center of this ruling was "compensation for arbitrary repudiation" (*ta'awid 'ala talaq ta'assufi*). The appeal was indeed rejected, but contrary to Qadi Zibdi's expressed opinion in his court decision, Qadi Zini ruled (and Qadi Zu'bi agreed) that the shari'a courts in Israel have no jurisdiction to deal with lawsuits concerning the compensation of a wife whose husband has repudiated her arbitrarily—that is, without her consent and without a proper *shar'i* justification.

I met Qadi Zibdi in the shari'a court in West Jerusalem several days after the appellate ruling was issued, and he was clearly disappointed, even though the appeal on his judgment was rejected. He approached me when I was standing in the secretariat area, told me that he had something interesting to show me and invited me to his chambers. I recount here what he said (in Hebrew) as I wrote it down soon after I left his room:

> I wanted to show you this ruling [of the appellate court. Qadi Zibdi shoved the text into my hands]. I had an idea: why should we not begin to grant compensation to divorced women who were repudiated arbitrarily by their husbands? We have here many many such cases,[33] and I thought—why must a woman in this position resort to the family court in order to be compensated for her sufferings? Wouldn't it be better to find a solution for this problem within the framework of Islamic law?
>
> *Q: Is there an Islamic solution to this problem? I thought that compensation may only be adjudicated in civil courts, according to civil law ...*

32 Qadi Zibdi admitted to me that he had been unaware that this type of order is included in his jurisdiction.

33 For a description of such a repudiation that took place in the courtroom itself, see Chapter 4.

No, no, no. You are wrong. In Jordanian law, for example, compensation for arbitrary repudiation may be up to one year of maintenance payments; and in Egyptian law, compensation is even larger—up to three years of maintenance payments. Anyway, I spoke with some lawyers, urging them to file lawsuits on behalf of their clients for compensation over arbitrary repudiation. Indeed, some such lawsuits have been filed, and I have begun to conduct hearings in these files.

I wanted to issue such a compensation ruling, and then to have that ruling reviewed by the shari'a court of appeal. Unfortunately, it went to the appellate court for the wrong reason. One of the lawyers who filed a compensation suit was not wise—I asked him if his client has proof that the repudiation was arbitrary, and he insisted that any repudiation without the consent of the wife is arbitrary. I told him that this was not the case according to the shari'a, but he simply repeated his argument. Finally I had no choice but to reject his suit.

Q: How can someone prove according to Islamic law that it was arbitrary repudiation?

You have to prove that there were no legitimate *shar'i* reasons for divorce. That the husband committed an injustice in divorcing his wife without *shar'i* justification. The problem is, that this lawyer appealed against my decision, and the shari'a court of appeal rejected his appeal on two grounds: that there is no proper clause in the Ottoman Family Rights Law to deal with such a lawsuit; and that the family courts already adjudicate in these cases according to penal and civil laws.

Q: This is what they said?

Yes. And it's a pity. So what if the family courts adjudicate according to civil law? This shouldn't prevent us from dealing with this problem in Islamic terms. And if we don't currently have an adequate clause in our law book—okay, so there is room for judicial *ijtihād*. It's a pity, because I will now have to reject all the lawsuits that were filed for lack of jurisdiction.[34]

(Conversation with Qadi Zibdi, October 19, 2003)

The attempt to introduce a new type of lawsuit—"compensation for arbitrary repudiation"—into the shari'a courts' routine thus failed, maybe due to the unfortunate circumstances under which the case came under review by the shari'a court of appeal. Another explanation, however, is that this initiative was rejected primarily because it was launched by a regional court, and not by the shari'a court of appeal itself.[35] Whatever the reasons for the failure, the episode clearly illustrates both the dynamism of the Israeli shari'a courts in general, and of the

34 Indeed, nine such lawsuits were deleted from the court schedule soon afterwards: ISC 1748/2002, 1860/2002, 2930/2002, 55/2003, 411/2003, 747/2003, 1207/2003, 2416/2003, 2654/2003.

35 On the attempts of the shari'a court of appeal to fortify its position vis-à-vis the regional, first instance courts, see Abu Ramadan (2003b).

shari'a court in West Jerusalem in particular, and the "competitive" frame of mind that brings about this dynamism.

Conclusion

To conclude this chapter, the 2001 legislation amendment intensified the "competitive impulse" that throbs in Israeli shari'a courts—the motivation to convince potential litigants that the shari'a courts offer them a "better bargain" than family courts. The court officials strive to attract more litigants because for them, more litigants means more legitimacy; and as non-profit organizations with dubious religious and national prestige, Israeli shari'a courts are in particular need of legitimacy. Since women constitute the largest pool of potential litigants for shari'a courts, and since the legislation amendment created a threat that women in particular will prefer the family courts—it was only reasonable that special efforts be made to improve women's status in shari'a courts.

As we have seen, the determination to attract potential litigants to the shari'a courts led to an organizational ideology of "user friendliness," that has become ever more salient in the shari'a court in West Jerusalem in recent years. Burdensome procedures were eased, and facilitative bureaucratic and judicial practices were adopted. More important, the process of bettering the position of women in Israeli shari'a courts continued to unfold, and even more pronouncedly than before: the amounts of maintenance payments continued to rise, and the shari'a courts incessantly broadened the "services basket" that they offer to women litigants.

No doubt, this process of continuous improvement in the status of women in shari'a courts is not unique to Israeli shari'a courts.[36] It would also be wrong to perceive it as resulting from the competition with the family courts alone.[37] Nevertheless the competition with the family courts drives qadis presiding in the

36 See for example the articles by Moore, Wurth, Welchman, Buskens, and Schultz, all published in a special issue of *Islamic Law and Society* (2003) on "Public Debates on Family Law Reform: Participants, Positions and Styles of Argumentation in the 1990s."

37 For example, other manifestations of the tendency to improve the status of women in court—that are not directly linked to the competition with the family court—are to be found with regard to obedience suits, and to dissolution of marriage on the initiative of the wife. While obedience suits (*ta'a zawjiyya*) have almost disappeared from court records (the last obedience judgment was issued by the shari'a court in West Jerusalem in 1998, and ever since that year, the court has systematically rejected all obedience lawsuits), a reverse process occurred with regard to "strife and discord" (*niza' washiqaq*) lawsuits. Such lawsuits, which enable wives to seek a divorce on grounds of disharmony in marriage life (in itself, a far reaching innovation in *Hanafī* law), have become, in recent years, the most popular mechanism for achieving a judicial dissolution of marriage. As argued by Abou Ramadan, the qadis presiding in the Israeli shari'a courts have adopted, in recent years, a particularly pro-women policy with regard to "strife and discord" lawsuits: not only have they eased the criteria for proving a situation of "strife and discord," they also tend to

Israeli shari'a courts to strive toward particular goals: they aim to become no less efficient than the civil family courts, and to provide similar services as provided by these courts. The next chapter will illustrate how these processes affect Muslim litigants—and particularly women—in Jerusalem.

---

adjudicate in favor of women with regard to the issue of financial rights following a judicial dissolution of marriage (see Abou Ramadan 2006a and Reiter 2009).

Chapter 11

Forum Shopping: Where to File a Maintenance Suit

As described in Chapter 10, the legislation amendment of November 2001 created a situation of deep or "strong" legal pluralism, from the point of view of Muslim litigants. Except for issues of marriage and divorce (which were left under the exclusive jurisdiction of the shari'a courts),[1] all other issues pertaining to personal status matters of Muslims in Israel can henceforth be dealt with either by shari'a courts or by family courts. Muslim men and women may now freely choose to appeal to either one of these forums in diverse matters such as child and wife maintenance, custody, and guardianship over minors. Furthermore, since a "connection principle" does not apply, filing a suit by one of the spouses in the shari'a court does not prevent the other party from filing a related suit in the family court, and vice versa.[2] Although the material laws that apply to personal status matters of Muslims are presumably similar in both tribunals, in effect, the differences in rules of evidence, in procedures, and in legal cultures—produce dissimilar judgments.

To illustrate the consequential implications of choosing to file a suit in one forum and not the other, this chapter delves into the complex considerations that Muslim Jerusalemite women who wish to obtain an *executable* maintenance order (should) take into account.[3] I added "should" in brackets, since—as we will

---

1 Issues related to *waqf* are also under the exclusive jurisdiction of the shari'a courts.

2 Notably, fully parallel suits (e.g. suits for child custody) may not be dealt with in both tribunals, due to the principle set by the High Court of Justice, according to which a tribunal shall not have jurisdiction over a matter that is already being dealt with by another tribunal (see HCJ 8497/2000). Yet, it is perfectly reasonable and occasionally happens that in response to a maintenance suit that a wife files in the family court, the husband files an obedience suit (*da'awat ta'a zawjiyya*) in the shari'a court. Such cases may result in a serious tangle, if the two tribunals issue contradictory rulings (e.g. the family court grants maintenance to the wife, while the shari'a court declares her a rebellious wife, and hence denies her entitlement to maintenance). As far as I know, no such contradicting court rulings were issued thus far (surely, this is also due to the attitude displayed in recent years by the shari'a court to dismiss obedience suits, as has been discussed in Chapter 10; see also Chapter 13, n. 19). For examples of cases of simultaneous hearings that took place in the Israeli shari'a court in West Jerusalem and in the family court in Jerusalem, see ISC 1751/2001, 621/2002.

3 They can also choose to file a claim in the Jordanian shari'a court or in a Palestinian shari'a court. However, the rulings of these courts are not recognized by the Israeli authorities, and consequently the maintenance order will not be very useful (see the discussion of this issue in Chapter 13).

see—in most cases litigants are not fully aware of the implication of their choice of forum, and their choice is therefore uninformed. Nevertheless, in some cases they do make a choice, and this choice is a complicated one, ridden with meanings, tensions, and conflicts.

Let us begin with a short excerpt taken from my field notes, written at the shari'a court in West Jerusalem on Tuesday, April 7, 2004: I arrived to the court in the morning. Hearings began at 09:00. At 11:00 Qadi Zibdi left the room and went to a meeting of all the judges at the shari'a court of appeal. Having nothing better to do, I sat on the green sofa in the court's waiting room and chitchatted with Akram al-Maliki, a *shar'i* advocate friend (…). When there was a moment of silence, a middle-aged man who sat nearby approached me and inquired who I am. I explained that I'm an anthropologist, conducting research in the court (…). I excused myself and went to talk with him. I asked him why is he there, and he replied that he is escorting his daughter, who should have a hearing concerning a maintenance claim that she had filed against her husband. He said that his daughter had left the marital home with her two young children (aged four and two) about a month ago, after she had been "viciously attacked" by her mother-in-law. I asked why it had happened, and he said:

> I don't know. This is how she's like. They [i.e. his daughter and her mother-in-law] quarrel all the time. She [the mother-in-law] doesn't like how she [his daughter] treats the children, she doesn't like how she cooks, she doesn't like how she dresses. One morning she assaulted her and tore her dress.
>
> *Q: And what did her husband do?*
>
> Her husband doesn't protect her. He's afraid of his mother […] so she ran away from there to me. […]
>
> *Q: Why did you choose to file the maintenance claim in this court?*
>
> I don't know. My uncle knows the lawyer Abu Sha'ban (*al-muhami Abu Sha'ban*), and he recommended him. We went to see him in his office, and he said that we should file a claim here. He is our lawyer.

While my interlocutor described Abu Sha'ban as a lawyer, this was not in fact the case. Apparently the man did not know that Abu Sha'ban was not a lawyer (*muhami*) but a *shar'i* advocate—a councilor allowed to represent clients in shari'a courts alone, and not in any other court.[4] This means that once my interlocutor decided to contact Abu Sha'ban, his ability to shop for a forum that would best serve the interests of his daughter was effectively reduced to zero.

This brief excerpt therefore brings up a very important point, which should be highlighted at the beginning of this analysis: many of the litigants whom I encountered in the shari'a court *did not*, in fact, practice forum shopping. These people were not well-informed as to the intricacies of the dual court system in the

4 On the difference between lawyers and *shar'i* advocates, and on the often tense relationship between them, see Chapter 6.

domain of family law, and some of them were not even aware of the possibility of choosing among different legal forums. Consequently, they had no practical ability, nor incentive, to shop for a forum. Rather, they were channeled to a specific forum by chance, coincidence, and no less important, social networks and references, such as the uncle's recommendation to contact his acquaintance, in the excerpt above.

And still, while some of those who represent litigants in the shari'a court are indeed *shar'i* advocates, others are lawyers—well familiar with both the shari'a and the civil courts. The lawyers often make sure that their clients are informed of the various options available to them. One of the lawyers who used to represent clients both at the shari'a court and at the family court, once told me:

> I recommend to my clients to appeal to the family courts, since rules of evidence are less restrictive there. [In the family court] it's enough to have a deposition [stating that the husband beat his wife] and a medical report signed by a doctor in order to obtain a maintenance judgment and a protection order. In the shari'a court you have to present evidence, to bring witnesses … it's much more difficult.
> (Conversation with *muhami* Mudhi al-Rishk, May 26, 2002)

Indeed, as indicated by ICS 509/2002, a wife appealing to the shari'a court may fail to substantiate her claims for maintenance payments due to insufficient evidence. In this particular case, a young woman sued her much older husband, claiming that he, together with his first wife and her adult children, had attacked her in the marital home and injured her so badly that she was forced to go to hospital several times for treatment. According to her statement of claim, she did not return to the marital home after this incident (that had occurred three and a half months earlier), and she stayed instead in a "state of anger" (*hardane*) in her father's house. Her husband, she further argued, had expressed no intention to bring her back to the marital home, for he has never sent a delegation of notables (*jaha*) in order to try and settle the dispute. She therefore asked the court to establish that she is entitled to maintenance, and to determine the sum of maintenance payments as it sees fit.

On the day of the hearing (April 29, 2002),[5] both husband and wife, who were represented by lawyers, attended the court. The young wife was covered from head to toe by a black robe, her face veiled by a *ḥijab*, and even her hands wrapped in black gloves; her husband, a man of about sixty years of age, was dressed in a plain-looking outfit, and a big white knitted skullcap on his bald head. Both the husband and the wife were accompanied by relatives (the husband by three of his

5 This was in fact the second hearing in this case. I did not attend the first one, which had taken place two and a half weeks earlier, on April 11. During the first hearing—according to the court minutes—the plaintiff made her statement of claim, and the defendant responded by denying that he ever beat his wife. He then argued that there was no proper *shar'i* justification for his wife's leaving of the marital home, and asked the court to determine, therefore, that she is not entitled to maintenance. The court ordered the wife to provide evidence supporting her claims in the next hearing, which was scheduled for April 29.

grown-up children, and the wife by her mother and brother), and the two parties expressed their mutual antagonism by constantly heckling and taunting each other. The difficulty faced by the wife was that the presumed beating had occurred in the marital home, and there were no witnesses to the event. Instead of witnesses, she tried to support her claim by presenting corroborating textual evidence: a signed confirmation that she had been taken by ambulance—at a specific time, from a specific location—to a hospital; some medical reports of her injury and treatment; and a copy of the complaint she filed against her husband at the police station.

The husband's attorney was not impressed by this evidence and claimed that none of it proved that the wife was indeed beaten by her husband. He further stated that for all we know, she could have done this physical damage to herself and then called an ambulance and filed a false complaint at the police station. In response to these suggestions, a small insurgency developed in the courtroom, as the parties began shouting and cursing each other. Only after several minutes of rumpus did the qadi—aided by the lawyers—manage to restore order in the courtroom. He rebuked the husband's attorney for suggesting that the wife fabricated her complaint, but he accepted his assertion that the evidence supplied by the plaintiff did not substantiate her claims. The qadi thus determined that the wife failed to prove her claims, and that the husband may now take an oath of innocence (on the *shar'i* oath, see Chapter 5). The husband took the oath, and the qadi ruled that the wife's suit for maintenance payments was hereby repelled.

This example demonstrates that the strict evidence rules applied in Israeli shari'a courts might indeed present difficulties to women and might prevent them from attaining maintenance payments—as argued by the lawyer cited above. Another disadvantage of shari'a courts from the perspective of women litigants has to do with the average sums of maintenance that these tribunals grant. It is common knowledge among attorneys, as well as among women litigants, that a maintenance suit filed in the family court will probably yield larger sums of maintenance payments than a similar suit filed in the shari'a court. Although there has been a significant increase in the average sums of maintenance granted by shari'a courts over the last decade (see Chapter 10), the family courts still have the upper hand. This gap can be explained, perhaps, by the socio-economic context: the population that attends the shari'a court (that is, the Arab-Muslim population in Jerusalem) usually comes from lower socio-economic strata than the population attending the family court (that is, a mostly secular Jewish population). As a result, the sums of maintenance payments—requested, and thence adjudicated—in the family court are necessarily higher.

But there is also another explanation for the larger sums of maintenance adjudicated by the family courts: unlike the shari'a courts, they have set a minimum sum of maintenance to be granted to entitled wives, regardless of their husbands' financial situation and of their capacity to pay such sums.[6] By contrast,

6 Conveniently, the minimum sums set by the family courts are exactly the sums of pensions determined by the NII. Sums paid by the NII in 2005 were as follows (in NIS): a

the shari'a courts that "do not wish to disintegrate families," as one of the lawyers told me, "find ways to reduce the sums of maintenance adjudicated to wives and minors."[7] The underlying assumption is that if the maintenance sums were higher, husbands would be motivated to divorce in order to avoid paying their wives.[8] Therefore, ideological preferences drive the shari'a courts to determine lower maintenance payments.

Thus far, we have recounted two very obvious advantages—from the viewpoint of Muslim women—of filing a maintenance suit in a family court, rather than in a shari'a court. And yet, there are also some noticeable advantages to shari'a courts. First of all, the family courts are often regarded as hostile and uninviting legal institutions for Muslim litigants, men and women alike. The language of litigation in these courts is Hebrew; security measures are stringent; and the procedural and material law is alien to Islamic norms. By contrast, the shari'a courts are perceived as much more familiar and accessible: litigation is held in Arabic; security measures are relatively loose; and procedural and material laws are based on traditional *shar'i* concepts.

Another, more concrete advantage of the shari'a courts in cases of maintenance suits has to do with their more efficient and speedy handling of such suits. As one of the attorneys told me:

> [I]f a client is [financially] strained, I recommend that she appeal to the shari'a court. Here you may get a temporary maintenance order (*qarar mu'aqqat bi'l-nafaqa*) within a day, while in the family court it may take a full month.
>
> (Conversation with Mudhi al-Rishk, May 26, 2002)

When I asked what may be the reasons for this difference between the two courts, the attorney explained that a maintenance order can be issued faster at the shari'a court since, unlike civil procedure, *shar'i* procedure does not require to inform

---

woman without children—1,393; a woman with one child—2,333; and a woman with two children or more—2,716. According to NII regulations, maintenance payments are made to women entitled to maintenance by court ruling. The NII pays the entitled woman the sum set by the court or the sum set by NII regulations—the smaller of the two. The NII pays entitled women a monthly payment, and then demands refunds from the husband. If the NII succeeds in collecting the full maintenance sum decided by the court, and this sum is larger than the sum paid by the NII, those entitled to the maintenance payment receive also the difference between these two sums. For the up to date sums, see the NII website (http://www.btl.gov.il/English%20Homepage/Benefits/Alimony/Pages/Alimony%20Payment.aspx [accessed: 10/1/2014]).

7 Interestingly, the same phenomenon seems to occur in the rabbinical courts as well. For statistical data indicating that sums of maintenance are significantly higher in family courts than in rabbinical courts, see Hacker (2003: 166, n. 63).

8 Article 150 OLFR determines that a divorcee is entitled to maintenance only for a period of three months, during which she is not allowed to remarry (the *'idda* period). After this period, she has no right to maintenance.

the plaintiff's husband about the suit before issuing a temporary order. As long as a guarantor (*kafil*) commits himself/herself to refunding maintenance payments made to the wife (in case it will eventually be decided that she had not been entitled to these payments), the court will issue a temporary maintenance order, solely on the grounds of the wife's deposition. Such a procedure is very common, and as far as I know, guarantors are seldom required to refund maintenance payments.

Finally, some differences between the shari'a court and the family court can be either advantageous to women or harmful to them—depending on their personal wishes and intentions. More specifically, the choice of a legal forum can exert, in itself, a significant influence on the matrimonial dispute and on the future of the marital life. While this effect could be desired by some women, it could be negative to others.

Although there are no credible statistical data in this regard, the general belief among attorneys working in the shari'a court is that matrimonial disputes that are adjudicated in the family court are much more likely to end in divorce. One of the lawyers explained:

> I ask my client [the wife], what do you want to achieve? Do you want reconciliation with your husband? Or do you wish for a divorce? If she says that she wants a divorce, I file a suit in the family court; if she says that she wants reconciliation, I file a suit here [the shari'a court].
>
> (Conversation with 'Ali Ghazlan, March 22, 2004)

And another lawyer told me:

> Every woman in Jerusalem whose husband "caressed" her, now goes to complain at the police station and to file a suit in the family court. She gets maintenance and a protection order, and the husband [gets] a criminal record, and sits in prison […]. I went to Luba [a police officer in charge of family violence cases in the Jerusalem district] and told her, "You divorce half of Jerusalem." She asked, "Why?" I told her, "Because you too easily charge husbands for beating their wives. You destroy Muslim families this way."
>
> (Conversation with Nawaf al-Salaymi, June 8, 2004)

These comments by lawyers illustrate that the considerations that guide litigants when shopping for a forum can indeed be very complex. Since estranged Muslim women in Jerusalem often find refuge among their agnatic families (that is, in the houses of their fathers, uncles or brothers), and since their agnatic families usually provide for their basic needs, it appears that a maintenance suit can sometimes serve not only as a cry for financial help, but also as an effective device for pressuring an obstinate husband. Indeed, if a woman dwells in "a state of anger" in her agnatic family house for a long period of time (let's say, several months), and if the husband does not seem to be in a hurry to end the dispute—that is, to divorce his wife or to invite her back to the marital home—then the wife will need some sort of "leverage" in order to push the husband into action.

The most effective leverage is a maintenance suit. It is an effective maneuver for pressuring husbands, since it is rather difficult to evade payments that were ordered by a court.[9] Thus, a maintenance order may force the husband either to reconcile with his wife or to divorce her. Many maintenance suits that are filed in the shari'a court are therefore pressuring devices, and all the more so, probably, when a Muslim woman files a maintenance suit at the family court.

But why is it that an appeal to the family court is more likely to bring about a divorce than an appeal to the shari'a court? There are three possible explanations. First, the shari'a court in West Jerusalem—perhaps like other shari'a courts in other places and times—maintains a strong preference for mediation and conciliation over adjudication. As noted by many observers of shari'a courts (e.g. Rosen 1989, Mir-Hosseini 1993: 61–2, Layish 1975: 106, 181), qadis often make extensive efforts to bring about reconciliation and compromise settlements between spouses.[10] In line with this agenda, the qadis in Israeli shari'a courts make extensive use of Article 210 of the codex of Qadri Basha (on the codex, see note 20 in Chapter 3). This article enables qadis to refer disputing parties to semi-institutional mediation: whatever the classification of the dispute, the qadi may offer the parties to withhold legal litigation, and to "give reconciliation a chance."[11] While a tendency for resolution without adjudication is also evident in family courts in recent years (see Arbel and Geifman 1997: 438–41), it seems that generally, the relatively pliable informal procedures of the shari'a court are more prone to bring about conciliation than the relatively formal procedures of the family court.

Second, as clearly reflected in the comments of the lawyers quoted above, the two courts draw on very different cultural and ideological assumptions with regard to the status and roles of men and women in the marital unit. While "occasional" beating of a wife (as long as it is not brutal beating, *darban mubarrihan*) is perceived by many Muslim Jerusalemites as a legitimate, although undesirable

---

9 Even if a husband refuses to pay maintenance, the wife may hand the court ruling to the NII and ask for an allowance. Based on the court order, the NII will provide the wife with a pension and try to collect the money from the husband with the aid of the Execution Office.

10 About the observed tendency of qadis—across times and geographical locations—to prefer conciliations and mutual agreements over issuing judgments, see Chapter 6, note 32.

11 If the parties agree, two mediators are nominated, and informal mediation begins. If reconciliation is achieved, the file is deleted from the court's schedule; if it fails, the parties return to legal litigation, to the exact point where it was halted. For examples of cases where mediation was employed, see ISC 104/2000, 162/2000, 110/2002, 2883/2003, 532/2004.

behavior,[12] it is perceived as an abominable, not to say criminal, behavior by the common family court judge. Now, even if the judges presiding in the two courts share exactly the same progressive views on gender relations, the fact that they serve different populations that embrace different values and norm systems, may produce very different judicial policies in such cases. Thus, it is reasonable to assume that family disputes that involve violence toward the wife have a much greater chance of ending in conciliation, if tried by the shari'a court, rather than by the family court.[13]

Third and last, filing a maintenance suit in the family court may be more likely to lead to a divorce due to the religious, cultural and political *meaning* attached to this act among the Muslim population of Jerusalem. As argued by many scholars in the field of law and society, "going to the law" (Engel 1980: 430), namely, filing a claim in a court, sometimes attests to a sharp escalation of the dispute, for it draws the marital problems between the spouses from the private sphere into the public one. As a result, people often postpone this extreme course of action as long as possible, hoping that their problems be solved in other ways (see e.g., Merry 1990: 3, Engel 1980: 429–31). Still, there are degrees of exteriorization of private problems, and appeals to different forums may be perceived as involving different degrees of "going public" and different degrees of defiance.

In the case of maintenance suits, a woman's decision to appeal to the family court rather than to the shari'a court might be perceived as more defiant and destructive due to the religious implications of this act. From a religious point of view, an appeal to a secular court rather than to a religious one is, of course, highly problematic. Indeed, among some sectors of the Palestinian population in East

12 This statement is based on my impression from dozens of conversations with litigants and legal professionals. Thus, for example, several of my male interlocutors paraphrased a well-known Qur'anic verse (*Surat al-Nisa'*, verse 34), which instructs husbands how to treat a "wrongheaded" wife. They explained to me that:

> if a husband has problems with his wife, what should he do? First, he should approach her and explain to her patiently and calmly what she did wrong. If this doesn't work, he should move to another bed for a couple of days, and refrain from sleeping with his wife. If this measure doesn't help either, he should seek the assistance of *ahl al-khair* [mediators], who will intervene in the dispute, trying to achieve reconciliation. If this doesn't help, and his wife is still rebellious and refuses to obey him, he may resort to the most persuasive method: educational beating (*darb ta'dibi*).

Of course, the fact that such views are held—again, to my impression—by the majority of the litigants (men and women alike) does not mean that there are no liberal and feminist circles among Muslim Jerusalemites that fiercely oppose such views.

13 My impression is that some acts of physical violence (e.g. slapping, shoving) are very common in the context of matrimonial disputes among the Muslim-Arab population of contemporary Jerusalem. Complaints of such behavior, as well as of "verbal abuse," can probably be found in nine out of ten statements of claim (although I have not checked this systematically).

Jerusalem, the religious legitimacy of the Israeli shari‘a court in West Jerusalem is also questionable. Nevertheless, in comparison with the total lack of legitimacy of its rival family court, it fares quite well.

Yet another reason why resorting to the family court may be perceived as radical is the meaning of this act from a national-Palestinian point of view. Although both courts—the shari‘a and the family courts—belong to the Israeli state legal system, the former has gained legitimacy and familiarity over the years. It is managed and presided by Palestinian Israelis, the language spoken in it is Arabic, and in many respects it is sympathetic to the Palestinians and their national identity and interests (see the discussion of this issue in Chapters 3 and 4). Preferring a "Zionist"-secular court over the shari‘a court can thus be perceived as insolent not only on religious grounds, but also on nationalist grounds. Muslim husbands in present-day Jerusalem may therefore perceive an appeal to the family court as a move that is intended to escalate the conflict. By contrast, recourse to the shari‘a court is more likely to be viewed as less radical and less offensive, leaving the "door of reconciliation" (*bab al-musalaha*) relatively open.

The combination of these three factors produces a sharp distinction between the two tribunals: the family court is notorious as a "family breaker," while the shari‘a court has a more moderate and neutral reputation in this regard. These images invite, in turn, active forum shopping on the part of Muslim women in Jerusalem, who must consider in advance what they wish to achieve by the legal procedures. In the rather scanty socio-legal literature on forum shopping, there is an ongoing debate over the social implications of this phenomenon. Scholars attempt to answer questions such as: who benefits from the ability to engage in forum shopping? Is it the strong, dominant side in the dispute (usually this means men), or is it the disadvantaged, subordinate side (mostly women)? (see e.g., Benda-Beckmann 1981, Molokomme 1991: 242–9, Baerends 1994: 84, Peletz 2002: 174–6).

In the case of contemporary Jerusalem, it appears that the answer is unequivocal: the greater freedom of choice that was granted to Muslim litigants by the 2001 legislation amendment works primarily to the advantage of women. The fact is that the family court rulings are usually more favorable to women than those of the shari‘a court. The investiture of parallel, concomitant jurisdiction to the family court in personal status matters of Muslims has therefore served to strengthen women in the context of family disputes.

Another interesting question that arises here has to do with the issue of divorce rates. How could the new option of recourse to the family court affect divorce rates among the Muslim-Arab population in Jerusalem? One possibility is that there is no impact at all. Indeed, if women decide in advance whether or not they wish to divorce, and then choose a court accordingly (as suggested in the quotation above), then the 2001 legislation would not make any difference: only women who would divorce anyway would appeal to the family court. In other words, if spouses decide in advance whether or not they wish to divorce, then the strategic choice to appeal to one court or another is not that important. Such a choice may determine, perhaps, the nature of the separation/conciliation arrangements, but not the continuation/ discontinuation of the marital relations. Such a conclusion is in line with the view of some researchers, who believe that the impact of formal law on divorce negotiations between spouses is negligible (see e.g., Erlanger et al. 1987, Jacob 1992).

However, based on countless observations of court hearings, and on numerous conversations with litigants (both men and women), I would estimate that many litigants do not know exactly, in advance, whether they want a dissolution of the marriage or matrimonial reconciliation. Often people are angry with their spouses; they may be vindictive, or they may want to teach them a lesson, but they have not made up their minds to divorce. Many litigants, as far as I can tell, are confused about the legal procedure. As a result, they tend to change their minds repeatedly; they are open to persuasion, and they are very much affected by the qadi's and the attorney's suggestions.[14] Moreover, they usually do not perceive the appeal to court merely in utilitarian terms: they want justice; they want recognition of their normative behavior; and they may want public acknowledgment of the maltreatment they suffered, in their view, at the hands of their spouses.

My impression of litigants' behavior in the shari'a court in West Jerusalem is therefore in line with the view that courts play a crucial role in determining the outcomes of disputes, and that the development of disputes tends to be still undetermined at the beginning of the legal procedures. In Mark Galanter's (1983: 34) words, "courts not only resolve disputes, they prevent them, mobilize them, displace them, and transform them." As argued above, for various reasons, the family court tends to mobilize litigants towards divorce much more than the shari'a court. Thus, we may hypothesize that the new option opened to Muslim women, of filing maintenance claims in the family court, will result in a rise in the divorce rate.[15]

To conclude, from the perspective of Muslim Jerusalemites, the strengthening of state-legal-pluralism following the November 2001 legislation amendment was anything but "socially insignificant." As we have seen, it opened new options to women involved in matrimonial disputes and thus improved their bargaining power in their negotiations with their husbands.[16] Even if a Muslim woman

14 Many studies have shown that divorce lawyers exert tremendous influence on their clients' decisions with regard to divorce settlements (see e.g., Relis 2002: 172, Sarat and Felstiner 1995: 17–20).

15 Indeed, data provided by the Israeli Bureau of Statistics indicates a slight rise in divorce rates among Israeli Muslims between the years 2002–07 (see http://www.news1.co.il/uploadFiles/224407374858857.pdf [accessed: 10/1/2014]). Internal statistics concerning divorce cases dealt with by the shari'a court in West Jerusalem are as follows: 1998–285 cases; 1999–297; 2000–245; 2001–250; 2002–301; 2003–299; 2004–294; 2005–322; 2007—399 (see http://index.justice.gov.il/Units/BatiDinHashreim/Pages/Report.aspx?WPID=WPQ7&PN=1 [accessed: 10/1/2014]).

16 It is important to note, however, that an appeal to the family court may turn out to be counterproductive in terms of a woman's interests. Not every lawyer is as attentive to his/

eventually chooses not to resort to the family court, the mere possibility of such a move works to her benefit. Indeed, as estimated by several of my informants (all lawyers), the absolute majority of maintenance cases of Muslim litigants in Jerusalem are still adjudicated by the shari'a court in West Jerusalem, and not by the family court.[17] Unfortunately, until today there is no systematic data concerning the "maintenance-suit choices" made by Muslim women in Israel that may corroborate, or else negate these estimations. Partial evidence suggests, however, that they are correct (see e.g., Algazi 2002).[18]

her client's wishes as the lawyer quoted above, and not every woman understands the full meaning of appealing to the family court. Consequently, it may very well be that an appeal that was primarily aimed to mobilize the husband to initiate matrimonial reconciliation leads eventually to an unnecessary divorce. In such cases, a wife's advantage might turn out to be a disadvantage, and she may find herself divorced inadvertently.

17 One lawyer estimated that 95 percent of the maintenance cases are filed in the shari'a court (conversation with I.'A., May 2, 2004). Other lawyers offered more moderate assessments, and estimated that the shari'a court deals with 70 to 90 percent of the cases.

18 A recent report by adv. 'Areen Hawari (2012) suggests that most Muslim and Druze women still view the religious courts as the most appropriate forums to deal with matrimonial disputes.

PART IV
A Tale of Three Courts and One City

Chapter 12
Three Shari'a Courts in Jerusalem

Whereas the Israeli shari'a courts and the family courts both operate under the aegis of the Israeli legal system, the Jordanian and the Palestinian shari'a courts belong to other state (or state-like, in the Palestinian case) legal systems. The parallel operation of several shari'a courts in present-day Jerusalem—an Israeli, a Jordanian and two Palestinian courts—should therefore be regarded as a clear case of "strong" legal pluralism, even in the sense that John Griffiths ascribes to the term (see Griffiths 1986a).

My main thesis in this chapter is that unlike the relations between the Israeli shari'a court and the family court, which are characterized primarily by *competition* over potential litigants (see Chapters 9 and 10), the relations between the Israeli shari'a court in West Jerusalem and the Jordanian and Palestinian shari'a courts in East Jerusalem are characterized primarily by *interdependency* and close interaction. Since the three courts occupy quite different positions in the religious-legal field, the competition between them is relatively limited. The Israeli shari'a court, with its inherent problems of legitimacy (see Chapter 2), does not threaten the religious and normative superiority of the Jordanian and Palestinian courts; and these courts, in turn, cannot seriously compete for litigants, since their rulings are not executed by the Israeli authorities.

In other words, these three courts may be likened to three suppliers of goods that operate in the same social field, but specialize in somewhat different niches. Since none of these courts threatens the dominance of the others in their specialized niches, competition is downplayed, and reciprocal relations for the benefit of all parties are promoted. Indeed, as I will try to show in this chapter, these three courts sustain dynamic relations with each other. These relations are based on a complex system of capital exchange: the Jordanian and Palestinian courts confer normative and religious legitimacy on the Israeli court, which in return provides these tribunals (and their staff) with institutional recognition and with substantial material benefits.[1] I argue that this complex arrangement of capital exchange is anything but stable and self-evident. In fact, during the first years of its existence, the Israeli shari'a court in West Jerusalem maintained a strained and even antagonistic relationship with the Jordanian and the Palestinian courts in East Jerusalem. It was only during the last decade or so that cooperation between these courts has evolved.

---

1 On various forms of capital, see Bourdieu (1986). See also *idem* (1998) for an illuminating discussion of capital exchange and "exchange rates."

The objective of this chapter is to review and to analyze the dynamic relations between these courts. My analysis focuses on the Israeli shari'a court in West Jerusalem, but I also characterize the positions that the other courts, the Jordanian and the Palestinian, occupy in the organizational network of legal institutions operating in contemporary Jerusalem. In the first section I thus provide some background information on the Jordanian and Palestinian shari'a courts. The second section tracks the history of the relations between these courts, as they have developed since the establishment of the Israeli shari'a court in Jerusalem.

The Jordanian and the Palestinian Shari'a Courts in Jerusalem

Since 1967 and until the establishment of the Palestinian National Authority in 1994, the operation of shari'a courts in the West Bank was arranged as follows: Jordanian courts were operating in all major Palestinian cities, and a shari'a court of appeal was in Jerusalem; the courts were administrated and financed by the Ministry of Awqaf in Amman, the Department of *Qadi al-Quda*, with the aid of the Supreme Islamic Board in Jerusalem; Israeli authorities allowed the shari'a courts to operate without interference, and the rulings of these courts were executed by Israeli execution offices, except for the rulings of the Jerusalemite courts.

These arrangements remained intact even when King Hussein of Jordan announced in July 1988 the formal severance of the administrative ties between Jordan and the West Bank.[2] According to the decision of the Jordanian Assembly, Jordan's administrative and legal disengagement from the West Bank was now complete, with the exception of the Ministry of Awqaf and the Department of *Qadi al-Quda*, which administered the shari'a courts (see Welchman 2000: 75). Thus, between the years 1988 and 1994 the shari'a courts and the *waqf* administration remained the last vestige of Jordanian direct influence in the West Bank. This influence was further reduced, however, following the signing of the Israel–PLO Declaration of Principles in September 1993, and the subsequent establishment of the Palestinian National Authority (PNA).

The "Jerusalem question" and the issue of control over the holy places on the Temple Mount appeared to be a hard nut to crack not only in the context of the Israeli–Palestinian negotiations, but also in the context of Jordanian–PNA relations.[3] King Hussein insisted that in light of the historic role that Jordan played in the Muslim holy shrines in Jerusalem, Jordan must be involved in the final

2 This announcement was made in the context of the first intifada (1987–92/3), and with the explicit purpose of assisting the Palestinian Liberation Organization (PLO)—"the sole legitimate representative of the Palestinian people"—in its struggle for freedom and independence. For King Hussein's statement, see *Palestine Yearbook of International Law* (1987/1988: 297–300).

3 For a detailed description of the triple struggle, Jordanian–Israeli–Palestinian, over control of the sacred places in Jerusalem, see Dumper (2002: 17–38).

negotiations concerning the future status of the city. Israel, for its own reasons, was willing to recognize the "special role of Jordan in Jerusalem" (see Klein 1996: 749–50), and thus the Israeli–Jordanian Washington Declaration (signed in July 1994) included a paragraph to this effect (quoted in Welchman 2000: 78).

Rumors of an Israeli–Jordanian deal designated to deprive the PNA of control over the Muslim holy places in Jerusalem (ibid.: 79) have inflamed a bitter struggle between Jordan and the PNA over strongholds in Jerusalem.[4] Due to the strained relations between the PNA and Jordan, the latter announced that it will cut all administrative ties with the shari'a courts and the *awqaf* departments in the West Bank as of October 1, 1994, with the exception of those in East Jerusalem. Consequently, the PNA took over responsibility for the employees of the *waqf* administration and the shari'a courts in the West Bank, who continued to work as before—only with Palestinian seals and stamps, instead of Jordanian ones (Welchman 2000: 79).

Negotiations between the PNA and Jordan concerning the resort of Palestinians from the West Bank to the shari'a court of appeal in Jerusalem failed, and in January 1995 Yasser Arafat issued a decision establishing a Palestinian shari'a court of appeal (ibid.: 81). The permanent seat of this court is supposed to be in Jerusalem, but in the meanwhile the court sits in Nablus and hears appeals from all West Bank shari'a courts, except for Jerusalem. To date, the Palestinian shari'a courts apply Jordanian substantive and procedural law, and despite the great efforts made both by civil society organizations and by Palestinian officials in order to draft a new Palestinian personal status law, this legislation has not yet materialized.[5]

As for Jerusalem, since the PNA is not allowed openly to act in the city, Palestinian shari'a courts have been established in Palestinian neighborhoods on the outskirts of the city, just outside its municipal borders as defined by Israel. These courts, situated in al-Ram and al-'Azariyya (see Figure 6.1), serve Muslim residents of the Palestinian district of Jerusalem. Within the city itself, the shari'a court of first instance administered by Jordan continues to hear cases and to register deeds of East Jerusalemite Muslims as before. However, the Jordanian appellate shari'a court now hears appeals only from that one court.

As explained in Chapter 8, I could not obtain access to the Jordanian and the Palestinian courts in East Jerusalem, and never had the opportunity to attend

4 For example, when the Jordanian-appointed Mufti of Jerusalem, Sheikh Suliman 'Ali al-Ja'abari, died (on January 10, 1994), the PNA and Jordan both sought to appoint his successor. The PNA appointed Sheikh 'Akrama Sabri, former Imam of al-Aqsa Mosque, whereas Jordan extended the mandate of Sheikh 'Abidin, acting *qadi al-quda* in Jerusalem, to the office of Mufti. For a short while the city had two muftis ostensibly doing the same job, but in the spring of 1995 the Jordanian appointee retired, leaving Sheikh 'Akrama Sabri as the sole "Mufti of Jerusalem and the Palestinian lands" (on this episode, see Welchman 2000: 81, Dumper 2002: 34).

5 On the heated public debate in Palestinian society over the issue of reform in personal status law, see Welchman (2003).

hearings in these courts. In the following, I will therefore provide some descriptions of these courts and their legal cultures as recounted by lawyers and litigants in the West Jerusalem shari'a court.

The Jordanian Shari'a Court of First Instance

The Jordanian court operating in Salah al-Din Street, near the Old City compound, was often mentioned by my interlocutors (litigants, legal professionals, and even court staff), and in different contexts. One lawyer, for example, while criticizing the Israeli shari'a court for a lack of observance of formal procedures, told me that:

> Here [in the Israeli shari'a court] there is no order (*nizam*). One day is like that, and the other day like that. One day they say that civil laws apply here, the other day they say they don't apply. This is no way to run a court.[6] You should go and see the shari'a court in Jerusalem (*al-mahkama al-shar'iyya fi al-quds*) [viz. the Jordanian shari'a court in East Jerusalem]; there you have order: they work by the book. They don't change their minds all the time.
>
> *Q: And is it good? Do they do justice to the litigants more than here?*
>
> Yes. Sometimes. There [in the Jordanian shari'a court] you know what to expect. They work by the book, as inscribed by the noble shari'a … [a moment of silence]. Sometimes it's good and sometimes not. They are very rigid there. Sometimes a person may be deprived of justice (*mazlum*), but he has no evidences. If you work by the book, you can't help him. But here the qadi [viz. Qadi Zibdi] is clement. He will meet this person half way; here there is leniency (*luyuna*), but sometimes leniency becomes lawlessness (*fawda*).
>
> (Conversation with N.S., June 8, 2004)

Another lawyer,[7] in response to my question concerning the difference between lawyers and *shar'i* advocates, argued that:

> Here [in the Israeli shari'a court] you have some *shar'i* advocates who became kings. One man [he tells me his name] was a close friend of Qadi Mudlij.[8] They were like this [he held his two index fingers close to each other, to indicate that Qadi Mudlij and that man were close as the two fingers …] This lowlife

6 The lawyer refers to the new directives issued by the Israeli shari'a court of appeal in recent years not to rely on civil ordinances (see discussion of this issue in Chapter 14). On the dynamic nature of the Israeli shari'a court, see Chapter 5.

7 The interviewee is a Jordanian lawyer—that is, he was educated in a Jordanian college, and he is a member of the Jordanian bar (on the tension between lawyers and *shar'i* advocates, see Chapter 6).

8 Qadi Zaki Mudlij was the first qadi to officiate in the Israeli shari'a court, in the years 1988–93. In 1993 he was promoted to the Israeli shari'a court of appeal and retired in 2004.

> man—here he is like a king […]. However, if he would dare to set a foot in the shari'a court in Salah al-Din Street, they would send him away in a second.
> (Conversation with A.A., March 25, 2002)

As illustrated by these excerpts, the Jordanian shari'a court is portrayed as an antithesis to the Israeli shari'a court in West Jerusalem. Indeed, whereas the former is described as a tribunal that fervently preserves "tradition," the latter is viewed as a tribunal that continuously adapts itself to the changing circumstances; whereas the former is described as uncompromising and rigid, the latter is portrayed as dynamic, not to say chaotic; and whereas the former is a prestigious, old fashioned institution, the latter has a dubious reputation.

In fact, the antithetic juxtaposition of the Jordanian and the Israeli shari'a courts is a recurring theme in my interlocutors' discourse. The two courts are described as poles apart, as almost antonymic institutions that differ from each other almost in every respect. In addition to the pairs of dichotomous images mentioned, the Jordanian and the Israeli shari'a courts are also depicted as contrasting in the following respects: the former is old and inefficient, and the latter new and friendly; the former serves the interests of men, whereas the latter promotes new ideas about gender-equality (see Shahar 2004); the former represents resistance to Israeli occupation, whereas the latter represents the occupation itself.[9]

Undoubtedly, there is a kernel of truth in these images.[10] They reflect the specialization of each of these courts in a specific "market niche," and the emergent "division of labor" between them. However, in my view, this set of binary oppositions also represents actors' attempts to make sense of the complex socio-legal reality surrounding them. They construct a mental map of the legal field, in which the Israeli and the Jordanian shari'a courts occupy contradictory positions and exhibit contradictory attributes.

The Palestinian Shari'a Courts

The Palestinian shari'a courts in the district of Jerusalem constitute the puisne element in the network of legal institutions described here. Compared to the three more prominent elements in the network—the Israeli and the Jordanian shari'a

---

9 Even in terms of working conditions the two courts were contrasted with each other. As one of the junior court employees told me:

> [I]t is better to work in the Jordanian court in Salah al-Din Street than here. We work like jackasses (*hmar*) all day long. There they have three officiating qadis, and a staff of 12 clerks. All this personnel—four times bigger than here!—is dealing with how many cases? Maybe 200 cases a year. They work only four days a week from 08:00 until 13:00, and they earn higher salaries than we do […].

10 As far as I can tell, at least with regard to the Israeli shari'a court in West Jerusalem, these images are not far from reality (see Chapter 5; see also Shahar 2000).

courts, and the Israeli family court—the Palestinian courts are indeed of secondary importance from the viewpoint of Jerusalemite Muslims. Not only are the PNA courts located outside the Israeli municipal borders of the city (and thus they are almost irrelevant for Israeli ID card holders), but they also lack both the normative and religious prestige of the Jordanian court and the practical effectiveness of the Israeli courts.

As noted by many observers, the PNA legal system (to which the PNA shari'a courts belong) suffers from very low credibility and accountability. Even before the decrease in the PNA's ability to govern in recent years,[11] it has been widely claimed that the implementation of "justice" in the Palestinian territories has become increasingly dependent upon patronage and violence (Frisch 1998, Robinson 1997). According to both Palestinian and international community commentators, the PNA legal system suffers from three major problems: corruption, pressures exerted on the judicial system by various security agencies and other power groups; and the inability to enforce court rulings (see e.g., Sayigh and Shikaki 1999, 'Ashrawi 2001, Kelly 2004).

This situation is reflected in the words of my interviewees in the Israeli shari'a court. One man—the father of a young woman, who was facing matrimonial problems with her husband—explained in emotional terms why there is absolutely no point in filing a lawsuit against his daughter's husband in the Ramallah shari'a court, even though the couple lives in Ramallah:[12]

> I don't know what to do. She [pointing at his daughter] has been living with me in a state of anger (*hardane*) for more than seven months, and I have no one to talk to. She is miserable, crying all day long, and I don't know what to do [he brings his hands to the fore in a gesture of helplessness].
>
> *Q: Why not?*
>
> Because her husband doesn't want her, but he refuses to divorce her unless she renounces all her rights.
>
> [Her mother intervenes in the conversation:] He [the husband] stole her gold jewelry (*masagh*)[13]—jewelry that is worth 5,000 Jordanian Dinars![14] He does

11 The PNA's ability to govern the Palestinian-administered territories in the West Bank has decreased following the second intifada and the Israeli measures taken to suppress it (see Klein 2003, More 2005).

12 The young woman and her parents were referred to me by Abu Zayd, the court's chief secretary. The conversation with them took place in the court's waiting room on June 23, 2004.

13 It is customary that the groom's family bestows the bride with gold jewelry (*masagh, siyagh*). This gift is regarded as a supplement of the dower (*tawabi' al-mahr*), and it is therefore the private property of the bride. This custom is so prevalent, that the Israeli marriage certificate (which is filled in by the *ma'adhun*) contains a special rubric for indicating the amount and the type of supplements to the dower.

14 A sum that equals about 7,000 US$.

not even deny that he took it. Why should he deny? He couldn't care less. Do you think that we can obtain a court order against him?

Q: If he does not deny that he took it, I'm sure that you can win the case in court. Why don't you file a lawsuit in Ramallah where they [the couple] got married?[15]

[the father gasps and speaks deridingly:] You think that I can win the case in the Ramallah shari'a court?

Q: No?

No! You know what does his [the daughter's husband's] brother do? He used to be a bodyguard of Marwan al-Barghuti![16] You think that the Ramallah qadi will rule in my favor? No chance.[17]

On another occasion, one of the *shar'i* advocates—a former police officer—was complaining about the deterioration in law enforcement in the Arab neighborhoods of Jerusalem. He told me (in Hebrew):

> You know that the police now refuse to enter the Arab neighborhoods if it is not for security reasons or for the purpose of demolishing houses?[18] I have a complicated case of bequest, and I need to summon an important witness. The qadi issued *habeas corpus* three times already, but the police ignore it. They refuse to bring him, since they say they don't have sufficient manpower for such tasks in the Arab neighborhoods […]. I'm telling you that in my time it was different. We weren't afraid to enforce the law. Now Jerusalem begins to look like Nablus or Hebron: you need to pay the police if you want them to enforce a court ruling. Maybe I need to pay a police officer [he rubs together his thumb

15 According to the Ottoman Law of Procedure for Shari'a Courts of 1917 (Article 9(a)), a lawsuit should be adjudicated by the shari'a court in the defendant's place of residence. Since the marital home of the couple is in Ramallah (and since the marriage was registered in the Ramallah shari'a court in the first place), the jurisdiction in this case should rest with this court. In addition, neither the wife nor her husband holds an Israeli ID card (the wife's family lives in the Shu'afat refugee camp, outside the municipal borders of Jerusalem, and the husband is a resident of Ramallah). It is therefore unlikely that the Israeli shari'a court in Jerusalem will rule that it has territorial jurisdiction (*salahiyya makaniyya*) to deal with this case. For an example of a case that was dismissed for lack of territorial jurisdiction, see ISC 958/2003.

16 Marwan al-Barghouti, head of the *Tanzim* (the paramilitary organization of the Fatah movement) in the West Bank, was considered—until his arrest and incarceration by Israel in 2003—one of the most powerful men in the West Bank.

17 Following my conversation with the woman and her parents, I told them that I am not sure whether the Israeli shari'a court will see fit to deal with their case (for the reasons specified in note 15 above). I therefore advised them to consult a professional attorney in this matter. Since this conversation took place during the last week of my fieldwork in the court, I have no knowledge of what became of their lawsuit.

18 For another description of this phenomenon, see below.

> and index finger in a gesture symbolizing the counting of money, and winks in my direction], in order to bring this witness to the hearing […].
>
> (Conversation with R.D., April 11, 2003)

As these quotations illustrate, the prevalent perception of the Palestinian legal system among my interlocutors is of a deeply corrupted system. Whether this image is justified or not is off the point here; what should be noted is that the Palestinian public (as well as Palestinian legal professionals) depict the PNA shari'a courts in terms of corruption, favoritism and "might is right." In this sense, the situation in the PNA resembles the situation in societies that lack a central mechanism of law enforcement (Kelly 2004).

Dispute resolution in two such societies—the Arusha of Northern Tanzania and the Ndendeuli of Sothern Tanzania—was described by legal anthropologist P.H. Gulliver (Gulliver 1963, 1971). According to Gulliver, in societies in which courts or court-like institutions do not exist (or otherwise, their judgments cannot be enforced), each disputant attempts to gain the support of influential personages and power groups. The resolution of the matter in dispute is then based on the assessed or demonstrated social strengths of the parties, and not on the enforcement of legal norms (Gulliver 1969: 25–6). This description, indeed, resembles the situation in the PNA-administered territories.[19]

After examining the prevalent public images of the courts, let us now turn to a diachronic review of the evolution of their interrelations over the last two decades.

From Antagonism to Interdependency

As described in Chapter 4, the Israeli shari'a court in West Jerusalem was established in 1988, only after it became clear to the Israeli authorities that their continuous efforts to co-opt the Muslim religious establishment in Jerusalem (including the shari'a courts in East Jerusalem) were in vain. Thus, the establishment of an Israeli shari'a court in West Jerusalem was rightly perceived by the Jordanian *waqf* functionaries, by the press, and by the general Palestinian public as yet another political act intended to strengthen Israeli rule in Jerusalem, and at the same time to decrease the

---

19 See the analysis of the "indigenous" forms of dispute resolution in the West Bank provided by the Palestinian lawyer George Bisharat (1989: 39–42). There are, however, some significant differences between the African societies studied by Gulliver and contemporary Palestinian society. For example, whereas among the Ndendeuli (and less so among the Arusha), "the use of coercion by force is abjured as a means of dispute settlement or of obtaining redress for injury" (Gulliver 1969: 27), in the Palestinian context the resolution of disputes by violent means is rather common (Kelly 2004; see also Brown 2003: 18–58). Moreover, in the Palestinian case, there does exist a system of tribunals whose operation is flawed, which may be attributable, at least in part, to the sweeping effects of the Israeli occupation.

Jordanian and Palestinian influence in the city (see Welchman 2000: 64). There is no wonder, therefore, that during its first years of operation the Israeli shari'a court in West Jerusalem suffered from a bad reputation, and consequently the number of East Jerusalemite litigants that resorted to it was relatively small (see Figure 6.1).

Between 1988 and 1993 the relations between the Israeli shari'a court in West Jerusalem and the Jordanian courts in East Jerusalem were characterized, therefore, by antagonism, lack of cooperation, and mutual de-legitimization. A radical illustration of the antagonistic relations that prevailed between the Israeli and the Jordanian Muslim establishments in Jerusalem can be found in a fatwa issued by the acting Jordanian *qadi al-quda* and Mufti of Jerusalem, the late Sheikh Sa'ad al-Din al-'Alami. According to some informants of mine, Sheikh al-'Alami issued a fatwa that literally permitted the killing of Sheikh Tawfiq 'Asliyya, then the president of the Israeli shari'a court of appeal, who was allegedly guilty of selling *waqf* property to Israeli official and semi-official elements. I was unable to locate the fatwa, but I heard this story from two different informants, who are both very familiar with the Islamic religious field in Jerusalem. One of my informants even claimed that in light of the fatwa, the Israeli General Security Services provided close quarters protection to Sheikh 'Asliyya.[20]

Nevertheless, it appears that the appointment of Qadi Ziad 'Asliyya—son of Sheikh Tawfiq 'Asliyya—to qadiship in the Israeli shari'a court in West Jerusalem in 1993 led to significant change. As described in Chapter 6, Qadi Ziad 'Asliyya enlisted several employees of the Jordanian *waqf* administration for mediation and arbitration assignments on behalf of the Israeli shari'a court, and also appointed some of them to the position of marriage registrars (*ma'adhuns*). These men were tempted, presumably by the material benefits of the job, and by agreeing to represent an Israeli tribunal they lent their respectability to this court. Moreover, personal contacts that were established between senior functionaries of the two establishments—the Israeli and the Jordanian—opened the door for cooperation between the two courts.

Within a few years, Qadi Ziad 'Asliyya, with the aid of Qadi Ahmad Natur (who was appointed president of the Israeli shari'a court of appeal in 1994), succeeded in developing productive relations with the Jordanian and Palestinian Islamic legal establishment in Jerusalem. As I was told by Qadi Natur, the turning point in the relations between the Israeli and the Jordanian shari'a courts occurred in 1995, when he issued an appellate ruling determining that the Jordanian qadi of Jerusalem should be considered "a religious scholar from among the scholars of the nation" (*'alim min 'ulama al-'umma*) and that hence rulings of the Jordanian court in Jerusalem must be recognized by Israeli shari'a courts.[21]

---

20 At the same time, other informants were unable to remember such a fatwa and raised doubts concerning the authenticity of the story. For a critical discussion of the role played by Israeli qadis in selling *waqf* property to Jewish elements, see Dumper (1994: 32).

21 Qadi Natur did not remember the number of this ruling, and I could not locate such a decision among the appellate shari'a court verdicts from 1995 that were published in

This new policy stood in sharp contrast to the policy adopted by the former president of the Israeli shari'a court of appeal (Sheikh Tawfiq 'Asliyya), who refused to recognize rulings of the Jordanian court.[22] Natur openly admits that the change of policy was meant to improve the relations between the Israeli shari'a courts and their Jordanian and Palestinian counterparts:

> Since the shari'a courts in East Jerusalem were excommunicated [by the Israeli authorities], the rulings of these courts were regularly taken to the shari'a court in Ramallah and recognized there. After this recognition, the rulings could be executed by the Israeli civil administration in the occupied territories. However, when they [the Israeli authorities] learned about this trick, they refused to execute [the rulings] even if they were formally recognized. Now they [the East Jerusalemite courts] had a problem, because they could no longer execute their rulings. My decision changed this situation entirely. I wrote it [viz. this decision] because there is no *shar'i* reason not to recognize their rulings,[23] and because I wanted to establish better relations with them. This [change of policy] altered their attitude altogether. Today we have good cooperation with them
>
> (Conversation with Qadi Natur, Tel Aviv University, March 24, 2005)

Indeed, the recognition of the Jordanian shari'a courts' rulings by the Israeli shari'a court in West Jerusalem,[24] literally enables the continuous functioning of the Jordanian courts in the city. In addition to this "generous" policy—that is, of course, highly instrumental—Qadi 'Asliyya, and later on Qadi Zibdi, employed a strategy of calculated self-effacement: they publicly acknowledged the normative and religious superiority of the Jordanian shari'a court. Thus, for example, Qadi 'Asliyya used to seek the advice of his Jordanian colleagues in the most prestigious cases that were brought before him—cases of dispute over *waqf*. As he once explained to me:

> They [the qadis presiding in the Jordanian court in East Jerusalem] are experts in *waqf*: they have a huge archive there, containing information about *waqf* property in Jerusalem, and they are also indigenous Jerusalemites. They

---

al-Kashshaf. Due to accessibility problems during the last months of my fieldwork, I was unable to search the appellate court archive for the ruling (on my accessibility problems, see Chapter 8).

22 The policy of Sheikh 'Asliyya (the father) was in line with the official directives of the Israeli authorities, which forbade the execution of any ruling issued by the Jordanian shari'a courts in East Jerusalem (see Chapter 4).

23 Qadi Natur's ability to decide on a "private" policy, which is in total contradiction to the official Israeli governmental policy, is yet another example of the broad judicial discretion of the qadis presiding in Israeli shari'a courts. On the lack of effective state supervision of the shari'a courts and the relative autonomy that results from this situation, see Chapter 2.

24 As described below, there are exceptions to this policy as well.

> have much better resources than I have at my disposal to deal properly with complicated *waqf* cases.
>
> (Conversation with Qadi Ziad 'Asliyya, May 16, 1998)

Likewise, when litigants in the West Jerusalem shari'a court relied on fatwas issued by the Jordanian (and later on, the Palestinian) Mufti of Jerusalem to support their claims, the Israeli qadis tended to refer to these fatwas with pronounced respect (see e.g., ISC 985/2002, 112/1998, 404/1999).

Apparently, all these efforts to gain the trust and cooperation of the Jordanian and Palestinian Muslim religious establishments gradually bore fruit. The Israeli qadis, who were once considered abominable (and may have been even targeted for assassination), have gradually become legitimate personages. In recent years, the Israeli qadis are regularly invited to pray in *al-Haram al-Sharif* as guests of their Jordanian and Palestinian colleagues on Muslim holidays and during the month of *Ramadan*. One of my informants, a lawyer, told me that Qadi 'Asliyya was asked—a few months after he had left the position of qadi in Jerusalem—to act as an arbitrator in a dispute between members of one of the most respected families in Jerusalem.

The growing personal legitimacy of the Israeli qadis was also accompanied by a growing legitimacy of the institution that they represent—the Israeli shari'a court in West Jerusalem. The status of this court has gradually changed during the last decade, from an almost excommunicated legal institution to the most popular court in Jerusalem. The most salient act, perhaps, of conferring legitimacy on this court took place, surprisingly or not, in the context of the struggle over the jurisdiction of the Israeli shari'a courts vis-à-vis Israeli family courts (see Chapter 9). As described, in response to an *istifta'* (query) presented to the Mufti of Jerusalem, Sheikh 'Akrama Sabri issued a fatwa declaring his utmost objection to the idea that Israeli (civil) family courts will be granted jurisdiction in personal status matters of Muslims. Implicit in this fatwa was the recognition of the Israeli shari'a courts as legitimate tribunals that properly implement the sacred shari'a. Thus, whereas only ten years earlier the Mufti of Jerusalem issued a fatwa permitting the assassination of the president of the Israeli shari'a court of appeal, the current Mufti of Jerusalem now issues a fatwa fully acknowledging the legitimacy of these courts (see Appendix 3).

The Jordanian and Palestinian Muslim establishments in Jerusalem have therefore gone a long way since their initial refusal to recognize the Israeli shari'a court in West Jerusalem. Nonetheless, the patterns of institutional recognition between the three tribunals still reflect the moral-religious and nationalistic superiority of the Jordanian and Palestinian courts. These hierarchical relations between the Jordanian and the Israeli shari'a courts can be illustrated by examining each court's treatment of marriage certificates issued by the other. Whereas the Israeli shari'a court recognizes marriage certificates issued by the Jordanian court almost automatically, the Jordanian court refuses to do so. Rather, it requires that the married couple repeat the marriage ceremony in the presence of a Jordanian-appointed *ma'adhun*. Thus, if a couple that was married by an Israeli-appointed *ma'adhun* wants their marriage to be recognized by the Jordanian authorities, they must either repeat the marriage ceremony or register the marriage in the Jordanian Embassy in Tel Aviv.[25]

As to the Palestinian shari'a courts: like the Jordanian courts, the Palestinian court of appeal in Ramallah ruled that judgments and registered deeds issued by the Israeli shari'a court in West Jerusalem "fall outside the competence of the [PNA] Execution Department" (Bakri 2000: 37). Yet, unlike the hierarchical relations between the Israeli and the Jordanian courts, the relations between the Israeli and the Palestinian shari'a courts are more egalitarian. This is because the Palestinian courts are facing some serious legitimacy problems of their own. Thus, on June 17, 2002, the president of the Israeli shari'a court of appeal, Qadi Ahmad Natur, issued an administrative directive stating that:

> Since we were informed that there are attempts to forge the seals of the Palestinian shari'a courts […], and in order to avoid reliance on such fabricated documents, you are requested [viz. the qadis presiding in Israeli shari'a courts] not to accept [the validity of] any document issued by a Palestinian shari'a court, unless it is ratified by the honorable acting *qadi al-quda*, Sheikh Taysir al-Tamimi.

The issuance of the administrative circular—and of course, its contents—brings to the fore some key features of the Palestinian and Israeli shari'a court systems: the corruption and the low credibility of the PNA legal system; the personification of the institutional relations between the two legal systems; and the far-reaching judicial agency displayed by the Israeli qadis (and by Qadi Natur, in particular), who may determine legal policies without resorting to any governmental or judicial external authority.

We may conclude that over the last two decades, the Israeli shari'a court in West Jerusalem, and the Jordanian and Palestinian shari'a courts in East Jerusalem have undergone a process of "relationship-building." Whereas initially the Israeli shari'a court's relations with its Jordanian and Palestinian counterparts were markedly antagonistic, the qadis and the other personnel in the three courts have managed during the last decade to develop personal acquaintance between them, as well as substantial cooperation between their institutions. This cooperation is based, as I argue, on an exchange of different capitals. The Israeli shari'a court offers to employees of the Islamic establishment in Jerusalem personal material

25 By filing a petition for the registration of the marriage in the Jordanian passport, the couple may escape the requirement to repeat the marriage ceremony. The Jordanian Ministry of Foreign Affairs recognizes registered deeds issued by Israeli courts after the Jordanian Embassy in Tel Aviv verifies these documents. However, despite the registration of the marriage in the Jordanian passport, this registration has no standing in Jordanian shari'a courts, and therefore the need to repeat the marriage ceremony will arise again in case the couple ever requires the services of a Jordanian shari'a court.

benefits—such as appointment to the position of *ma'adhun*. In return, these individuals confer on the Israeli court their legitimacy and respectability among the Palestinian community in Jerusalem. In addition, by recognizing registered deeds issued by the Jordanian and the Palestinian shari'a courts, the Israeli court turns these deeds into legal acts that are also recognized by Israeli state institutions. In return, the Jordanian and Palestinian courts grant the Israeli court more legitimacy and recognition—as exemplified by the 2001 *fatwa* issued by the Mufti of Jerusalem, in which the Mufti actually sides with the Israeli shari'a court in its struggle against the encroachment of its jurisdiction.

From an organizational perspective, it may be argued that the growing cooperation and interdependence between these courts are a result of the relatively low competition between them. Each specializes in a different "niche," and they generally do not compete over litigants. The interactions between the courts occur on a daily basis, across various domains, and at both formal and informal levels. In fact, as we will see in the next chapter, not only the formal legal arrangements between the courts affect the unfolding interactions between them, but also the personal, informal relationships between their personnel. Likewise the choices made by the "joint clientele" of these courts—Jerusalemite Muslims—also affect the form of relationship that the three courts maintain with each other.

benefits, such as appointment to the position of qadi or mazun, many individuals enter on the Israeli court their legitimacy and specialty among the Palestinian community in Jerusalem. In addition, by recognizing legal deeds issued by the Jordanian and the Palestinian shari'a courts, the Israeli courts turn these deeds into legal acts that are also recognized by Israeli state institutions. In return, the Jordanian and Palestinian courts grant the Israeli court legitimacy and recognition—as exemplified by the 2010 *fatwa* issued by the Mufti of Jerusalem, in which the Mufti actually stressed the Israeli shari'a court['s] [illegible] its status against the encroachment of its jurisdiction.

From an organizational perspective, it may be argued that the ongoing cooperation and interdependence between these courts are a result of the relatively low competition between them, each specializing in different fields and usually potentially do not compete over litigants. Participation between these courts occurs on a daily basis, across various domains, and at both formal and informal levels. In fact, as we will see in the next chapter, not only the formal legal arrangement between the courts affects the unfolding of each court's [illegible] but also the personal, informal relationships between their personnel [illegible] mainly by the "epistemic circle" of these courts [illegible] also affect the form of relationship that the three courts maintain with each other.

Chapter 13
Forum Shopping between Shari'a Courts

As we have seen, a complex system of interdependency has developed in recent years between the three shari'a courts operating in Jerusalem. These relations find expression in close interactions between these courts, on a daily basis and across various domains. The most salient encounter between these courts undoubtedly occurs in the domain of registered deeds (e.g. marriage and divorce certificates and inheritance deeds).

The different and asymmetric policies of the three courts with regard to the mutual recognition of registered deeds naturally create a strong incentive to appeal first to the Jordanian or Palestinian courts, and only later to the Israeli court. The logic is simple: if registered deeds issued by more than one court are needed, and if court *A* routinely recognizes the deeds issued by court *B* and *C*, whereas the latter courts refuse to recognize the deeds issued by court *A*—it makes sense to appeal first to courts *B* or *C*, and only later to court *A* for a recognition of the deeds issued by courts *B* or *C*. Indeed, this is exactly what happens in Jerusalem: about half of the files in the Israeli shari'a court in West Jerusalem are actually requests for the recognition of deeds registered by the Jordanian or the Palestinian shari'a courts (see Figures 7.1 and 7.2).

Another reason for preferring Jordanian (or Palestinian) *ma'adhun*s is the significant differences in the material laws that are applied by the courts and by the *ma'adhun*s they appoint. Whereas the Jordanian Law of personal Status of 1976 allows the marriage of a girl aged 15 to 17 and of a boy aged 16 to 18,[1] Israeli legislation considers the marriage of minors (girls under 17; boys under 18) a criminal offence.[2] In other words, while the Jordanian *ma'adhun*s are allowed to marry off minors aged 15 to 17 (girls) and 16 to 18 (boys), the Israeli *ma'adhun*s are not allowed to do this, and unless they want to risk criminal prosecution, they will certainly refrain from performing such marriages. In a similar vein, while the Israeli Knesset criminalized polygamy (see Chapter 3), the Jordanian law does not forbid it. Thus, a man who wishes to marry a second wife will surely register his polygamous marriage with a Jordanian *ma'adhun*, rather than with an Israeli one (who is anyhow likely to refuse registering such a marriage).

1 Such minor marriages are allowed on proof of sufficient maturity and physical development (see Welchman 2000: 62–3).

2 Only a civil judge, not a qadi, nor any other religious judge, is allowed, under special circumstances, to permit the marriage of a 16-year-old girl (see the discussion in Chapter 3).

Indeed, the calculated choice of a *ma'adhun* for the purpose of performing and registering a marriage constitutes the most prevalent form of forum shopping in Jerusalem. Since the Israeli shari'a court recognizes Jordanian and Palestinian marriage certificates, even in cases of clearly illegal acts (by the standards of Israeli statutory law—such as minor or polygamous marriages), the strategic maneuvering between the various legal systems usually proves worthwhile. In the past, when Israeli qadis encountered a case of minor or polygamous marriage, they used to recognize the marriage, but add a note to the file stating that a felony had been committed. They also used to send the file to the shari'a courts administration for further handling.[3] However, in recent years the Israeli shari'a court of appeal has determined in several rulings that it is not for the shari'a courts to make any notes or indications concerning violations of Knesset legislation. The shari'a court of appeal stressed that the shari'a courts are merely obliged to rule according to Islamic principles; and thus, as long as shari'a rules have not been violated, any offence against "worldly" legislation is of no interest to these courts.[4]

Marriage and divorce certificates issued by a Jordanian or a Palestinian court are therefore recognized in Israeli shari'a courts, even in cases of minor or polygamous marriages, or of unilateral repudiation of wives.[5]

Safeguarding the Rights of Orphaned Grandchildren

A more complicated situation arises in cases of inheritance deeds (*hasr 'irth*), as illustrated by the following example, an event that occurred in May 17, 2004: One afternoon, several hours after the hearings of that day had ended, I was sitting in the court secretariat, preparing (at the request of Abu Zayd, the acting chief secretary) some Hebrew summonses for prisoners who were requested to appear in court. The summonses were to be sent by fax to the Israeli Prison Authorities, and therefore had to be written in legible Hebrew.[6] The court building was empty of litigants and lawyers, and even the typists had already left. Only Abu Zayd and

3 Moreover, until 1998 the Israeli shari'a courts used to issue an annual report on cases in which offences against state law were committed. It is noteworthy, though, that there were usually no legal steps taken in such cases (see Shahar 2004: 204–5).

4 See e.g., SCA 31/1995, 128/1997, 9/1999, 263/2003. This new policy is of course another manifestation not only of the far-reaching judicial agency enjoyed by the qadis presiding in the Israeli shari'a courts, but also of the qadis' attempt to distance the shari'a courts from the Israeli legal system (see Chapter 14).

5 As explained in Chapter 3, the Israeli legislator criminalized the act of unilateral repudiation that is divorce without the wife's consent.

6 Unlike previous chief secretaries, Abu Zayd does not speak or write Hebrew (in fact, this "deficiency" has prevented him from becoming the formal chief secretary in the Jerusalem shari'a court). He therefore needs the assistance of others when Hebrew communication is required, and when I was present in court he often asked me to write Hebrew summonses for prisoners. See more about my fieldwork in Chapter 8.

Abu 'Uday (Abu Zayd's aide) were with me in the secretariat; also Qadi Zibdi was still there—working in his chambers. During my years of fieldwork in the Israeli shari'a court in West Jerusalem, I have learnt to cherish such relaxed times, when I could chit-chat with Abu 'Uday and Abu Zayd, or discuss with them interesting cases that I witnessed during the day.

As I was sitting there, Qadi Zibdi entered the room, sat down and started to discuss with Abu Zayd a dilemma that he had encountered earlier that day. He recounted that a family had come to the court, asking for the recognition of a certificate of inheritance (*hasr 'irth*) issued by the shari'a court in Salah al-Din Street [viz. the Jordanian court in East Jerusalem]. He was about to recognize this deed as he always does, when he suddenly observed that orphaned grandchildren were also among the legatees. Qadi Zibdi explained:

> It suddenly occurred to me that there is a difference between the Jordanian law of succession and our policy as determined by the judicial circular.[7] Whereas the Jordanian law distinguishes between agnate grandchildren (*awlad al-zuhur*) and cognate grandchildren (*awlad al-butun*), here we do not differentiate between them. Now I have a problem, I cannot automatically recognize Jordanian inheritance deeds. I need to check first that no orphaned grandchildren are involved.

Qadi Zibdi and Abu Zayd then discussed the implications of this problem, and Qadi Zibdi asked Abu Zayd to survey all the bequest deeds that were recognized by the court during the years 2003 and 2004—to find out whether there were any other cases of this kind. Reluctantly,[8] Abu Zayd agreed to do so, and Qadi Zibdi departed.

This example illustrates the complexity of the legal situation in Jerusalem, which often creates genuine problems and dilemmas. It also demonstrates that the qadis presiding in Israeli shari'a courts are keener to sustain the reforms introduced by their own initiative (e.g. by the judicial circulars) than they are to sustain Israeli Knesset legislation. Thus, whereas the Israeli qadis are actively directed to disregard (and therefore to conceal) instances of offences against state law, they demonstrate considerable sensitivity to breaches of regulations set up by

7 Qadi Zibdi refers here to the third judicial circular issued by Qadi Natur, the president of the Israeli shari'a court of appeal. This circular, titled "The Obligatory Bequest," deals with the issue of bequests in favor of orphaned grandchildren—a well-known problem in Islamic law of succession (see Coulson 1971: 33). In this circular, Qadi Natur chooses to follow the Egyptian Law of Testamentary Disposition of 1946, which does not distinguish between agnate grandchildren (that is, children born to the sons of the deceased) and cognate grandchildren (that is, children born to the daughters of the deceased). In contrast to the Egyptian law, the Syrian and the Jordanian laws of personal status (of 1953 and 1976 respectively) exclude the cognate grandchildren from the compulsory bequest (see A. Natur 1996; see also Abou Ramadan 2003b, Zahalka 2009).

8 In 2003 the court dealt with more than 160 cases of succession and bequests. About two thirds of these were recognitions of deeds issued by Jordanian or Palestinian courts. Reviewing these files was therefore not an easy task for the court's secretariat.

the judicial circulars,[9] to the extent that Qadi Zibdi instructed the court secretariat to review hundreds of cases in order to see that no other mistakes had been made.

The event described here should be viewed, however, as it is: an exceptional occurrence that testifies to the norm. As a rule, the Israeli shari'a court in Jerusalem tends to recognize legal documents issued by Jordanian or Palestinian courts. References to rulings or documents issued by these courts can be found in countless cases deliberated by the Israeli shari'a court. To mention just two common examples: in many cases, power-of-attorney registrations (*wikalat*) are signed by qadis presiding in Palestinian or Jordanian courts (see e.g., ISC 746/2000, 1603/2001, 510/2003); and in some cases, Israeli qadis request the assistance of qadis officiating in shari'a courts in the West Bank, and ask them to hear and validate the testimonies of witnesses who cannot come to the Israeli court in West Jerusalem due to travel restrictions (see e.g., ISC 1543/2001, 107/2004).

A Venue for Divorce, Another for Maintenance

It is also rather common that legal procedures in the Israeli shari'a court in West Jerusalem come to an end after a Jordanian or a Palestinian court has achieved agreement between the disputants. In particular, a considerable number of "strife and discord" cases (*niza' washiqaq*) were deleted from the Israeli shari'a court's schedule following the issuance of a divorce certificate by either a Jordanian or a Palestinian shari'a court.[10] The following example may serve as an illustration.[11]

A middle-aged couple from one of the Arab neighborhoods inside the municipal borders of post-annexation Jerusalem encountered problems in their marital life. As usually happens in such cases, the wife left the marital home and sojourned in her father's house for several months. The couple's youngest child accompanied her, while the other children—some of them grown-ups—remained with the father. The couple was apparently unable to resolve the dispute by themselves, and despite some attempts to achieve reconciliation, the quarrel persisted.[12]

9 In itself, a mechanism with a dubious legal status. See discussion of the judicial circulars in Chapter 9.

10 See e.g., ISC 751/2000, 1018/2000, 1054/2000, 1428/2000, 80/2001, 1629/2001, 1758/2001, 734/2002, 1563/2002, 469/2003, 510/2003, 786/2003. Notably, the legal procedures in requests for the dissolution of marriage on the grounds of "strife and discord" are usually quite lengthy and troublesome. There is no wonder that in many such cases a parallel legal procedure unfolds in another shari'a court, and that this parallel procedure often ends in a divorce.

11 The following description is based on two hearings that I witnessed at the end of the summer of 2003, and on a conversation with the defendant in this case (i.e. the husband). This man explicitly asked me not to expose any personal details of his, nor to mention the file number of the case.

12 As the husband later told me, he and his (ex-)wife are blood-relatives—they are second-degree cousins. For that reason, presumably, the grave dispute between them was

In the summer of 2003, after several months of unresolved dispute between husband and wife (and their families), the wife filed a "strife and discord" lawsuit in the Israeli shari'a court, asking for the judicial dissolution of the marriage. She claimed that due to their "impaired marital life (*su' al-mu'ashara*), the mutual hatred and discord between them are permanent and irresolvable."

In the first hearing in the case, both the wife and the husband attended the court. The wife was represented by a *shar'i* advocate, the husband by a lawyer, and both were accompanied by agnate relatives. Also present in court were five of their children (while three other children did not appear). As usual, the hearing began with a presentation of the statement of claim by the wife's legal representative. Then the qadi addressed the husband's legal representative, asking for his response to the statement of claim. The husband's lawyer responded by denying the existence of strife and discord between the spouses, and claiming that the wife had left the marital home without any *shar'i* justification. The lawyer therefore asked the court to reject the wife's lawsuit, and to order her to pay the trial costs.

The qadi ended this very brief hearing by stating that since the defendant denied the statement of claim, the burden of proof rests with the claimant. He therefore ruled that the wife must provide the court with evidence in the next hearing, which was scheduled—after consultation between the qadi and the legal representatives—for three weeks later. Throughout the hearing neither the wife nor the husband spoke a word.

I did not attend the second hearing, but from the court minutes I learned that the wife described in detail two cases of quarrels with her husband that deteriorated to physical violence on his part (she claimed that on one occasion he pushed her and banged her head against the wall). She also brought evidence that her husband recently filed an obedience lawsuit (*ta'a zawjiyya*) in the Jordanian shari'a court, and argued that this is a spiteful lawsuit (*da'wa kaydiyya*), which clearly indicates that a state of discord and strife does exist between them. In addition, the wife summoned to court three witnesses—neighbors living in close vicinity to the disputing couple—who testified that there are problems in the couple's marital life. One of the witnesses was apparently an agnatic uncle of the husband, and yet he testified on behalf of the wife: he said that the couple had been living in conflict for a long time, and that loud shouting was frequently heard from their house.[13]

---

particularly harmful and painful to their families. The statement of claim describes several attempts to settle the dispute with the assistance of a "delegation of notables" (*jaha*), sent by the husband's family to the wife's family. All these efforts, nevertheless, did not yield a solution.

13 I later asked the husband how come his uncle testified in the court against him. He answered that his uncle was involved in some attempts of reconciliation. When he realized that the couple's problems were real, he came to the conclusion that the dispute must be resolved in court, and he therefore gave testimony in support of the wife, who demanded the intervention of the court.

The husband's lawyer tried to undermine the witnesses' testimonies. He also responded to the claim of the wife's representative that filing an obedience suit indicates the existence of "strife and discord." It is exactly because the husband denies such a state of affairs, he argued, that he demands the return of his wife to the marital home and her obedience to him. Nevertheless, it appears that Qadi Zibdi was convinced that strife and discord do exist between the couple.[14] He gave a resolution to this effect, and ordered the parties to provide the court with names of arbitrators within ten days.[15]

The next hearing took place ten days later.[16] The purpose of the hearing was to appoint arbiters. Nevertheless, when the hearing began, the wife's representative rose and said that there will be no need to appoint arbiters, for an agreement on a divorce had been achieved in the shari'a court in Salah al-Din Street [viz. the Jordanian shari'a court]. The advocate then handed to the qadi a signed ruling of "divorce by consent with mutual waiving of all financial obligations" (*talaq bi'al-ibra'*), issued just three days earlier by the Jordanian court. He said that the spouses had agreed to reciprocally renounce any financial claims that they may have, except for the *'idda* and the minor child maintenance payments.[17] They even agreed on the maintenance amounts: the husband will pay monthly child maintenance of 1,200 NIS, and during the *'idda* period additional 800 NIS for his wife.

The advocate then asked that the details of the maintenance agreement be noted and registered in the court ruling. Qadi Zibdi, who was not at all surprised by this new development, dictated a ruling, stating:

---

14 In recent years, the Israeli shari'a court of appeal has led a minor revolution with regard to lawsuits of "strife and discord." The court determined in several cases (e.g. SCA 165/2000, 162/2002, 114/2003) that the most important proof to the existence of strife and discord between spouses is the qadi's conviction. In other words, the substantiation of a claim to strife and discord depends not so much on specific *shar'i* evidence, but rather on the ability to convince the qadi that the dispute is real and substantial. These precedent rulings of the shari'a court of appeal brought about a significant change: if previously the substantiation of strife and discord was quite difficult—and thus demanded much time and effort on behalf of the parties and the court—this phase is now relatively short and unproblematic (see Abou Ramadan 2006).

15 According to Article 130 OLFR, in cases of "strife and discord" the court should nominate two arbiters—one on behalf of each party. These arbiters must first try to reconcile the disputing spouses, but if they conclude that reconciliation is impossible, they may determine that the marriage should be dissolved. It is the qadi, however, who has the authority to dissolve the marriage, and not the arbiters.

16 I was present in this hearing. The two legal representatives were present, of course, as well as the husband. The wife, however, did not attend the court that day.

17 According to all schools of Islamic law, a husband must pay his divorcee wife maintenance during the *'idda* period—the time span during which a divorcee or a widow is not allowed to remarry. The length of this period changes according to the type of marriage and the reasons for the dissolution of the marriage (see Layish 1975: 177–8).

> in due date, the representative of the plaintiff [his name indicated] and the representative of the husband [his name indicated] and the husband [his name indicated] were present in court. Before the hearing began, the plaintiff's representative declared that a divorce in agreement had been achieved in the shari'a court in Salah al-Din Street. The litigants agreed that the husband will pay child maintenance of 1,200 NIS, and *'idda* maintenance of 800 NIS. In light of what was described above, I hereby delete this file from the court's schedule […].

The court's scribe (Salih) printed the ruling, and the qadi, the legal representatives of the parties, as well as the husband, all signed the document. The hearing thus ended, and a new hearing in a different case immediately began.

After this hearing I had a long conversation with the husband outside the courtroom. He was much more relaxed and calm than the first time I saw him, and was therefore quite talkative. I inquired what the real reason for the dispute was, and he said that the main reason for the deterioration of the marital life was his wife's new Islamic devotedness. In his words, she has become a "religious fanatic" (*mutatarifa*) in recent years, and since he maintained his former way of life, they could no longer live together.[18] He was therefore content with the divorce and the financial settlement that had been achieved.

The most revealing aspect of this case is the functional division of labor between the Jordanian and the Israeli shari'a courts. As one could expect, it was the wife—sojourning in her father's house for several months—who first initiated a legal procedure. If she wanted to achieve a divorce (and apparently, she did), the most reasonable thing to do was indeed to file a "strife and discord" lawsuit in the Israeli shari'a court. As mentioned, the Israeli shari'a courts have adopted in recent years a particularly facilitative approach with regard to "strife and discord" suits (see Abou Ramadan 2006a, Reiter 2009). Thus, even if her husband were to cling to his objection to the divorce, she would still have a fair chance to win the case and to have the qadi dissolve the marriage. Similarly, it was quite reasonable on the part of the husband to file an obedience lawsuit in the Jordanian shari'a court in Salah al-Din Street. This court is much more inclined than the Israeli shari'a court to issue an obedience ruling, and the husband's prospects of winning such a case there are much higher.[19]

---

18 Indeed, during her visit to the court, the wife appeared covered from head to toe with a black robe (*nikab*).

19 To the best of my knowledge, between 1998 and 2006 the Israeli shari'a court in West Jerusalem has refrained from issuing obedience rulings. I have no statistical data concerning the Jordanian shari'a court's policy in this matter, but I know of at least two cases of matrimonial disputes in recent years, in which an obedience ruling was issued by this court (see e.g., ISC 1078/2001). One needs to remember, though, that the significance of gaining an obedience ruling in the Jordanian shari'a court is symbolic rather than material (since the rulings of this court are disregarded by Israeli authorities). Nevertheless, such a

The described matrimonial dispute was thus dealt with by the two shari'a courts—the Israeli and the Jordanian—each in the manner and style that could be expected of it. To be sure, *shar'i* advocates and lawyers who work in the realm of family law are well aware of the differences between the courts and advise their clients to choose the most appropriate legal recourse for their purposes (see also the discussion of this issue in Chapter 11). Both the wife and the husband have made strategic choices along the dispute and opted for the tribunal—and for the type of appeal—that best served their interests.

As is most common in "strife and discord" lawsuits, this particular case ended in the dismantling of marital life.[20] Nonetheless, in their separation arrangements the parties continued to strategically employ the advantages that each court offers. Apparently, they chose to perform the divorce ceremony in the Jordanian court,[21] the most prestigious court in Jerusalem, which confers its respectability on their separation agreement (and on each of them as God-fearing Muslims). Whereas respectability was earned by the association of the divorce with the Jordanian shari'a court, the more earthly aspects of this separation were handled in the Israeli shari'a court. Not only was the divorce recognized and registered by this court—thus making sure that Israeli authorities will be notified of the change in the litigants' personal status—but the qadi even took upon himself to mention in his ruling the maintenance agreement between the (ex)husband and wife, thus bestowing the status of a court ruling on the agreement. Based on the court ruling, the secretariat of the Israeli shari'a court soon issued two important documents: a divorce certificate and a Hebrew translation of the maintenance agreement.[22] The

---

ruling may constitute an important leverage in the context of a matrimonial dispute. See also the description of such a case in Chapter 5.

20 The absolute majority of strife and discord lawsuits end in divorce. For example, of 107 "strife and discord" files that were dealt with by the Israeli shari'a court in West Jerusalem in 2002, only 12 cases ended in reconciliation (ISC 38/2002, 78/2002, 615/2002, 832/2002, 1467/2002, 1578/2002, 1597/2002, 1869/2002, 2327/2002, 2478/2002, 2620/2002, 3036/2002). In addition to these cases, 17 other cases were deleted from the court schedule after the parties did not return to court for more than six months. Notably, the fact that they have not returned to court does not necessarily mean that they have reconciled, but even if we presume that most of these couples have reconciled, still, 78 cases out of 107 ended either in divorce or in judicial dissolution of the marriage.

21 When a couple agrees on separation with mutual remission of *shar'i* rights (*talaq bi'l-ibra'*), the spouses perform the divorce act in front of the qadi.

22 The issuance of Hebrew translations of maintenance awards is another innovation that has been introduced in the Israeli shari'a court in West Jerusalem in recent years. Since many Muslim women were facing difficulties dealing with non-Arabic speakers in the NII, Qadi Zibdi decided to prepare a Hebrew form for maintenance awards. Such forms are filled in regularly by the court secretariat, and stamped with the court's official stamp. This procedure has proved particularly rewarding—both for the women and for the shari'a court—for it has significantly reduced the number of "clarification requests" from the NII to the shari'a court concerning maintenance rulings.

latter is a document of utmost importance for the divorced woman, for it ascertains that the Israeli NII will grant her and her minor child maintenance allowance.

The relations between the Israeli shari'a court in West Jerusalem and the Jordanian court in East Jerusalem, as illustrated by this case, appear to be not only close, but also complementary. Whereas one court confers respectability and religious legitimacy on the parties, the other provides them with executable rulings. This "symbiosis" works perfectly due to the facilitative policy of the Israeli shari'a court with regard to rulings and registered deeds issued by the Jordanian court. We may further speculate that the complementing functions of the courts were taken into consideration by the parties and their legal representatives when they agreed on a legal solution. It is reasonable to assume that had it not been taken for granted that the Israeli shari'a court would recognize the ruling of the Jordanian court, the divorce would not have been performed in the Jordanian court. Rather, the wife—as pious as she might be—would have preferred the divorce to take place in the Israeli shari'a court instead.

Fastest Way to Remove Impediments to Marriage

In the following I describe another example of close cooperation between courts for the benefit of Muslim Jerusalemites. In this case the cooperation occurs between the secretariats of the Israeli shari'a court in West Jerusalem and the Palestinian shari'a court in al-'Azariyya:

One vernal Sunday (April 17, 2004), late in the morning, a young girl accompanied by her elder brother and by Sheikh GH.N.D.—a senior *ma'adhun* of the Israeli shari'a court in West Jerusalem and an employee of the Jordanian *waqf* administration in *al-Haram al-Sharif*—arrived to the court. Sheikh GH. approached Abu Zayd, and the two men hugged each other and exchanged kisses on both cheeks. I was standing near Abu Zayd, inside the secretariat, holding two cups of coffee that I had just prepared in the court's tiny kitchen. When the greetings ended, I handed Abu Zayd one of the cups, and offered the other to Sheikh GH. He gladly took it, greeting as well as thanking me.

I then remained standing beside Abu Zayd, while Sheikh GH. started "talking business:" he told Abu Zayd that the girl here is in trouble. She is going to travel tomorrow to Amman in order to get married. Her family arranged the marriage that is supposed to take place in ten days. Sheikh GH. explained:

> The problem is that they [the girl's family] did not know that in order to get married, the girl must have a formal certificate testifying that there are no impediments (*mawani'*) to her marriage.[23] They only learned about this

23 This procedure is intended to make certain that there are no impediments that might prevent the marriage from taking place, or make the marriage contract invalid (on possible impediments to marriage, see Schacht 1995: 28).

yesterday and came to me to issue the certificate. Now, I'll be happy to issue the required document—she is a good girl from a good family—but it will not do. They will have to take this document to the Jordanian Embassy that will then send it to the Jordanian Ministry of Foreign Affairs. It takes at the least two months to obtain the recognition of documents in this manner. [Directing the question to Abu Zayd:] Now, what do you think that we can do? It's a pity (*haram*), we have to help her.

[*Abu Zayd*:] Ammm … . a problem [moment of silent]. But what can we do? Perhaps it's better for her to go to a Jordanian or a Palestinian *ma'adhun* and to get the no-impediments-to-marry certificate (*khulu' mawani'*) from him.

[*Sheikh GH.*:] You are right. Perhaps we can call the Palestinian court in al-'Azariyya and ask them if they can give her this certificate?

[*Abu Zayd*:] You want me to call them? [Without waiting for a reply, Abu Zayd picks up the phone and calls the chief secretary of the Palestinian court in al-'Azariyya. He converses with the man in a familiar and very friendly tone, and indeed, his interlocutor apparently agrees to help. Abu Zayd, still holding the telephone receiver, tells the Sheikh and the girl:] two witnesses will have to testify, of course, that there are no impediments to marriage. Do you have witnesses?

[*Sheikh GH.* replies instead of the girl, saying:] she has one witness, and I will testify as well. We will go there right away. I will drive her.

[*Abu Zayd*, speaking to the man on the other side of phone:] okay my dear (*tayyib habibi*), they will be with you in 30 minutes. Sheikh GH. is bringing her, so take good care of him […].

This case exemplifies not only another instance of cooperation between two shari'a courts operating in contemporary Jerusalem, but also the very informal, personal nature of the social interactions taking place in the Israeli shari'a court of West Jerusalem. As illustrated by the described events, the cooperation between the courts goes way beyond a mere legal and functional "division of labor" between the institutions. Rather, the interrelations between the various shari'a tribunals in Jerusalem are based, first and foremost, on personal ties and informal connections between officials and personnel. In other words, despite—and perhaps, because of—the complex bureaucratic and legal apparatus that seemingly defines the relations between these institutions, it is, in the end, informal networks of clientele and patronage that strongly influence their interrelations.

Police Incompetence and Contradictory Custody Rulings

Such instances of inter-organizational cooperation—formal and informal—between the Israeli and the Jordanian or Palestinian shari'a courts are not rare, but they represent, nevertheless, only one side of the coin. The other (dark?) side of the relations between these courts is revealed in cases of directly contradictory rulings. Here is an example of such a case,[24] which occurred in 2002:

On a cold winter day, I arrived in court at about 08:00. There were almost no litigants and visitors present at this early hour, but I was surprised to find that Qadi Zibdi was already working, and that hearings had already begun. The door of the courtroom was closed, so I knocked, apologized, and asked whether I can enter. Qadi Zibdi invited me in and introduced me to the two women who were sitting inside. He told them that I am a university researcher (*bahith min al-jami'a*), who conducts research in the court. I entered the hearing room and sat to the right of the two women (apparently they were mother and daughter), while Qadi Zibdi commented in Hebrew that it's good that I came, for this is an interesting case. He continued,[25] saying (still in Hebrew):

> This young woman here has a difficult problem. Several months ago, after a long struggle with her husband, she was granted [by the Israeli shari'a court] custody over her two minor children, aged four and three. Nevertheless, it appears that six months earlier her husband kidnapped the children, and that he refuses to return them to their mother. The problem is that the husband's family lives in Area B,[26] and the [Israeli] police will not enter this area in order to bring the children back.
>
> *Q: Is that really so?*
>
> [*Qadi Zibdi*, in Arabic:] Yes. And you can imagine, of course, that if these were Jewish children, the security forces would have made every possible effort to rescue them. But this is how things are done around here: what is obvious with regard to Jewish children is incomprehensible with regard to Palestinian children.
>
> [*Qadi Zibdi* continues, returning to the Hebrew:] Now, a few weeks ago she [viz. the children's mother] came here and told me that her husband and his mother filed a lawsuit in the Jordanian shari'a court in Salah al-Din Street, asking for custody over the children. I contacted the Jordanian court and asked them to repel his [viz. the husband's] petition and not to deal with this case, because I have already issued a ruling in this matter. I think that they shouldn't deal with it, but I don't know what they'll decide. [He then turned to the young woman and her mother and asked in Arabic]: Did you hear from them?

---

24 The following description is based on my presence in a hearing on February 7, 2002. The file number is ISC 26/2002.

25 The following conversation shifted from Arabic to Hebrew and back.

26 According to "Oslo II (interim)" Agreement of 1995, Area B includes 450 Palestinian towns and villages in the West Bank. In these areas, as in Area A, the Palestinian Authority holds all civil authority. However, it differs from Area A in that Israel maintains overriding security authority in it "in order to safeguard its citizens and to combat terrorism" (see http://www.palestinefacts.org/pf_1991to_now_oslo_accords_2.php [accessed 10/13/2014]).

[*The young woman*:] Yes. We have a hearing on the twelfth of the month, next week.

[*Qadi Zibdi*:] So they do deal with the case. What can we do?!

Q [to the women]: Perhaps you can present Qadi Zibdi's ruling to them. Will it help?

[*The woman*, speaking to me in Arabic:] Yes. My lawyer takes care of that. I put my trust in God Almighty (*la hawla wala quwwa illa bi-Allah*).

Q [after moment of silence]: And why are you here today?

[*Qadi Zibdi*, in Arabic:] Because she filed a petition for the issuance of a stay-of-exit order [an order prohibiting a person from leaving the country] against her husband, on the grounds that he stole from her some gold jewelry (*masagh*) as well as some clothes and other personal stuff. I've already issued the order […].

This case illustrates that the relations between the Israeli and the Jordanian shari'a courts are not always characterized by harmonious cooperation. Rather, sometimes the competition between these courts surfaces, and each court strives to undermine the rulings issued by the other. In this particular case, it was the qadi officiating in the Jordanian shari'a court who chose to ignore an explicit request of his Israeli colleague and continued the deliberation in a matter that has already been adjudicated by the Israeli shari'a court.

Although we could speculate that the Jordanian qadi's decision reflects his low esteem of the Israeli shari'a court's rulings, it is noteworthy that on several similar occasions that I witnessed, the Israeli qadis (both 'Asliyya and Zibdi) also chose not to concede their right to adjudicate. Thus, in cases in which litigants claimed that the Israeli shari'a court in West Jerusalem lacks jurisdiction because another shari'a court—either Jordanian or Palestinian—has already dealt with it (or is still dealing with it), the qadis usually rejected the claim and ruled that they do have the jurisdiction to deal with the case.[27] It is, therefore, more likely that such instances of encroachment into the jurisdiction of another court emanate more from unwillingness to waive power than from a lack of respect for the procedures or rulings of another court.

Conclusion

As illustrated in this chapter, from the viewpoint of Muslim Jerusalemites, the simultaneous operation of several shari'a courts in contemporary Jerusalem facilitates a rather sophisticated type of forum shopping. Litigants take advantage of the substantial differences in the laws applied by each court, and manage to

27 See e.g., ISC 368/1995, 395/1998, 1078/2001. See, in contrast, ISC 404/1999, in which Qadi 'Asliyya decided that the Israeli shari'a court has no jurisdiction to deal with a dower case, since the Jordanian court has already adjudicated the case.

sustain in this manner some "traditional mores," such as minor and polygamous marriages.[28] Moreover, we have seen that each of these courts is characterized by a different legal culture, which also contributes to their significantly different rulings. Thus, whereas men have much better prospects of winning an obedience lawsuit in the Jordanian or Palestinian courts than in the Israeli court, women have much better chances to gain a judicial dissolution of marriage in the Israeli court than in the Jordanian or Palestinian courts.

For Muslim litigants in Jerusalem, the three shari'a courts operating in the city constitute a unified system of tribunals, dealing with family dispute resolution and with the personal status of Muslims. Whether there is cooperation and harmonious division of labor between these courts or competition and contradictory rulings—the litigants, advised by their legal representatives, have learnt to maneuver in this system and to make the most of the legal possibilities that it opens to them.

28 In fact, it may very well be that these "traditional mores" are reinforced in Jerusalem due to the special political, economic and legal situation in the city. The relatively improved economic and social situation in East Jerusalem in comparison to other areas in the West Bank (primarily due to the safety net provided by the Israeli NII in annexed East Jerusalem) attracts many West Bank residents to the city. Many Palestinian women from the West Bank are apparently willing to marry Jerusalemite men even as second wives (or otherwise, their guardians are willing to marry them off as second wives) for the purpose of acquiring an Israeli ID card, or at least a temporary resident permit, which allows sojourn within Israel. Such marriages are therefore dubbed "blue marriages"—to indicate that they are motivated by the desire to gain a blue Israeli ID card (see Abed Raboh 2012). It may be argued that this phenomenon caused polygamous marriage, in the past prevalent only among the rich and wealthy, to become widespread among broad echelons of the Muslim population in Jerusalem.

PART V
Concluding Discussion

Chapter 14
Israeli Shari'a Courts as Pluralistic Organizations: A New Institutional Perspective

As elaborated in the introduction, the organizational approach to legal pluralism developed in this book entails three levels of analysis: the level of *interrelations between single organizations*, the level of litigants' agency and forum shopping, and the level of the *organizational field*. The previous five chapters all focused on the first two levels of analysis, namely the interrelations between the shari'a court in West Jerusalem and other courts that operate parallel to it (the Israeli family court, and the Jordanian and Palestinian shari'a courts), and the phenomenon of forum shopping among Muslim Jerusalemites, who may maneuver between these courts. The analyses of these organizational relations have yielded many insights: We have seen how dyadic inter-court relations may develop and transform over time; how competitive and/or cooperative relations between courts may unfold, and how these relations affect both the judicial policies of the involved courts, and the choices of potential litigants.

In this chapter I would like to complement this dual perspective on organizational relations, by adding an institutional dimension to the analysis. For that purpose I will review some of the developments encountered in previous chapters, discussing them now from an institutional perspective. This discussion will draw on one of the most influential organizational theories in the last four decades—*new institutional theory*.[1]

The chapter unfolds as follows: The next section briefly introduces the basic tenets of new institutional theory in organization studies and discusses the applicability of this theory to the study of the Israeli shari'a courts. The bulk of the analysis then dwells on two judicial reforms that were introduced in these courts in recent years. I argue that these reforms may be traced back to contradictory influences and pressures, exerted on the shari'a courts within the two organizational fields to which they belong. Finally, the empirical and theoretical implications of this perspective are elaborated.

1 Indeed, its influence may also be detected in the law-and-society field of research (see e.g., Suchman and Edelman 1996). Several scholars employed the new institutional theoretical framework for the study of courts of law (e.g. Epstein et al. 1989, Hall and Brace 1989, Brace and Hall 1995, Cohen 2002), yet, as far as I know, this approach was never applied in the context of legal pluralism.

New Institutional Theory in Organization Studies

At the core of new institutional theory lies an underlying skepticism toward atomistic explanations of social processes (Wooten and Hoffman 2008) and a belief that organizations, like individuals, are constituted through their embeddedness within broader systems of meanings and networks of relationships. Accordingly, a central construct in new institutional theory is the notion of "organizational field." Each organization, so goes the argument, operates within one or more organizational fields, and cannot be understood outside of this context. An organizational field is defined as "a community of organizations that partakes of a common meaning system and whose participants interact more frequently and fatefully with one another than with actors outside of the field" (Scott 1995: 6).[2]

A basic tenet of new institutional theory is that organizations within an organizational field are under constant pressure to conform to the rules and models that prevail within this field. Such conformism is necessary for an organization to gain legitimacy as a rational, effective and well-managed organization, whereas failure to conform to accepted rules, norms and models means loss of legitimacy. Since organizations depend on their environments for obtaining resources, they, or more precisely, the staff or the personnel working in them, cannot afford to lose their legitimacy in the organizational field.[3]

According to DiMaggio and Powell (1983), organizations are therefore exposed to strong *isomorphic* pressures operating within the organizational field. They identify three different sources of isomorphism in organizational fields:

2 A different conceptualization was suggested by DiMaggio and Powell (1983: 148), who define an "organizational field" as consisting of "those organizations that, in the aggregate, constitute a recognized area of institutional life: key suppliers, resource and product consumers, regulatory agencies, and other organizations that produce similar services or products." Obviously, there are no objective, absolute boundaries to organizational fields; rather, the demarcation of the boundaries in specific cases is relative and operational, and depends on both empirical investigation and the researcher's goals and perspectives.

3 Researchers have often debated the relationship between the theoretical construct of "organizational field" and other sociological notions of fields, especially that of Bourdieu (e.g. Fourcade 2007, Emirbayer and Johnson 2008). Unlike Bourdieu's notion of field, the construct of "organizational field" naturally focuses on organizations as predominant field actors. In recent years, however, this focus has somewhat eroded, and today the term "institutional field" is often used interchangeably with "organizational field" (as will also be done here). Another major difference has to do with underlying assumptions concerning power and conflict: while for Bourdieu the field is a terrain of ongoing contestation and struggle for domination, early versions of new institutional theory tended to draw attention away from conflict within organizational fields. Instead, they were interested primarily in the processes whereby fields stabilize and coalesce around accepted, taken for granted structures, norms and "rules of the game" (see Wooten and Hoffman 2008). This tendency has been somewhat mitigated, however, in recent new institutional literature (see e.g., Greenwood et al. 2008).

(1) *Coercive isomorphism* results "from both formal and informal pressures exerted on organizations by other organizations upon which they are dependent and by cultural expectations in the society within which organizations function" (DiMaggio and Powell 1983: 67). (2) *Mimetic isomorphism* is based on imitation and is intensified under conditions of uncertainty: "[W]hen organizational technologies are poorly understood, when goals are ambiguous, or when the environment creates symbolic uncertainty, organizations may model themselves on other organizations" (ibid.: 69). Such mimetic modeling occurs when other organizations in the organizational field are perceived as more legitimate or more successful. (3) *Normative isomorphism* is related to the diffusion of norms in organizational fields and attributed primarily to the presence of professionals and of professional networks in such fields. Professionals share common formal education and common codes of behavior, and are connected by professional networks that span organizational boundaries. They therefore constitute a significant conduit for the dissemination of rules, norms and cultural models between organizations. According to DiMaggio and Powell (1983), these isomorphic pressures, in turn, push organizations pertaining to an organizational field toward becoming increasingly similar to one another; they also push the organizational field as a whole to homogenization and stabilization as it matures.

Yet, what happens when an organization is active in more than one organizational field? This question has attracted growing attention among organizational scholars in recent years. Kraatz and Block (2008) observe that some organizations operate in environments characterized by "institutional pluralism:" they are active in multiple institutional spheres, are subject to multiple regulatory regimes, must conform to multiple normative orders, and are constituted by more than one "institutional logic." This situation poses many challenges in terms of the legitimacy of these organizations, their identity and status within the different organizational fields to which they belong, and the consistency of their actions and policies.

As explained in the introduction, I contend that the Israeli shari'a courts constitute such "institutional hybrids:" they are located at the intersection of two different organizational fields, and thus operate within two different institutional settings. On the one hand, they belong to a broad organizational field structured around the Israeli legal system. This organizational field includes other courts (e.g. magistrate's courts, district courts, the High Court of Justice, religious courts); state organizations such as the State Advocacy, the Ministry of Justice, and the Israeli parliament (the Knesset); state agencies outside the strict boundaries of the legal system that interact with it and affect it, such as the police, the prison administration; professional associations such as the bar; and civil society groups such as human rights and women's rights organizations.

On the other hand, and at the very same time, Israeli shari'a courts belong to another organizational field, constructed around Palestinian-*shar'i* organizations and institutions. In comparison to the Israeli state-law organizational field, this second field is not so well-defined. It is constructed around institutions related to Islamic law, Islamic education and "Islamic religious affairs" in Israel/Palestine, but since it includes institutions that operate in three distinct political environments (Israel, the West Bank and the Gaza Strip), its boundaries are rather blurred. This field, as I define it, includes Islamic institutions in Israel such as Israeli shari'a courts, shari'a colleges and universities,[4] muftis, imams and preachers (who may be regarded as religious institutions, and not only as individuals), the *waqf* establishment in Israel, Islamic charity associations and non-governmental Islamic organizations such as the Islamic Movement in Israel. It also includes, however, similar institutions that operate in the West Bank, in East Jerusalem and to some extent in the Gaza Strip as well.

As shown by many scholars studying Palestinian society, the national, familial and political ties between the Palestinians in Israel and their compatriots in the West Bank and the Gaza Strip were reestablished after the 1967 War (Rouhana 1989, Rekhess 1989, Smooha 1992). These ties were particularly close in the case of Islamic religious services and Islamic institutions, as the development of such institutions within Israel was held at bay by the authorities until the late 1980s (Peled 2001). Some of the leaders of the Islamic movement in Israel, for example, were educated in Islamic universities in the West Bank in the 1970s and 1980s and still maintain very close relationships with various Islamic elements in the West Bank (see Rekhess 1993, Louër 2007: 70, 158). Moreover, as we have seen, the Israeli qadis in Jerusalem have managed to develop close relations with their Palestinian and Jordanian counterparts over the last decade or so.

We may therefore conclude that from the point of view of Israeli qadis, the two fields—the Israeli state-law and the Palestinian-*shar'i* organizational fields—are both important and tangible. These two fields nurture, however, very different values, norms, bureaucratic traditions, organizational cultures and, of course, political inclinations. Whereas the first field nurtures a strong Zionist, civil, and gender-equalizing ethos, the second—the Palestinian-*shar'i* field—is characterized by a national-Palestinian, religious-Islamic, and patriarchal ethos.[5] In terms of their "institutional logics" (Thornton and Ocasio 2008), the two fields are thus almost diametrically opposed to one another, and it is not surprising that an organization that pertains to both of them would face opposing isomorphic pressures.

This structural positioning of Israeli shari'a courts at the intersection of two different organizational fields, poses exceptional challenges. Simply put, in order to continue functioning, the qadis and personnel of these courts need to maneuver between the contradictory influences, pressures and expectations originating from

4 For example, the Umm al-Fahm College of Preaching and Canonic Studies (*Kuliyyat Umm al-Fahm li'l-Da'wa wa'l-'Ulum al-Shar'iyya*).

5 This is not to say, however, that these organizational fields should be seen as monolithic, well-defined, and static. Undoubtedly, each of these fields comprises not only diverse organizations, but also diverse legal philosophies, bureaucratic traditions, and political tendencies. And yet, as assumed by new institutional theorists, these organizational fields are characterized by "dominant" or commonly accepted "institutional logics," and organizations that belong to them are expected to conform to these commonly accepted logics.

the two opposing organizational fields, to which these courts belong. To exemplify how such maneuvering may look, let us turn now to an analysis of two judicial reforms which have been introduced in these courts in recent years. Both these reforms have already been discussed above, but here they are analyzed in the theoretical framework of new institutional theory.

Coping with Contradictory Isomorphic Pressures

From the many judicial reforms that have been implemented in the Israeli shari'a courts in recent years (see Chapter 4; see also Abou Ramadan 2003a, 2003b, Layish 2006, Reiter 2009, Zahalka 2009), I focus in this section on two specific judicial reforms: one pertaining to maintenance claims, and the other to the treatment of Israeli statutes. At first glance, these two reforms—when viewed together—seem to indicate an incoherent judicial policy. However, I will show that they represent, in fact, a persistent effort to accommodate to conflicting demands exerted within two very different organizational fields.

Reform in Maintenance Claims

As explained in Chapter 9, the Israeli shari'a court system found itself under mounting pressure in the mid-1990s: an efficient coalition of liberal and feminist organizations joined hands and initiated a draft bill that threatened to strip the shari'a courts of most of their exclusive jurisdiction. The feminist activists argued that Muslim women are discriminated against in comparison to other women, and that the reason for this discrimination is the patriarchal and old-fashioned conduct of the Israeli shari'a courts. They thus demanded that jurisdiction in personal status matters of Muslims be conferred upon the family courts.

As the issue of maintenance stood at the center of the feminist activists' campaign, the qadis tried to appease their critics by initiating a reform of their own, meant to close the gap with the family courts and to enlarge the maintenance sums allocated to women in their courts. For that purpose they employed a unique mechanism—the judicial circular—that allowed them to reform the manner by which sums of maintenance were being evaluated and determined. As we have seen, the qadis' efforts were in vain, and after a bitter struggle that lasted six years, the Knesset passed a legislation amendment granting family courts parallel jurisdiction in most personal status matters of Muslims (except for marriage and divorce).

The implications of the legislation amendment—the ensuing intensification of legal pluralism—were discussed in Chapter 10. Here I would like to delve deeper into the *institutional context* of the reform in maintenance suits that was introduced by the judicial circular. In this respect, the most important aspect of this episode is the direct link between the pro-women judicial reform initiated by the qadis, and the pressures exerted on shari'a courts within the Israeli state-law organizational field. As we have seen, the judicial reform led by Qadi Natur was a direct response to a threat to the status of Israeli shari'a courts within this field, namely the danger of losing a part of their jurisdiction. The threat was created by civil society organizations belonging to the Israeli state-law organizational field, as defined above. These organizations tried to mobilize the field, and eventually the Knesset, for improving the status of women in Israeli shari'a courts. Put differently, they sought to harness the state legislature for promoting their agenda.

To avert the danger, shari'a courts had to accommodate to the dominant norms, values and logics of the Israeli state-law organizational field, and especially to its gender-equalizing ethos. Such an adjustment was deemed necessary for shari'a courts to maintain their legitimacy and status within the field. Moreover, to achieve this goal these courts had to become *more similar* to the family courts, which are more central actors in the field and represent its ethos better. In terms of new institutional theory, processes of mimetic isomorphism also contributed, therefore, to the pro-women judicial reform initiated by Israeli shari'a courts. These courts were pushed to imitate family courts and allot similar maintenance sums to women, as a means for gaining legitimacy within the Israeli state-law organizational field. The fact that even this incredibly effective internal reform could not prevent the diminution of the shari'a courts' jurisdiction, testifies, perhaps, to their relatively marginal position in the state-law organizational field, and to their relative lack of political power.

Ignoring "Worldly Laws" in Shari'a Court Rulings

During the second half of the 1990s—at about the same time that the shari'a court system was entangled in the bitter struggle over jurisdiction, and not at all unrelated to that struggle—the shari'a court of appeal began promoting a surprising new judicial policy. Under the leadership of Qadi Natur, the shari'a court of appeal embarked on an effort to distance the shari'a court system from Israeli law. In numerous appellate decisions, phrased in sharp rhetoric, the shari'a court of appeal admonished shari'a courts of first instance for relying in their rulings on Israeli law. Thus, for example, Qadi Natur stated with regard to a decision concerning temporary maintenance:

> [I]t should be mentioned that the civil law that the lower court draws on, with regard to temporary maintenance, is unrelated to the law applied by shari'a courts. The lower court ruling does not apply to Muslims, given that the shari'a court is prohibited from ruling in accordance with laws that are not grounded in Islamic law, and must only rule in accordance with the shari'a law.
>
> (SCA 191/1997, quoted in Abou Ramadan 2003b: 277)

And in another decision,[6] dealing with the Capacity and Guardianship Law:

---

6 For similar statements, see also SCA 294/1998, 194/1999.

> The shari'a courts must not rely on the Capacity and Guardianship Law, 1962 […] the noble shari'a constituted a complete judicial system before [this law was promulgated], and will remain such after [it will change or disappear]. The shari'a does not require any positive secular rules.
>
> (SCA 55/2001, quoted in Abou Ramadan 2003b: 278)

This new emphasis on Islamic sources—and only on Islamic sources—stands in sharp contrast to the judicial policy of previous generations of Israeli qadis, who had no reservations in drawing on Israeli statutes in their rulings (Layish 1975).

These new directives resulted in substantial confusion, and yet this did not deter the shari'a court of appeal. It was determined, so it seems, to create a symbolic—if not real—buffer between the shari'a court system and Israeli law. This policy was taken a step further when the shari'a court of appeal directed qadis that even when they learn during their hearings that litigants have violated Israeli statutes, they should avoid mentioning these violations in their rulings. As mentioned, this policy stood in direct contradiction to the previous policy of inserting special notes in the shari'a courts' files, whenever a felony (according to Israeli statutes) had been committed (e.g. polygamy, unilateral repudiation of a wife).

This new policy, totally contradicting previous practices, highlights the far-reaching judicial agency enjoyed by qadis presiding in Israeli shari'a courts. The question how courts operating under the aegis of the Israeli legal system can decide to completely disregard Israeli statutes, is less interesting for the present purpose than the question of why they introduced such a policy. The answer to the latter question, I argue, is that this reform constitutes an attempt, led by the Israeli shari'a court of appeal, to gain support and legitimacy in the Palestinian-*shar'i* organizational field. I contend that there is a close link between the pressure exerted on Israeli shari'a courts in the state-law organizational field during the mid-1990s and the (almost) unconcealed effort made by the shari'a court of appeal to gain status and legitimacy in the opposing, Palestinian-*shar'i* field. In other words, the more alienated Israeli shari'a courts became within the Israeli state-law field, the more prone they were to seek legitimacy and support within the Palestinian-*shar'i* organizational field.

Gaining legitimacy in the latter field was not a trivial task for Israeli shari'a courts. During the 1970s and 1980s, these courts were usually seen by Islamic elements—even within Israel—in highly critical terms (see the discussion in Chapter 9), and all the more so in the eyes of non-Israeli constituencies. A good illustration of the hostility toward Israeli shari'a courts in the Palestinian-*shar'i* organizational field can be found, I believe, in a fatwa issued in the mid-1980s by the Mufti of Jerusalem. As mentioned in Chapter 12, the Mufti—surely, a respectable and highly esteemed functionary, holding a senior position in the Palestinian-*shar'i* field—issued a fatwa that literally permitted the killing of the president of the Israeli shari'a court of appeal, for allegedly selling *waqf* property to Jewish elements.

It may be argued, therefore, that Israeli shari'a courts suffered from a chronic lack of legitimacy in the Palestinian-*shar'i* organizational field. Seeking to improve their reputation within this field, Natur and other qadis did exactly what new institutional theorists would predict them to do under conditions of uncertainty and loss of legitimacy: they imitated other, more prestigious organizations in the field, and tried to implement practices perceived in the field as worthwhile and normative. Indeed, it appears that the very same policy—a refusal to mark offenses against state law—had been employed in this field before. Specifically, following the Israeli occupation in 1967, the Jordanian shari'a courts in the West Bank declared that they would not cooperate with the Israeli authorities. Whereas prior to the occupation these courts used to inform the Jordanian authorities of breaches of civil statutes that came to light during *shar'i* proceedings,[7] after the occupation they refrained from such action, to avoid Israeli persecution of litigants (see Welchman 2000: 73–4).

The directives of the Israeli shari'a court of appeal to stop basing rulings on Israeli statutes and to stop noting breaches of these statutes should be seen, therefore, as a case of mimetic isomorphism, designed to increase the legitimacy of Israeli shari'a courts in the Palestinian-*shar'i* organizational field. Indeed, as we have seen, this policy was quite successful: since the mid-1990s, slowly but surely, the reputation of Israeli shari'a courts—and particularly of the shari'a court in West Jerusalem—improved, and these courts gained considerable legitimacy within the Palestinian-*shar'i* field.

The Benefits of Institutional Pluralism and its Price

As we have seen, the Israeli shari'a court in West Jerusalem, and in fact, the Israeli shari'a courts in general, may be described as "pluralistic organizations" (Kraatz and Block 2008) that operate within a pluralistic, complex and bifurcated organizational environment. As such, they are exposed to very different, often contradictory, influences and demands originating from the two organizational fields to which they belong. While they need to maintain their legitimacy in both of these fields, any accommodation to the norms and expectations in one field might put at risk their status in the other.

How do these courts handle the conflicting demands and expectations of their bifurcated organizational environment? While they cannot exit any of the organizational fields they partake in, they can certainly maneuver between them as need arises. In fact, as argued by Kraatz and Block (2008: 244), this ability to maneuver between conflicting demands is a critical organizational capability of pluralistic organizations.

7 Like the Israeli law, the Jordanian law criminalized certain deeds related to family law, such as non-registration of a divorce pronounced out of court, and involvement in the marriage of an under-aged woman (see Welchman 2000: 73–4, n. 136).

It appears that the Israeli shari'a courts maneuver between these two organizational fields in a way that is reminiscent of the maneuvering of individual litigants in conditions of legal pluralism. In their search for normative anchors such litigants may choose from among the various normative orders available to them (Pospisil 1958: 102–3; see also Benton 2002), or shop for a suitable forum in their search for favorable rulings (Benda-Beckmann 1981). Similarly, "pluralistic organizations" like the Israeli shari'a courts appear to be able to shift, in their quest for legitimacy and resources, from conformity to one organizational field to conformity to the other.

This maneuvering capacity turns the Israeli shari'a courts into exceptionally dynamic, adaptive, and pliable organizations. Since these courts serve as meeting points not only between normative orders and organizational fields, but also between "the state" and its Muslim population, their pliability and adaptive dynamism is extended to these relations as well. In other words, for Muslim Palestinians in Israel the courts constitute an organizational example for accommodating to—and benefiting from—the Israeli state apparatus. In the context of Jerusalem, in particular, the inherent dynamism of the West Jerusalem shari'a court is an important source of social, political and cultural adaptations, far beyond the court itself. Indeed, the shari'a court in West Jerusalem maintains its "friendly" and communal character, and most litigants regard an appeal to the court as instrumental and beneficial.

This dynamism does not come cheap, however. From the point of view of the pluralistic court (or more accurately, from the point of view of its staff), there are two noticeable drawbacks for this positioning betwixt and between organizational fields. First, pluralistic organizations that "play simultaneously in two games, with two different sets of rules," to use a metaphor suggested by Kraatz and Block (2008: 243), might end up marginalized on both game boards. In other words, they might suffer from low status and weak legitimacy in both organizational fields. This might occur when an act of compliance with the demands originating from one field entails estrangement from the other. In such cases, the pluralistic organization that by definition needs to maneuver between opposing demands, will inevitably be seen as dubious in both organizational fields. Moreover, as argued by new institutional theorists, the weaker the legitimacy of an organization, the stronger its tendency to adapt to the rules and requirements set by its environment (Scott and Mayer 1991). Thus, the pluralistic organization may find itself in a vicious circle: the more it is marginalized within its surrounding organizational fields, the more exposed it is to contradictory isomorphic pressures; and the more it strives to conform to these contradictory pressures, the more marginalized it is.

The second price to be paid for "excessive" dynamism has to do with the danger of losing one's organizational integrity. Indeed, the conspicuous dynamism displayed by the Israeli shari'a court in West Jerusalem was perceived as irrational, incoherent, and arbitrary not only by some academic critics of the shari'a court system (e.g. Abou Ramadan 2003a, 2003b), but also by some of my interlocutors during my fieldwork at the court. This is what one of the lawyers, working regularly in this court, had to tell me in this regard:

> Here [in the Israeli shari'a court] you have no order (*nizam*). One day is like this, and the other day like that. One day they say that civil laws apply here, the other day they say they don't apply. This is no way to run a court.
>
> (Conversation with N.S., June 8, 2004)

From a new institutional perspective, however, the judicial policy of the Israeli shari'a court in West Jerusalem is far from being erratic or irrational. Rather, its policy is perfectly explainable in the context of its pluralistic organizational environment, and of its simultaneous belonging to two different organizational fields. New institutional theory thus provides us with useful conceptual tools enabling a more sophisticated analysis that goes beyond dyadic inter-court relations and highlights the institutional context within which the various courts operate and interact. In doing so, new institutional theory also helps connecting the organizational approach to legal pluralism, developed and exemplified in this book, and to the vast body of literature on legal pluralism. As mentioned in the introduction, most studies of legal pluralism to date have focused on encounters between normative orders or legal systems, and emphasized, therefore, the broad systemic aspects of the phenomenon. These aspects are absent in the dyadic organizational investigation presented in previous chapters, or in the discussions of litigants' forum shopping, but new institutional theory brings them back into the analysis.

Chapter 15
Empirical and Theoretical Implications

This book examined the origins and consequences of legal pluralism in Jerusalem, or more precisely, among the Muslim population of Jerusalem. It did so by closely observing one focal organization—the Israeli shari'a court in West Jerusalem—and tracing its relations with several other courts that serve the Muslim population in the city. Ethnographic fieldwork in this court was combined with historical reviews and legal analyses, to produce a picture of the complex and dynamic interrelations between this court and other courts in its environment.

In this concluding chapter, I integrate the research findings by discussing the quadruple organizational network, comprising the Israeli, the Jordanian, and the Palestinian shari'a courts, and the Israeli family court.[1] In congruence with the book's logic, the discussion focuses on two complementing vantage points: that of Muslim Jerusalemite litigants who may maneuver between these courts and engage in meaningful forum shopping; and that of the courts as organizations operating in an environment of legal pluralism. I begin with a discussion of the litigants' point of view, which focuses on two related issues: a) the implications of legal pluralism in the context of the Israeli–Palestinian national struggle in Jerusalem; and b) the implications of legal pluralism in the context of gender relations among Muslim Jerusalemites. The chapter then shifts the focus to the organizational point of view and discusses the effects of legal pluralism on the characteristics displayed by each of the four courts.

Legal Pluralism in Jerusalem and the Israeli–Palestinian National Struggle

In the politically charged atmosphere of present-day Jerusalem, the question that naturally arises when discussing legal pluralism in the city is: *whom does it serve?* Does it serve the dominant, occupying side in the struggle (i.e. Israel), or perhaps the underprivileged, occupied side (i.e. the Muslim-Palestinian residents of East Jerusalem)? Does legal pluralism facilitate the imposition of Israeli rule in the city, or otherwise, does it actually facilitate Palestinian and/or Jordanian resistance to that rule?

1 There are of course other tribunals operating in Jerusalem (e.g. the Israeli district court; labor courts, juvenile courts, etc.) that also interact with the Israeli shari'a court in West Jerusalem. Nevertheless, these courts do not deal primarily with matters pertaining to the personal status of Muslims, and consequently they are not included in the organizational network described here.

As always in such complex and multi-faceted situations, the answer to such questions is equivocal. On the one hand, it may be argued that inter-state legal pluralism—that is, the simultaneous operation in Jerusalem of three types of shari'a courts, each belonging to a different state legal system—does undermine Israel's claim to exclusive sovereignty in the unified city after the annexation. To take, for example, the Jordanian court: as described in Chapter 4, the Israeli authorities were genuinely determined to thwart and prevent its "normal" operation in East Jerusalem (see Welchman 2000: 64). The fact that this court continues to adjudicate cases, and that rulings and registered deeds issued by this court are usually recognized by an Israeli institution (the Israeli shari'a court of West Jerusalem), may be regarded as a manifestation of successful resistance to Israeli rule.

On the other hand, it may also be argued, and with no less conviction, that Israeli authorities actually allow legal pluralism in the relatively marginal domain of personal status for the purpose of pacifying nationalistic and religious grievances and creating an illusion that Israeli rule in the city is liberal and enlightened. Indeed, several commentators described Israel's policy in East Jerusalem in exactly such terms: they contend that Israel manages to achieve quiescence in Jerusalem by providing a very thin social security network (primarily via the NII) as well as a convenient (and not dangerous) leeway for national and religious sentiments (see Lustick 1980b: ch. 3, La Tendresse 1995: 12, Tamari 2003: 124).

Both of these opposing arguments seem plausible, and it is difficult to determine which one is more valid. The answer to the question very much depends on personal inclinations and interpretations. It remains, therefore, for each observer—according to his or her own theoretical and empirical predilections—to choose whether to highlight hegemony or counter-hegemony, mechanisms of control or modes of resistance. My own inclination, however, is toward a focus on resistance and counter-hegemony: I tend to believe that the state of legal pluralism in Jerusalem helps Muslim litigants to manage their relations with Israeli state agencies more successfully, and hence assists them in obtaining material benefits that make their lives in the city more bearable. In this sense, at least, legal pluralism improves their capability to resist Israeli dominance in the city.

In this context, the "intra-state" legal pluralism within the framework of the Israeli legal system is even more important than the inter-state legal pluralism in Jerusalem. I refer, of course, to Muslim litigants' ability to choose to resort—in matters pertaining to their personal status—to either the Israeli family court or the Israeli shari'a court. As argued in Chapter 14, the "rationale of operation" that guides the Israeli shari'a court in West Jerusalem often diverges from the "Zionist" or perhaps "Jewish" rationale, which usually guides the operation of Israeli governmental institutions (among them, naturally, the family court). In my MA thesis I have shown, for example, that during the late 1990s, Muslim Jerusalemites, who were struggling to maintain their rights of residence in the city,[2]

2 As briefly mentioned in Chapter 5, during the late 1990s the Israeli authorities waged a semi-official campaign designed to reduce the Arab-Palestinian population in

could resort to the Israeli shari'a court in West Jerusalem and find there sympathy and a genuine will to help. Such litigants could occasionally obtain rulings and documents from this court that were designed—first and foremost—to assist them in their conflictual encounters with other Israeli official agencies (see Shahar 2000: ch. 8).

In this sense, the role of the Israeli shari'a court in West Jerusalem—as an institution that serves the interests of Muslims in the city, even to the detriment of official Israeli policy—is crucial. From the viewpoint of Muslim litigants, this court is a culturally familiar and relatively sympathetic legal institution that may even assist them in their interactions with other Israeli state agencies. It may therefore be argued that legal pluralism in Jerusalem benefits the occupied and the underprivileged side, that is, the Palestinians. By maneuvering between the various legal institutions, and by taking advantage of the "subversive" policy enacted by the Israeli shari'a court in West Jerusalem, Jerusalemite Muslims manage to undermine Israel's claims to exclusive sovereignty in the city.

Legal Pluralism and Gender Relations among Muslims in Contemporary Jerusalem

The question "*Whom does legal pluralism serve?*" does not have a clear and unequivocal answer, not only in the context of the national conflict in Jerusalem, but also in the context of gender relations in the Palestinian community in Jerusalem. Indeed, how should we evaluate the consequences of legal pluralism in this regard? Does the ability to engage in forum shopping and to choose a tribunal from among several options, promote the cause of equal rights for women? Or does it actually thwart legal reforms designated to equalize the status of men and women, and thus contribute to the preservation of the patriarchal social order?

As described in Chapter 9, a legislation amendment passed by the Israeli parliament in November 2001 resulted in a strengthening of legal pluralism within the Israeli legal system. The amendment granted family courts jurisdiction over some matters pertaining to the personal status of Muslims (apart from marriage and divorce), and opened the way for Muslim litigants to appeal to these courts for various purposes. As we have seen, the reform certainly improved the status of Muslim women in matrimonial disputes, since they could now take advantage of the more lenient evidence rules and more egalitarian material laws applied in Israeli family courts (see Chapter 11).

The new venue allowing Muslim women to choose between these two legal options has provided them with a greater degree of freedom and accorded them some concrete leverage against their husbands. Moreover, since the 2001 amendment brought Israeli shari'a courts into direct competition with family courts over potential litigants, some changes in favor of women have been introduced

---

Jerusalem. This policy came to be dubbed the "quiet deportation" (see Chapter 5, note 5).

in shari'a courts as well. Consequently, legal pluralism has also improved the situation of women who eventually prefer to appeal to Israeli shari'a court, and not to family court.

It appears, therefore, that the feminist and liberal goals that motivated the promoters of the 2001 legislation amendment were by and large realized. Nevertheless, as illustrated in Chapters 10 and 11, legal pluralism has various kinds of consequences, some of which definitely do not work in favor of women. Parallel procedures that take place in family courts and in Israeli shari'a courts also involve delays, hindrances, and legal setbacks,[3] which usually benefit the party that is less in need of a court ruling (that is, in the context of family disputes, usually men).

Furthermore, the parallel operation in Jerusalem of other shari'a courts—Jordanian and Palestinian—also does not necessarily improve the position of Muslim women in the city. In addition to setbacks that may result from parallel appeals to more than one tribunal, the fact that Israeli progressive legislation does not apply in the Jordanian and Palestinian shari'a courts facilitates the circumvention of some very important gender-equalizing principles introduced by Israeli law. Thus, as argued in Chapter 13, "traditional mores" such as minor marriage and polygamy—though prohibited by Israeli law—continue to exist and may even have become more prevalent in contemporary Jerusalem. As we have seen, Israeli restrictive legislation is easily circumvented with the assistance of the Jordanian and Palestinian shari'a courts (and the *ma'adhun*s they appoint); and the Israeli shari'a court, on its part, contributes to the prevalence of these mores by systematically turning a blind eye and by granting formal recognition to illegal (according to Israeli law) marriage contracts.

It may be argued, therefore, that in Jerusalem, as elsewhere, legal pluralism also has a "dark side" (Dane 1991: 964). As noted by Halperin-Kaddari (1997: 739–41), the inherent tension between liberalism and pluralism is often revealed in legal pluralist situations. Whereas legal pluralism facilitates the recognition and legitimization of particular communal norms, it may very well be that these norms also entail a violation of the liberties/rights of individuals in these communities.[4] While legal pluralism in Jerusalem is not the result of an intended

3 Such interferences with the "efficient" implementation of a unitary rule of law brought many legal scholars to express their objection to the phenomenon of forum shopping (see e.g., Clermont and Eisenberg 1995, Norwood 1996; see also the discussion of this issue in Shahar 2013).

4 The most famous case of such a clash of values in the United States is *Santa Clara Pueblo v. Martinez* 436 US 49 (1978). The subject at issue in this case was the exclusion from the Santa Clara tribe, of children who were born to tribeswomen who married exogamously. According to the tribe's laws, whereas children born to tribesmen who married non-tribe women were regarded as tribe members, children-born to tribeswomen married to non-tribe men were not regarded as tribe members. In the case, a tribeswoman who married exogamously and her daughter appealed to the court, asking for the annulment of this rule and for a verdict that orders to accept the daughter as a member in the tribe. The appellants relied in their appeal on the Indian Civil Rights Act (1968), which applied the principles

pluralist ideology (but the outcome of unique political and legal circumstances), confrontation between values does occur. In this case, Islamic and nationalistic values appear to collide with liberal and feminist values. Thus, whereas resort to the Jordanian or Palestinian shari'a courts may serve the purpose of resistance to the Israeli occupation and annexation of East Jerusalem (as well as the principle of religious adherence to "non-contaminated" Islamic law), it may also serve the "unholy" purposes of performing polygamous marriages or of marrying off minors. Similarly, whereas an appeal to the Israeli family court may undoubtedly improve the status of a Palestinian woman in a matrimonial dispute, this same act may also weaken the Palestinian and Islamic elements in Jerusalem.

We may conclude, therefore, that legal pluralism in Jerusalem is not necessarily "good" or "evil;" it does not necessarily serve the underprivileged or the dominant and hegemonic elements in society. Rather, it seems that the consequences of legal pluralism are contingent on particular circumstances and constellations. The complexity of the political and the legal situation in Jerusalem makes it all the more difficult to evaluate the consequences of legal pluralism in the city and to trace the various routes that Muslim litigants may take in order to manipulate the legal system(s)—for good or for bad.

The Consequences of Legal Pluralism in Jerusalem: An Organizational Perspective

Legal pluralism in Jerusalem—in the realm of personal status matters of Muslims—is indeed uniquely conspicuous and powerful. As we have seen, the four courts that operate in this realm maintain complex patterns of interaction between each other. In fact, it may be argued that the relations between the legal institutions constituting our organizational network exemplify almost all the types of relations defined by Woodman (1999: 15–18) in his typology of the relations between bodies of law.[5] Thus, we may find in Jerusalem *conflict* between bodies of law—a situation in which different bodies of law impose contradictory norms on the population;[6] we may find *integration* of bodies of law—a situation in which legal procedures pertaining to different bodies of law complement each other;[7]

---

of equality before the law and of fair proceedings to Indian tribes. The US Supreme Court of Justice rejected their claim, relying on the principle of Indian cultural autonomy (see Halperin-Kaddari 1997: 740 n. 197).

5 For a similar typology between "justice systems," see, Forsyth 2007.

6 E.g. the contradictory norms imposed by the Israeli and the Jordanian shari'a courts with regard to bequests in favor of orphaned grandchildren (see Chapter 13).

7 As we have seen, there are cases in which the legal procedures in the Israeli and in the Jordanian shari'a courts complement each other. In one case, for example, a couple chose to perform an act of divorce in the more prestigious Jordanian court, but at the same time made sure that the financial arrangements that were agreed upon were formally

we may find *separation* of bodies of law—a situation in which a population acquires independence and creates its own separate legal system;[8] and we may find the whole spectrum of *recognition/non-recognition* between bodies of law—ranging from mutual non-recognition, to unilateral recognition (when one body of law recognizes another, but the latter does not recognize the former), to mutual recognition.[9]

Woodman's typology, as his conceptualization suggests, refers to relations between different bodies of law at the doctrinal level or at the level of the legal systems. The organizational approach adopted in this book, however, advances a different conceptualization: Not the encounters between bodies of law or legal systems are examined, but the encounters and interrelations between courts as organizations. As illustrated in previous chapters, this is not a semantic sophistry: although each of the studied courts belongs to a state (or state-like) legal system, the organizational motives/ideologies/practices of each court may very well stand apart from the motives/ideologies/practices of the "system" to which it belongs. In other words, the interrelations between the courts may not be reduced to interrelations between legal systems—these are different levels of analysis that should not be conflated.

Indeed, the close diachronic examination of dyadic relations between the Israeli shari'a court in West Jerusalem and its various judicial counterparts (Israeli shari'a court/family court; Israeli shari'a court/Jordanian shari'a court; Israeli shari'a court/Palestinian shari'a courts), have yielded some interesting insights about the dynamics of legal pluralism. For example, a new type of relations that may be found in situations of legal pluralism, and that was not observed by Woodman, has been identified: Competition and cooperation between courts (see Chapters 10 and 12). Moreover, I believe it was convincingly shown that the relations between the courts shape and affect the courts themselves, at all levels of their operation—at the judicial policy level; at the procedural level; and at the organizational level. Hence, in order to understand these courts it is imperative to understand their interrelations with other courts.

In the following, I discuss the manner in which the various courts are influenced by their positioning in the quadruple network, and their different responses to

---

recognized by the Israeli shari'a court in West Jerusalem. In this manner, they turned the financial agreement into an executable court ruling, recognized by Israeli authorities (see Chapter 13).

8 The creation of a separate Palestinian *shar'i* legal system after the establishment of the Palestinian National Authority may be regarded as such a case (see Chapter 12).

9 Mutual non-recognition exists between the Israeli family court and the Jordanian and Palestinian shari'a courts; mutual recognition exists, naturally, between the Israeli shari'a court and the Israeli family court; lastly, the relations between the Israeli shari'a court and the Jordanian and Palestinian shari'a courts have developed from mutual non-recognition to unilateral recognition (when the Israeli court changed its policy and began recognizing the rulings issued by its counterparts—see Chapter 12).

the state of legal pluralism in which they operate. My analysis refers to all four tribunals—the Israeli, the Jordanian, and the Palestinian shari'a courts, and the Israeli family court—but the focus will obviously be on the Israeli shari'a court in West Jerusalem, which will therefore be discussed last.

The Jordanian Shari'a Court

The Jordanian shari'a court of first instance in Salah al-Din Street is a remnant of the old, defeated regime. Due to political considerations made by the new sovereign (i.e. Israel) it was allowed to continue operating in the unified city after the annexation, but the very same considerations also led the Israeli authorities to avoid recognizing this court and its rulings. Since there is not much point in resorting to a legal institution whose rulings are not enforced, the court's very existence was compromised because of this deliberate Israeli policy. The status of the Jordanian shari'a courts in Jerusalem (the court of first instance and the appellate court) deteriorated even further after the establishment of an independent Palestinian shari'a court of appeal. This court took away all the appeals originating in the shari'a courts of the West Bank from the Jordanian shari'a court of appeal in Jerusalem. Since January 1995, the Jordanian appellate court deals only with appeals on the decisions of the Jordanian court of first instance in the city (see Chapter 12).

Nevertheless, as we have seen, the Israeli shari'a court in West Jerusalem adopted a "private" policy of granting formal recognition to registered deeds and even of court rulings issued by the Jordanian court. This, of course, improved the status of the Jordanian court, and yet this court still has very little to offer in terms of material benefits. That is to say, potential litigants who consider resorting to the Jordanian court must bear in mind that any ruling issued by this court will not be executable in itself.

Lacking ability to enforce its rulings, the only thing that is left for the Jordanian shari'a court to trade with is its reputation—its repute as a respectable religious institution that is not as corrupt as the Palestinian courts and not as "contaminated" with non-Islamic statutes as the Israeli shari'a court. The only advantage that this court enjoys in comparison to the other tribunals operating in Jerusalem is therefore its standing as an organization that opposes the Israeli occupation and at the same time implements relatively "pure" Islamic law.

With such a problematic position (in terms of the inability to enforce its rulings) on the one hand, and with such a leading position (in terms of religious and normative prestige) on the other, it is easy to understand why the officials working in the Jordanian shari'a court in East Jerusalem have opted for "conservatism." Sustaining an image of an old-fashioned, traditional, unchanging shari'a court highlights the supposed strengths of the court, and concomitantly conceals its weaknesses. The image conveys a message of religiosity, piety, and tradition and at the same time legitimizes inefficiency, ineffectiveness and restricted ability to adapt to changing circumstances.

Its positioning in the organizational network and the ensuing constrains and opportunities have led the Jordanian shari'a court to nurture an ideology of legal and cultural conservatism. As illustrated in Chapter 12, the response of the Jordanian shari'a court to pressures exerted by the legal pluralistic environment is diametrically opposed to the response of the Israeli shari'a court in West Jerusalem: whereas the former reacted by adopting an ultra-conservative legal culture, the latter reacted by adopting a pronounced "culture of change" and an orientation of "user-friendliness;" whereas the former was pushed to cling to tradition and to the past, the latter developed a highly dynamic culture with relatively few barriers to change.

The fact that the Israeli shari'a court in West Jerusalem recognizes registered deeds issued by the Jordanian shari'a court, whereas the latter does not recognize the former—what Woodman (1999) would call "unilateral recognition"—also reflects the different positions that these institutions occupy in the organizational network. The less prestigious court (i.e. the Israeli shari'a court) recognizes and ratifies almost automatically the decisions issued by its more respectful counterpart (i.e. the Jordanian shari'a court), while the latter refrains from recognizing decisions issued by the former and requires for registered deeds reenactment under its own supervision.

Of course, as we have seen, the described network structure is not static, but has gradually evolved over the years. The relations between the Israeli and the Jordanian shari'a courts in Jerusalem developed over several years, until they reached the current state of "functional interdependency" and capital exchange between the courts. Bearing in mind the significant dependency of the Jordanian shari'a court on the Israeli shari'a court,[10] it may not be far-fetched to estimate that more symmetrical relations of mutual recognition might develop between these two institutions in future.

The Palestinian Shari'a Courts

As argued in Chapter 12, the Palestinian shari'a courts are undoubtedly the less important element in our quadruple organizational network. These courts are located on the outskirts of Jerusalem, outside the Israeli-defined municipal borders of the city, and with the construction of the "separation barrier" they are becoming almost inaccessible to Muslim Jerusalemites dwelling inside Jerusalem, that is on the Israeli side of the barrier.[11] In addition to problems of accessibility, the

10 I believe that it would not be too much of an exaggeration to argue that by employing a "private" policy of recognition, contrary to official directives of the Israeli authorities, the Israeli shari'a courts have practically resuscitated the Jordanian court in Jerusalem that was facing rapid decline.

11 On the implications of the construction of the "separation barrier" in the Jerusalem area, see Kimhi (2006). On the general controversy concerning this barrier, see B'Tselem report (2003).

widespread perception of the Palestinian courts as corrupt and unreliable—as exemplified by the remarks made by my interlocutors in the Israeli shari'a court in West Jerusalem—makes them an undesirable choice for most litigants. Still, some litigants may have no other choice but resorting to these courts, or otherwise, they may choose to appeal to these courts if they feel confident in their ability to gain a favorable ruling.

All in all, it may be said that the Palestinian shari'a courts occupy a marginal position in the organizational network of tribunals dealing with personal status matters of Jerusalemite Muslims. Their ability to compete with other institutions over litigants is relatively limited, and their impact on the operation of the other courts is therefore negligible. Indeed, the relations of these courts with the Israeli shari'a court in West Jerusalem reflects their puisne position in comparison with the Jordanian shari'a court: whereas the Jordanian court is able to maintain asymmetric relations of unilateral recognition with the Israeli shari'a court, more egalitarian relations have evolved between the Israeli and the Palestinian courts.[12]

The Israeli Family Court

The Israeli family court is indisputably the exceptional member in the organizational network of tribunals dealing with personal status matters of Muslims in Jerusalem. Not only is this court a "newcomer" to this exclusive club of tribunals,[13] it is also the only member that is a civil court, and not a religious Islamic one. Thus, whereas all the other tribunals in this network apply very similar Islamic codes (originally compiled by Ottoman reformers at the beginning of the twentieth century), the Israeli family court applies Israeli civil legislation. Furthermore, whereas the main language in all the other courts is Arabic, the main language in the family court is Hebrew; whereas all the other courts serve *only* Muslim litigants, the family courts serve litigants of all religious affiliations, and among them, only a relatively small number of Muslims.

The legislation amendment that granted the family court jurisdiction over personal status matters of Muslims was not initiated by the Israeli legal establishment, but rather by liberal and feminist groups in the Palestinian community in Israel (see Chapter 9). We may speculate that among judges and other officials working in these courts, dealing with this domain of the law and with the Palestinian-Muslim population is considered more of a burden than a privilege: not only does it necessitate complex bureaucratic arrangements (e.g. translation to and from Arabic), it also adds significant judicial workload and opens

12 As we have seen, problems of corruption in the PNA shari'a courts led the Israeli shari'a courts to restrict the recognition of rulings issued by these courts (see Chapter 12).

13 As described in Chapter 9, it was only in November 2001, after the legislation amendment passed in the Knesset, that the family court in Jerusalem joined the network of tribunals at issue here.

a whole new range of unresolved juridical problems.[14] Moreover, the Israeli family court—unlike the Israeli shari'a court—does not suffer from dubious normative status or from problems of legitimization, and therefore does not strive to enlarge its pool of potential litigants.

Thus, unlike the other three tribunals in our quadruple network—that all thrive on the domain of personal status matters of Muslims—the Israeli family court treats cases pertaining to this domain as an unnecessary load. We may further speculate that functionaries in the family courts would be glad to relieve themselves from this burden. If this is indeed the case, then it is easy to understand the manifest indifference with which the family courts responded to the 2001 legislation amendment. As described in Chapter 10, there was no reorganization in the family courts following the passing of the legislation amendment (contrary to earlier promises made by the Ministry of Justice), and no efforts whatsoever were made to attract Muslim litigants.

We may conclude, therefore, that the 2001 legislation turned the Israeli shari'a court and the civil family court into "direct competitors," but it appears that only the former responded strongly to the competition, whereas the latter did not exhibit any interest in it. Nevertheless, we have seen that despite this indifference, and despite the fact that only a relatively small number of Muslims have appealed to the family court to date, its entry into the scene in 2001 was very consequential.

The Israeli Shari'a Court in West Jerusalem

Finally we come to discuss the court that stands at the center of this book—the Israeli shari'a court in West Jerusalem. I contend that this court constitutes, in fact, the central axis of the studied network of courts. If we analyze the relations between the courts in the network (namely, between the different courts in Jerusalem that adjudicate personal status of Muslims), it is evident that the Israeli shari'a court is the only one that openly interacts with all the other courts: the Jordanian and Palestinian shari'a courts do not directly interact with the Israeli family court, and vice versa. In structural terms, therefore, the Israeli shari'a court constitutes the center point of the network.

The central position of the Israeli shari'a court in the network of tribunals also highlights its liminal location in/between the Israeli and the Palestinian arenas. Indeed, as argued in Chapter 14, this court simultaneously belongs to two different organizational fields: the Israeli state-law organizational field and the Palestinian-

14 The legislation amendment of 2001 granted the family court jurisdiction over personal status matters of Muslims, but by no means did it resolve all the statutory, jurisdictional and juridical problems emanating from the application of Muslim religious laws in Israeli family courts. Thus, many crucial issues relating to the division of labor between family courts and shari'a courts are still unresolved. These problems are left to the discretion of the judges, who are not always too keen to deal with them.

shar'i organizational field. Its central position in the network is due to the fact that it provides a connection between these two organizational fields.

And yet, the court's situation is rather paradoxical, since it is marginal in each of the two organizational fields despite its centrality in the network. If we compare it with the Jordanian shari'a court—a prestigious member in the organizational field of Islamic legal institutions in Palestine/Israel—the Israeli shari'a court is clearly inferior: both its Islamic character and its commitment to the Palestinian national cause seem doubtful. In a similar vein, if we compare it with the Israeli family court, the Israeli shari'a court is inferior in this context as well: whereas it constitutes a marginalized "legal transplant" within the Israeli legal system, the family court constitutes an organic part of the system; whereas the shari'a court in West Jerusalem deals with a religious and national minority that is in constant confrontation with other state institutions, the family court in the city deals primarily with the dominant, Jewish sector of the population.

The inherent ignobility and marginality of the Israeli shari'a court in West Jerusalem in both organizational fields may explain its conspicuous need to secure legitimacy and its constant search for approval and acceptance (this is true, in fact, for all shari'a courts in Israel). Indeed, of all the institutions constituting the organizational network under study, the Israeli shari'a court in West Jerusalem is the one most in need of litigants. From the point of view of Israeli qadis, more litigants mean more legitimacy; if more litigants choose to appeal to the court, it indicates not only that the Muslim population needs its services, but also that it regards the court as a reasonably legitimate and just legal institution.

No wonder, then, that Israeli shari'a courts in general, and the Israeli shari'a court in West Jerusalem in particular, invest great effort in attracting litigants. Unlike the family court, which—to put it bluntly—could not care less whether or not Muslim litigants choose to appeal to it, (Muslim) litigants are literally "the air that the Israeli shari'a courts breathe." Thus, as we have seen, these courts' response to the new competition posed by the family courts (following the 2001 legislation amendment) was highly competitive. The qadis were quick to introduce administrative reforms and adjustments that were designed to make their courts more "user-friendly" and thus more appealing to litigants. Moreover, taking advantage of their far-reaching judicial autonomy, the qadis introduced some legal reforms that substantially improved the status of women in shari'a courts. By these measures they undoubtedly intended to prevent the gradual migration of litigants to the new competitor (i.e. the family court).

We may therefore discern three different responses of courts in the network to pressures exerted by the legal pluralistic environment. The family court responded to the 2001 legislation amendment by plain indifference; the Jordanian shari'a court responded to changes in the legal pluralistic environment by clinging to Islamic conservatism; and the Israeli shari'a court responded to pressures and competition by adopting a strategy of dynamism, constant change, and adaptability. The responses of the Israeli and the Jordanian shari'a courts are similar in the sense that they both try to accentuate and nurture their strengths, while downplaying their limitations. Hence, the Israeli shari'a court in West Jerusalem emphasizes its user-friendliness and judicial leniency, while downplaying its relatively dubious Islamic and nationalistic credentials.

From the point of view of Jerusalemite Muslims, it is the Israeli shari'a court's ability to maneuver between opposing legal codes, cultural perceptions, and organizational principles that makes it so effective,[15] and therefore this is the attribute that is highlighted. The Israeli shari'a court in West Jerusalem merely needs to convince Muslim Jerusalemites that it is worthwhile to appeal to it, that it provides them with legal aid that is at once effective, convenient, and just—much more than any other alternative court. And indeed, the Israeli shari'a court is very successful in this task: the number of cases it adjudicates is currently several times larger than the cases adjudicated by all the other courts in the network taken together.

Conclusions

What are our conclusions, then, concerning the effects of legal pluralism on courts as organizations? It appears that we can safely determine that legal pluralism does not necessarily yield any particular organizational reaction. It has been shown that each of the courts in the studied organizational network responded differently to the environmental pressures entailed by legal pluralism, and that their responses were influenced by their positioning in the network. Legal pluralism can promote organizational dynamism, or organizational conservatism, or neither—depending on the circumstances.

Quite a different set of questions arises concerning the possibility of generalizing from our findings in the West Jerusalem shari'a court to other shari'a courts, in other times and places. Of the two diametrically opposed responses of the Israeli and the Jordanian shari'a courts—one adopting a "culture of change," the other clinging to conservatism—it is the response of the latter that is more in line with the general view of shari'a courts as old-fashioned, traditional, even stagnant institutions. Nevertheless, I would like to suggest that this view may be erroneous. Contrary to prevalent views, it is actually the reaction of the Israeli shari'a court that is perhaps more representative of the "usual" reactions of shari'a courts to pressure created by legal pluralism—at least since the *tanzimat* reforms in the nineteenth century.

I contend that ever since the *tanzimat* reforms in the Ottoman Empire (and in most of the Middle Eastern nation states that were established after the demise of the Empire), shari'a courts had to adopt not only to state-driven processes of "modernization," "rationalization," and "bureaucratization," but also to

15 Actually, this ability to maneuver is exactly what gives cultural hybridity its generativity and productivity (see Chapter 5).

contradictory isomorphic pressures, exerted within two distinct organizational fields: the field of the state legal system and the field of the *shar'i* legal system.

These two organizational fields were formally separated from each other by Ottoman reformers, who established a "modern" court system (the *nizami* courts) that operated parallel to the shari'a courts. The *nizami* court system soon became the more dominant and influential judicial system, encroaching upon the "old-fashioned" shari'a court system, which fell out of grace. Although both systems operate under the general auspices of the state, the shari'a court system does retain, in almost all states,[16] at least some level of autonomy and separation from the state legal system (see Balz 1995, Berger 1999), and we may therefore still speak of two distinct organizational fields.

Thus, it may be argued that "modern" shari'a courts—that is, shari'a courts in the last 150 years or so—are liable to contradictory isomorphic pressures, exerted upon them by the two organizational fields they belong to. If this is indeed the case, then the exceptional legal institution is not the Israeli shari'a court in West Jerusalem, but rather the Jordanian court in East Jerusalem. It appears that the latter court, presumably due to its severance from the Jordanian state legal system, has found itself in the unusual situation of being affiliated with one organizational field only—that of the *shar'i* establishment.[17] As a result, this court exhibits a monolithic and perfectly coherent policy of *shar'i* conservatism.

Contrary to the unique political and administrative circumstances of the Jordanian shari'a court in contemporary Jerusalem, the more common situation of shari'a courts is the affiliation with two organizational fields. We should therefore expect to find in them dynamic, adaptive legal cultures, rather than conservatism—just as we have seen in the shari'a court in West Jerusalem. Indeed, as illustrated by several historical and ethnographic studies of shari'a courts in the modern era, dynamism and continuous transformation appear to be the rule, rather than the exception (see e.g., Messick 1993, Welchman 2000, Wurth 2003, Peletz 2002, Rosen 2000: ch. 6, Agmon 2006). Nevertheless, despite the recent scholarly focus on the dynamic, transformative nature of Islamic law in the modern era, the organizational aspects of this dynamism have not yet been examined systematically. The organizational perspective proposed in this book may therefore serve to fill up this lacuna and enrich our understanding and explanations concerning transformation processes in shari'a courts.

Although we may certainly generalize from the Israeli shari'a court in West Jerusalem to other shari'a courts, the uniqueness of this court should not be played down. This book portrayed a singular institution, which operates in unique

16 Except, of course, for those states that abolished shari'a courts altogether (e.g. Turkey, Egypt, and Libya).

17 As mentioned in Chapter 12, following the signing of the Oslo Accords and the establishment of the Palestinian National Authority, Jordan cut off all its governmental and bureaucratic ties with the West Bank, except for its ties with the *waqf* administration in Jerusalem, headed by the office of *qadi al-quda* in Amman.

political and legal circumstances and under conditions of a particularly strong and conspicuous legal pluralism. Most significantly, this shari'a court belongs to the legal system of a non-Muslim state (Israel) and serves a Palestinian population that opposes and resists Israeli rule. Consequently, the two organizational fields to which the court belongs are particularly far apart, and the isomorphic pressures exerted in them are especially contradictory and conflictual. In this sense, the shari'a court in West Jerusalem represents an unusual case, indeed. This book aims, therefore, not only to enhance our general understanding of legal pluralism and its organizational aspects (in Islamic contexts and elsewhere), but also to present a rich historical and ethnographical picture of this exceptional legal institution in present day Jerusalem.

Appendix 1
Shari'a Court Fees

بسم الله الرحمن الرحيم

מדינת ישראל
משרד המשפטים
إدارة المحاكم الشرعية

sharia courts management **הנהלת בתי הדין השרעיים**

التاريخ: 24-3-2004

حضرات سكرتيري المحاكم الشرعية

تحية وبعد

الموضوع: <u>رسوم المحاكم الشرعية</u>

نعلمكم بهذا ان رسوم المحاكم الشرعية تغيرت حسب انظمة المحاكم الشرعية (رسوم) لسنة 1968, للمبالغ المبينة ادناه ابتداءاً من يوم 1.1.04 كالتالي:

.1	عن دعوى تتعلق بزواج , طلاق, طاعة , وصاية , حضانة, تبني, إرث, تركات , وصيات, وقف وتغيير ديانة	201.34
.2	عن تجديد النظر في دعوى من الدعاوي المذكورة أعلاه في الفقرة (1) بعد النظر فيها	141.35
.3	عن استئناف واستئناف مضاد او اعتراض على قرار صدر بحضور طرف واحد	161.56
.4	عن إجراء مؤقت وطلبات مساعدة لم تطلب حين تقديم الدعوى الأصلية	100.95
.5	عن رخصة سنوية لمرافع شرعي	403.84
.6	عن تسجيل عقد زواج	201.34
.7	عن تصديق مستندات لكل صفحة	4.00
.8	عن كل موضوع او عمل او اجراء لم يتعين له رسم في هذه الانحة	141.35
.9	عن تبليغ وثائق بصورة شخصية حسب عنوان معروف	40.34

النفقة معفاة من الرسوم وهي تشمل اجرة المسكن.

ارجو العمل بهذه التعريفة اعتبارا من 1.1.2004 .

باحترام ,

اياد زحالقة. محام
القائم بأعمال مدير المحاكم الشرعية

7 Kanfey nesharim st. Jeruselem شارع كنفي نشريم7- القدس רח' כנפי נשרים –7- ירושלים
fax. 02-6588226 **02-6588220** **Tel . 02-6588220**

Appendix 2
Form for Court Petition

A form of an *istid'a'* (petition), asking for the court's recognition of a Jordanian marriage. The court' acting secretary, Abu Zayd, provided me with this handwritten form, and I assisted petitioners in filling it.

Translation of the form:

In the shar'i hearing that was held with us,

petitioner (male) ________

and petitioner (female) ________

were present.

They both confirmed the existence of a proper (shar'i) marriage [between them]

that was registered by marriage contract no. _______ issued by the court in Salah

al-Din street [the Jordanian shari'a court in East Jerusalem], date _________.

We herby request that this marriage be recognized by this court.

___________	___________	___________
Petitioner	Petitioner	Qadi

محضر

[illegible]

في المجلس الشرعي المعقود لدينا حضر

المدعي

والمدعية

وتصادقا على قيام الزوجية الشرعية

الصحيحة بموجب عقد زواج صادر

عن محكمة ش صلاح الدين. بحسب الحكم

تاريخ والتمسا تثبيت حصول

الزواج لدى هذه المحكمة .

تحريراً

المدعي المدعية القاضي

Appendix 3

Fatwa by the Mufti of Jerusalem, Sheikh ‘Akrama Sabri, issued on July 31, 2001, in response to an istifta’ (query) presented on July 26, 2001

The fatwa was issued in support of Israeli shari‘a courts in their struggle to retain exclusive jurisdiction in matters related to Muslims’ personal status.

31.JUL.2001 10:43 GRAND MUFTI JERUSALEM NO.650 P.1

بسم الله الرحمن الرحيم

DAR AL-FATWA
And ISLAMIC RESEARCH
Expounder of the Islamic Religious Law
Al-Quds

ار الفتوى
بحوث الإسلامية
للقـــدس
الديار الفلسطينية

ـم : [illegible]

يخ : [illegible] هـ

فق : [illegible] م

الموضوع : فتوى شرعية

سماحة مفتي القدس والديار الفلسطينية الدكتور الشيخ عكرمة سعيد صبري المحترم

السلام عليكم ورحمة الله وبركاته .

نوع الفتوى : عامة . بشأن صلاحيات المحاكم الشرعية .

سيدي : تبت المحاكم الشرعية بأمور الأحوال الشخصية للمسلمين ، ولكن هناك اقتراح قانون جديد يقضي بتحديد صلاحية المحاكم الشرعية حيث يكون لها وحدها صلاحية البت بأمور الزواج والطلاق ، أما في باقي الأمور (النفقة – الوصاية _ الوقف .....الخ) لسيكون " سباق صلاحيات "، أي في حالة تقدم الطرف المشتكي بالشكوى الى المحكمة المدنية (محكمة شؤون العائلة) فأن المحكمة الشرعية تخسر صلاحيتها في البت في القضية وتكون الصلاحية فقط بيد المحكمة المدنية ، وبالعكس ففي حالة تقدم الطرف المشتكي بالشكوى الى المحكمة الشرعية فتكون هي المخولة الوحيدة في البت في القضية ، فما رأى الشرع الحنيف في ذلك .

المستفتي

المحامي زاهي الجيدات

بسم الله الرحمن الرحيم

الحمد لله رب العالمين والصلاة والسلام على اشرف المرسلين سيدنا محمد الأمين وعلى آله وصحبه أجمعين وبعد:–

الأخ الفاضل المحامي زاهي الجيدات – سكرتير جمعية الميزان .

السلام عليكم ورحمة الله وبركاته:–

بالإشارة الى سؤالك المثبت أعلاه والمؤرخ في ٢٦/٧/٢٠٠١م بخصوص صلاحيات المحاكم الشرعية ابين لك ما يأتي :–

١– لقد شرع الله تبارك وتعالى التقاضي بين الناس احقاقاً للحق واعطاء لكل ذي حقه يقول تعالى " واذا حكمتم بين الناس ان تحكموا بالعدل " .

٢– ان الاحتكام الى الشرع الشريف بالنسبة للمسلمين واجب لا بد منه وعليهم ان يحتكموا الى القرآن الكريم والسنة المطهرة قال تعالى " ومن لم يحكم بما أنزل الله فأولئك هم الكافرون " .

٣– اذا فرض على المسلمين نظام غير نظام الإسلام في التحاكم والتقاضي فلا يجوز لهم الرضا والقبول به بل عليهم رفضه والاعتراض عليه بكل الوسائل المتوفرة .

القدس هاتف : ٠٢-٦٢٦٠٥٨٢ فاكس : ٠٢-٦٢٨٥٠٨٢ هاتف متنقل : ٠٥٠-٣١١٤٨٩ ص . ب : ٥٤٨٢٥

P.O. Box 54825 M. Ph. 050-311489 Fax : 00 628[illegible]

The Fatwa ... And ISLAMIC RESEARCH
Expounder of the Islamic Religious Law
Al-Quds

... الفتوى
... البحوث الإسلامية
... للقدس
... الديار الفلسطينية

الموضوع : فتوى شرعية

٤- الاصل في بلاد المسلمين ان تكون جميع القوانين والأنظمة مستمدة من الشريعة الإسلامية الغراء لأن ذلك ادعي للحق وفي الامر عبادة لله يتقرب بها المسلم الى خالقه .

٥- لقد اجازت الشريعة الإسلامية لغير المسلمين في بلاد الإسلام أن يحتكموا في احوالهم الشخصية وامورهم التعبدية الى دياناتهم انطلاقا من قوله تعالى " لا إكراه في الدين " .

٦- إن الأحوال الشخصية التي تشمل الطلاق والزواج والنفقات والميراث والولاية والوصاية ...الخ) بالإضافة الى أمور الوقف هي من الأمور التي ترتبط بالعبادات بحيث يحرم على المسلم ان يخالفها فالنفقة والميراث مثلا يجب على المسلم ان ينفذ حكم الله فيها كما ينفذ فريضة الصلاة والزكاة والحج حتى ولو كان يعيش في بلاد غير إسلامية .

بناء على ما تقدم فإنني أقول بأن المسلم يجب عليه السعي الى تطبيق أحكام الله في كل أمر من أموره .
اما بالنسبة لتطبيق غير قوانين الإسلام في قضايا الأحوال الشخصية فإن هذا الأمر يعتبر اعتداء سافرا على العبادات وتدخلا في حرية العبادة ولا يجوز القبول بذلك مطلقا ويحرم على المسلم أن يحتكم الى المحاكم التي تحكم بخلاف رأي الإسلام في هذه القضايا التعبدية ، وينبغي المحافظة على بقاء المحاكم الشرعية، والسعي لتوسعة صلاحياتها وليس الى تقليصها لتشمل جميع جوانب الحياة .

والله يقول الحق وهو يهدي السبيل
والسلام عليكم ورحمة الله وبركاته .

المفتي العام للقدس والديار الفلسطينية

الدكتور الشيخ عكرمة سعيد صبري

القدس هاتف : ٠٢-٦٢٦٠٥٨٢ فاكس : ٠٢-٦٢٨٥٠٨٢ هاتف متنقل : ٠٥٠-٣١١٤٨٩ ص . ب : ٥٤٨٢٥
Al-Quds Tel. : 02-6260582 Fax : 02-6285082 M. Ph. 050-311489 P.O. Box 54825

Bibliography

Laws and Regulations Cited

Ottoman

Law of Family Rights [OLFR] (1917)—*Dustur*, 2nd series, vol. 9, 762–83.
Law of Procedure for Shari'a Courts (1917)—*Dustur*, 2nd series, vol. 9, 783–94.
Law of Succession (1913)—*Dustur*, 2nd series, vol. 5, 145.
Majalla (1869–76)—Mecelle-i Ahkam Adliye. Atif Bey, Istanbul: Mahmut Bey Matbaasi, 1909.

British Mandate

Criminal Code Ordinance (1936), *Palestine Gazette*, no. 652, supp. 1, 399.
Establishment of a shari'a court of appeals (October 10, 1918, and August 1, 1919)—*Official Gazette*, 1919–22, 12, 14.
Moslem Family Law Ordinance (September 25, 1919)—*Laws of Palestine*, vol. 2, ch. 96, 1014.
Palestine Order in Council (1922–47), *Laws of Palestine*, vol. 3, 2569.
Proclamation No. 42 (June 24, 1918), issued by the O.E.T.A (south) Headquarters—*Official Gazette*, 1919–22, 10. Amendment, No. 81 (November 1918)—*Official Gazette*, 1919–22, 13.
Succession Ordinance (1923), *Laws of Palestine*, vol. 2, ch. 135, 1378.

Israeli

Abolishment of the Majalla Law (5744–1984)—*Sefer Ha-Chukim* (5744–1984), 1119, 156.
Absentee Property Law (5710–1950)—*Sefer Ha-Chukim* (5710–1950), 37, 86.
Age of Marriage Law (5710–1950)—*Sefer Ha-Chukim* (5710–1950), 57, 286.
Basic Law: The Judiciary (5743–1983)—*Sefer Ha-Chukim* (5743–1983), 1110, 78.
Capacity and Guardianship Law (5722–1962)—*Sefer Ha-Chukim* (5722–1962), 380, 120.
Civil Wrongs Ordinance (new version) (5728–1968)—*Sefer Ha-Chukim* (5728–1968), 529, 101.
Court Regulations (Suspension of Leaving the Country) (5717–1957)—*Regulations Book* (5717–1957), 222, 104.

Establishment of a Shari'a Court in Jerusalem—*Yalkut HaPirsumim*, (5749–1989), 3624, 1762.

Family Court Law (5755–1995)—*Sefer Ha-Chukim* (5755–1995), 1537, 393–400. Amendment No. 5 (5761–2001)—*Sefer Ha-Chukim* (5761–2001), 1810, 16.

Law and Administration Ordinance, no. 1 (5708–1948)—*Laws of the State of Israel*, vol. 1, 9. Amendment No. 11 (5727–1967)—*Sefer Ha-Chukim* (5727–1967), 499, 74.

Municipalities Ordinance (Amendment No. 6) Law (5727–1967)—*Laws of the State of Israel*, vol. 21, 75.

Nationality Law (5712–1952)—*Sefer Ha-Chukim* (5712–1952), 95, 146.

Penal Law (5737–1977)—*Sefer Ha-Chukim* (5737–1977), 864, 226.

Prevention of Violence in the Family Law (5751–1991)—*Sefer Ha-Chukim* (5751–1991), 1352, 138.

Qadis Law (5721–1961)—*Sefer Ha-Chukim* (5721–1961), 339, 118. Amendment No. 10 (July 2002)—*Sefer Ha-Chukim* (5762–2002), 1860, 505.

Rabbinical Courts Jurisdiction (Marriage and Divorce) Law (5713–1953)—*Sefer Ha-Chukim* (5713–1953), 134, 165.

Regulations regarding *shar'i* advocates (1963), issued by Minister of Religious Affairs—*Kovetz Ha-Takanot*, 1440 (April 18), 1374.

Regulations regarding shari'a court fees (1968), issued by Minister of Religious Affairs—*Kovetz Ha-Takanot*, 2259 (July 25), 1955.

Religious Courts (Assistance Units) Law (5711–2011)—*Sefer Ha-Chukim* (5711–2011), 2297, 918.

Religious Courts (Prevention of Disturbance) Law (5725–1965)—*Sefer Ha-Chukim* (5725–1965), 452, 115.

Religious Courts (Summons) Law (5716–1956)—*Sefer Ha-Chukim* (5716–1956), 200, 40.

Shari'a Courts (Validation of Appointments) Law (5714–1954)—*Sefer Ha-Chukim* (5714–1954), 139, 43.

Spouses (Property Relations) Law (5733–1973)—*Sefer Ha-Chukim* (5733–1973), 712, 267.

Succession Law (5725–1965)—*Sefer Ha-Chukim* (5725–1965), 446, 63.

Women's Equal Rights Law (5711–1951)—*Sefer Ha-Chukim* (5711–1951), 82, 248.

Others

Egyptian Law of Testamentary Disposition (1946)—Act no. 71/1946, *al-Jareeda al-Rasmiyya*, 52, 525–7.

Jordanian Law of Family Rights (1951)—Law no. 92/1951, *Official Gazette* 1081, May 16, 1951.

Jordanian Law of Personal Status (1976)—Law no. 61/1976, *Official Gazette* 2668, December 1, 1976.

Jordanian Law of *Shar'i* Procedure (1959)—Law no. 31/1959, *Official Gazette* 1449, November 1, 1959.

Syrian Personal Status Law (1953)—Law 95/1953, *Official Gazette* no. 63, October 8, 1953.
[US] The Indian Civil Rights Act (1968)—(ICRA), 25 U.S.C. §§ 1301–4.

Court Rulings Cited

Israeli High Court of Justice

HCJ 282/61, Al-Sarouji *v.* The Minister of Religious Affairs, P.D., 17 (1), 188.
HCJ 1/62, ‘Abd al-Qadir Abu Angle *v.* The Population Registration Officer, P.D., 17 (4), 275.
HCJ 106/79, P.D., 34 (1), 825.
HCJ 250/83, Sahr Umri and others *v.* ‘Abd al-Fatah Ibrahim Zu’bi and others, P.D., 39 (2), 113.
HCJ 1842/92, Bloigrond *v.* The Rabbinical Court, P.D., 46 (3), 438–9.
HCJ 6452/96, Custodian of Absentee Property *v.* The Shari‘a Court of Appeal, P.D., 55 (4), 363.
HCJ 8497/00, Feig-Felman *v.* Felman, P.D., 57 (2), 118, 132.
HCJ 891/01, Zo’bi Ubaid *v.* Minister of Religious Affairs, P.D., 58 (3), 857.
HCJ 7052/03, Adalah, et al., v. Minister of Interior, et al., P.D., 61 (2), 202.

Israeli Shari‘a Court of Appeal

106/1994	294/1998	44/2002
31/1995	9/1999	162/2002
128/1997	194/1999	114/2003
191/1997	165/2000	259/2003
203/1997	55/2001	263/2003

Israeli Shari‘a Court of First Instance in West Jerusalem

260/1990	1428/2000	78/2002
368/1995	80/2001	110/2002
215/1996	171/2001	509/2002
112/1998	1078/2001	615/2002
395/1998	1543/2001	621/2002
404/1999	1603/2001	721/2002
104/2000	1629/2001	734/2002
162/2000	1751/2001	832/2002
746/2000	1758/2001	985/2002
751/2000	2295/2001	1467/2002
1018/2000	26/2002	1563/2002
1054/2000	38/2002	1578/2002

1597/2002	469/2003	2379/2003
1748/2002	510/2003	2416/2003
1860/2002	747/2003	2438/2003
1869/2002	786/2003	2564/2003
2327/2002	958/2003	2654/2003
2478/2002	1198/2003	2878/2003
2620/2002	1207/2003	2883/2003
2930/2002	1731/2003	107/2004
3036/2002	1744/2003	532/2004
55/2003	1935/2003	552/2004
411/2003	1974/2003	

Others

[USA] *Santa Clara Pueblo v. Martinez* 436 U.S. 49 (1978)

Newspapers

Al-Quds, Jerusalem.
al-Sha'ab, Jerusalem.
Ha'aretz, Tel Aviv.
Sawt al-Haqq wa'l-Hurriyya, Nazareth.

Books, Articles, and other References

Abd Al-Jawad, S. (ed.) 1998. *Nahu Istrategiya Filastiniya Tujah Al-Quds* [Toward a Palestinian Strategy in Jerusalem]. Bir Zeit: Jamiat Bir Zeit.

'Abed Rabho, L. 2012. Blue ID instead of Love: Instrumental Marriages of Palestinian Men with Muslim Women in Israel. *Migdar*, 1, 155–74 [Hebrew].

Abir, M. 1975. Local Leadership and Early Reforms in Palestine, 1800–1834, in *Studies on Palestine during the Ottoman Period*, edited by M. Maoz. Jerusalem: The Magnes Press, 284–310.

Abou Ramadan, M. 2003a. The Transition from Tradition to Reform: The Shari'a Appeals Court Rulings on Child Custody. *Fordham International Law Journal*, 26 (3), 595–655.

______2003b. Judicial Activism of the Shari'a Appeal Court in Israel 1994–2001: Rise and Crisis. *Fordham International Law Journal*, 27 (1), 254–303.

______2006a. Divorce Reform in the Shari'a Court of Appeals in Israel (1992–2003). *Islamic Law and Society*, 13 (2), 242–74.

______2006b. Islamic Legal Reform: The Alimony of Muslim Wife in the Shari'a Court of Appeals. *HAWWA: Journal of the Women of the Middle East and the Islamic World*, 4 (1), 29–75.

_____2008. Notes on the Anomaly of the Shari'a Field in Israel. *Islamic Law and Society*, 15 (1), 84–111.

Abu Lughod, L. 1991. Writing against Culture, in *Recapturing Anthropology: Working in the Present*, edited by R. Fox. Santa Fe, NM: School of American Research Press, 137–51.

Abu Zahra, M. n.d. *Al-Ahwāl al-Shakhiyya*, Cairo.

Adalah. 1998. *Legal Violations of Arab Minorities in Israel: A Report on Israel's Implementation of the International Convention on the Elimination of all Forms of Racial Discrimination*, Adalah, the Legal Centre for Arab Minority Rights in Israel, http://www.adalah.org/eng/publications/violations.htm [accessed: 10/14/2014].

Agmon, I. 2004. Recording Procedures and Legal Culture in the Late Ottoman Shari'a Court of Jaffa, 1865–1890. *Islamic Law and Society*, 11, 333–77.

______2006. *Family and the Courts: Legal Culture and Modernity in Late Ottoman Palestine*. Syracuse, NY: Syracuse University Press.

Akiba, J. 2003. A New School for Qadis: Education of Shari'a Judges in the Late Ottoman Empire, *Turcica*, 35, 125–63.

______2005. From *Kadi* to *Naib*: Reorganization of the Ottoman Shari'a Judiciary in the Tanzimat Period, in *Frontiers of Ottoman Studies: State, Province and the West*, (2 vols) edited by C. Imber and K. Kiotaki. London: I.B. Tauris, 1, 43–60.

Akif Aydin, M. 2000. The Codification of the Islamic-Ottoman family Law and the Decree of 'Hukuk-I Aile,' in *The Great Ottoman Turkish Civilization*, edited by K. Çiçek. Ankara: Yeni Türkiye, 3, 705–13.

Al-Faqih, Y. 1989. *Al-Ahwāl al-Shakhsiyya fī Fiqh Ahl al-Bayt* [Personal Status in the Jurisprudence of the People of the House]. Beirut: Dar al-Adwa'.

Algazi, J. 2002. The Qadis' Status is Deteriorating, but Slowly. *Ha'aretz*, 15 September, B3 [Hebrew].

Al-Kashshaf. 1999. *Al-Kashshaf 'an Qararat al-Isti'naf al-Sadira 'an Mahkamat al-Isti'naf al-Shar'iyya al-'Ulya fi al-Quds al-Sharif* [A Spotlight on the Appeal Decisions Issued by the Shari'a Court of Appeals in Jerusalem] (6 vols), Herzeliyya: The Interdisciplinary Center [no author/editor].

Al-Kayyali, 'A. 1970. *Ta'arikh Filastin al-Hadith* [Modern History of Palestine]. Beirut: al-Mu'asasah al-'Arabiyya li'al-Dirasat wa'al-Nashr.

Al-Qattan, N. 1999. Dhimmis in the Muslim Court: Legal Autonomy and Religious Discrimination. *International Journal of Middle East Studies*, 31, 429–44.

Amirav, M. 2003. *The Palestinian Struggle in Jerusalem*. Jerusalem: The Jerusalem Institute for Israel Studies [Hebrew].

______2009. *Jerusalem Syndrome: The Palestinian-Israeli Battle for the Holy City*. Eastbourne: Sussex Academic Press.

Arbel, D. and Geifman, Y. 1997. Family Court Law, 1995—Critical Analysis. *Hapraklit*, 43 (3), 431–52 [Hebrew].

Ashcroft, B. 2001. *Post-Colonial Transformations*. London: Routledge.

Ashcroft, B., Griffiths, G., and Tiffin, H. 2003. *Post-Colonial Studies: The Key Concepts*. London: Routledge.

‘Ashrawi, H. 2001. Lawlessness and the Rule of Law, published online, January 19 at http://www.miftah.org/Display.cfm?DocId=152&CategoryId=1 [accessed: 10/13/2014].

Baerends, E. 1994. *Changing Kinship: Family and Gender Relationships in Sub-Saharan Africa*. Leiden: Women and Autonomy Centre, Leiden University.

Bakri, ‘A. 2000. *Al-Ab‘ad al-Qanuniyya wal-Idariyya wa’l-Taghyirat ala al-Mahakim al-Shar‘iyya fi Filastin, 1995–2000* [Legal and Administrative Measures and Changes in the Shari‘a Courts in Palestine, 1995–2000], Background paper for The Birzeit University Women’s Studies Center, Comparative Islamic Family Law Project.

Balz, K. 1995. Shari‘a and Qanun in Egyptian Law: A Systems Theory Approach to Legal Pluralism. *Yearbook of Islamic and Middle Eastern Law*, 2, 37–53.

Bate, P.S. 1997. Whatever Happened to Organizational Anthropology? A Review of the Field of Organizational Ethnography and Anthropological Studies. *Human Relations*, 50, 1147–75.

Bauman, R. and Briggs, C.L. 1990. Poetics and Performance as Critical Perspectives on Language and Social Life. *Annual Review of Anthropology*, 19, 59–88.

Benda-Beckmann, F. von. 2002. Who’s Afraid of Legal Pluralism? *Journal of Legal Pluralism*, 47, 37–82.

Benda-Beckmann, K. von. 1981. Forum Shopping and Shopping Forums—Dispute Settlement in a Minangkabau Village in West Sumatra. *Journal of Legal Pluralism*, 19, 117–53.

Benda-Beckmann, F. von and Benda-Beckmann, K. von. 2006. The Dynamics of Change and Continuity in Plural Legal Orders. *Journal of Legal Pluralism*, 53/4, 1–44.

Benda-Beckmann, F. von, Benda-Beckmann, K. von, and Griffiths, A. (eds). 2005. *Mobile People, Mobile Law: Expanding Legal Relations in a Contracting World*. London: Ashgate.

Benton, L. 2002. *Law and Colonial Cultures: Legal Regimes in World History, 1400–1900*. New York: Cambridge University Press.

Bentwich, N. 1926. *Legislation of Palestine, 1918–1925* (2 vols). Alexandria: Whitehead Morris Limited.

Benvenisti, M. 1976. *Jerusalem: The Torn City*. Minneapolis: University of Minnesota Press.

_______1983. *Jerusalem: Study of Polarized Community*. Jerusalem: West Bank Data Project.

_______1995. *Intimate Enemies: Jews and Arabs in a Shared Land*. Berkeley, Los Angeles, and London: The University of California Press.

_______1996. *City of Stone: The Hidden Story of Jerusalem*. Berkeley: University of California Press.

Benziman, U. 1980. Israeli Policy in East Jerusalem after Reunification, in *Jerusalem: Problems and Prospects*, edited by J.L. Kraemer. New York: Praeger, 110–30.

Berger, M.S. 1999. The Shari'a and Legal Pluralism: The Example of Syria, in *Legal Pluralism in The Arab World*, edited by B. Dupret, M. Berger, and L. al-Zwaini. The Hague, London, Boston: Kluwer Law International, 113–24.

Berman, P.S. 2009. New Legal Pluralism. *Annual Review of Law and Social Sciences*, 5, 225–42.

Bernard, M. 1993. s.v. mu'amalat, *EI2*, VII, 254a.

Bhabha, H. 1990. The Third Space: Interview with Homi Bhabha, in *Identity, Community, Culture, Difference*, edited by J. Ratherford. London: Lawrence and Wishart, 207–21.

Bishara, S. and Toma-Suliman, A. 1997. Personal Status and Family Laws, in *NGO Report: The Status of Palestinian Women Citizens of Israel*, The Working Group on the Status of Palestinian Women in Israel, 66–73 at: http://www.adalah.org/eng/intladvocacy/pal_women1.pdf [accessed: 10/13/2014].

Bisharat. G.E. 1989. *Palestinian Lawyers and Israeli Rule: Law and Disorder in the West Bank*. Austin: University of Texas Press.

Bohannan, P.J. 1957. *Justice and Judgment among the Tiv*. London: Oxford University Press.

Bollens, S.A. 2000. *On Narrow Ground: Urban Policy and Ethnic Conflict in Jerusalem and Belfast*. Albany: SUNY Press.

Bornstein, A. 2001. Ethnography and the Politics of Prisoners in Palestine-Israel. *Journal of Contemporary Ethnography*, 30 (5), 546–74.

Botiveau, B. 1993. *Loi islamique et droit dans les sociétés arabes. Mutations des systèmes juridique et droit du Moyen-Orient*. Paris: Karthala.

Bourdieu, Pierre. 1986. The Forms of Capital (trans. by R. Nice), in *Handbook for Theory and Research for the Sociology of Education*, edited by J.G. Richardson. New York, Westport, CT and London: Greenwood Press, 241–58.

______1998. The Economy of Symbolic Goods (trans. Randal Johnson), in *Practical Reason: On the Theory of Action*. Cambridge: Polity Press, 92–123.

Bowen, J.R. 2003. *Islam, Law and Equality in Indonesia: An Anthropology of Public Reasoning*. Cambridge: Cambridge University Press.

Brace, P. and Hall, M.G. 1995. Studying Courts Comparatively: The View from the American States. *Political Research Quarterly*, 48 (1), 5–29.

Brecher, M. 1978. Jerusalem: Israel Political Decisions, 1947–1977. *Middle East Journal*, 32 (1), 13–34.

Brown, N.J. 2003. *Palestinian Politics after the Oslo Accord*. Berkeley, Los Angeles, and London: The University of California Press.

Brunschvig, R. 1960. s.v. Bayyina, *EI2*, I, 1151b.

B'Tselem Report. 1997. *The Quiet Deportation: Revocation of Residency of East Jerusalem Palestinians*, Joint Report with Hamoked—Center for the Defense of the Individual. http://www.btselem.org/Download/199704_Quiet_Deportation_Eng.doc [accessed: 10/12/2014].

______1998. *The Quiet Deportation Continues: Revocation of Residency and Denial of Social Rights of East Jerusalem Palestinians*, Joint Report with Hamoked—Center for the Defense of the Individual. http://www.btselem.

org/Download/199809_Quiet_Deportation_Continues_ Eng.doc [accessed: 10/12/2014].

______2003. *Behind the Barrier—Human Rights Violations as a Result of Israel's Separation Barrier*, Position Paper. http://www.btselem.org/Download/200304_Behind_The_Barrier_Eng.pdf [accessed: 10/13/2014].

Burawoy, M. 1998. The Extended Case Method. *Sociological Theory* 16 (1), 4–33.

Buskens, L. 2003. Recent Debates on Family Law Reform in Morocco: Islamic Law as Politics in an Emerging Public Sphere. *Islamic Law and Society*, 10 (1), 70–131.

Cattan, H. 1981. The Status of Jerusalem under International Nations Resolutions. *Journal of Palestine Studies*, 10 (3), 3–15.

Chanock, M. 1985. *Law Custom and Social Order: The Colonial Experience in Malawi and Zambia*. Cambridge: Cambridge University Press.

Choshen, M. and Assaf-Shapira, Y. 2005. *Jerusalem: A City in Transition.* Jerusalem: The Jerusalem Institute for Israel Studies. http://www.jiis.org.il/jerusalem-in-transition.pdf [accessed 10/12/2014].

Clarke, K.M. 2010. Toward a Critically Engaged Ethnographic Practice. *Current Anthropology*, 51 (2s), s301–s312.

Clermont, K.M. and Eisenberg, T. 1995. Exorcising the Evil of Forum-Shopping. *Cornell Law Review*, 80, 1507–72.

Cohen, A. 1984. *Jewish Life under Islam: Jerusalem in the Sixteenth Century*, Cambridge, MA: Harvard University Press.

______1994. *A World Within: Jewish Life As Reflected in Muslim Court Documents from the* Sijill *of Jerusalem (XVIth Century)*, Philadelphia: University of Pennsylvania Press.

Cohen, A., Ben Shimon-Pikali, E., and Ginieo, E. 1993–2003. *Jews in the Muslim Religious Court: Society, Economy and Communal Organization in the Sixteenth Century. Documents from Ottoman Jerusalem*, 3 vols, Jerusalem: Yad Izhak Ben-Zvi.

Cohen, J.M. 2002. *Inside Appellate Courts: The Impact of Court Organization on Judicial Decision Making in the United States Courts of Appeal*. Ann Arbor: The University of Michigan Press.

Comaroff, J.L. 1994. Foreword, in *Contested States: Law Hegemony and Resistance*, edited by M. Lazarus-Black and S.F. Hirsch. New York and London: Routledge, ix–xiii.

Coulson, N.J. 1971. *Succession in the Muslim Family*. Cambridge: Cambridge University Press.

Cuno, K.M. 2015. *Modernizing Marriage: Family, Ideology, and Law in Nineteenth and Early Twentieth Century Egypt*. Syracuse: Syracuse University Press.

Dane, P. 1991. The Maps of Sovereignty: A Meditation. *Cardozo Law Review*, 12, 959–1006.

Davison, R.H. 2000. s.v. "Tanzimat," *EI2*, X, 200.

DiMaggio, P.J. and Powell, W.W. 1983. The Iron Cage Revisited: Institutional Isomorphism and Collective Rationality in Organizational Fields. *American Sociological Review*, 48, 147–60.
Doumani, B. 1985. Palestinian Islamic Court Records: A Source for Socio-economic History. *Middle Eastern Studies Association Bulletin*, 19, 155–72.
Dumper, M. 1994. *Islam and Israel: Muslim Religious Endowments and the Jewish State*. Washington, DC: Institute for Palestine Studies.
______2002. *The Politics of Sacred Space: The Old City of Jerusalem in the Middle East Conflict*. London: Lynne Rienner.
Edelman, M. 1994. *Courts, Politics and Culture in Israel*. Virginia: University Press of Virginia.
Ehrlich, E. 1936. *Fundamental Principles of the Sociology of Law*, (trans. W.L. Moll), Cambridge, MA: Harvard University Press.
Eisenman, R.H. 1977. *Islamic Law in Mandate Palestine and Modern Israel: A Study of the Survival and Repeal of Ottoman Legislative Reform*. Ann Arbor, Michigan: University Microfilms International [PhD dissertation, Columbia University].
Emirbayer, M. 1997. Manifest for a Relational Sociology. *The American Journal of Sociology*, 103 (2), 281–317.
Emirbayer, M. and Johnson, V. 2008. Bourdieu and Organizational Analysis. *Theory and Society* 37 (1), 1–44.
Engel, D.M. 1980. Legal Pluralism in an American Community: Perspectives on a Civil Trial Court. *Law and Social Enquiry*, 5 (3), 425–54.
Epstein, L., Walker, T.G., and Dixon, W.J. 1989. The Supreme Court and Criminal Justice Disputes: A New Institutional Perspective. *American Journal of Political Science*, 33, 825–41.
Erlanger, H., Chambliss, E., and Melli, M. 1987. Participation and Flexibility in Informal Processes: Cautions from the Divorce Context. *Law and Society Review*, 21, 585–604.
Farhi, D. 1979. The Islamic Board in East Jerusalem and in Judea and Samaria since the Six Days War. *Hamizrah Hehadash* [The New East], 28, 3–21 [Hebrew].
Findley, C.V. 1980. *Bureaucratic Reforms in the Ottoman Empire: The Sublime Porte 1879–1922*. Princeton: Princeton University Press.
______1991. s.v. Madjalla, *EI2*, VI, 971–5.
Forsyth, M. 2007. A Typology of Relationships between State and Non-State Justice Systems. *Journal of Legal Pluralism*, 56, 67–112.
Foucault, Michel. 1979. *The History of Sexuality*. London: Allen Lane.
______1982. The Subject and Power, in *Michel Foucault: Beyond Structuralism and Hermeneutics*, edited by H.L. Dreyfus and P. Rabinow. Brighton: Harvester Press, 202–26.
Fourcade, M. 2007. Theories of Markets and Theories of Society. *American Behavioral Scientist*, 50, 1015–34.
Friedland, R. and Hecht, R. 1996. *To Rule Jerusalem*. Cambridge: Cambridge University Press.

Friedman, M. 1995. The Structural Foundation of Religio-Political Accommodation in Israel: Fallacy and Reality, in *Israel: The First Decade of Independence*, edited by I.S. Troen and N. Lucas. New York: SUNY Press, 51–82.

Frisch, H. 1998. Modern Absolutism or New-Patrimonial State Building? Customary Law, Extended Families and the Palestinian Authority. *International Journal of Middle East Studies*, 29 (3), 341–58.

Galanter, M. 1974. Why the "Haves" Come Out Ahead: Speculations on the Limits of Legal Change. *Law and Society Review*, 9 (1), 95–160.

______1981. Justice in Many Rooms: Courts, Private Ordering and Indigenous Law. *Journal of Legal Pluralism*, 19, 1–47.

______1983. Reading the Landscape of Disputes: What We Know and Don't Know (and Think We Know) about our Allegedly Contentious and Litigious Society. *UCLA Law Review*, 31, 4–71.

Galanter, M. and Krishnan, J. 2001. Personal Law Systems and Religious Conflicts: A Comparison of India and Israel, in *Religion and Personal Law in Secular India: A Call to Judgment*, edited by G.J. Larson. Bloomington: Indiana University Press, 270–300.

Garner, B.A. (ed.). 2001. *Black's Law Dictionary*, 2nd Pocket Edition, West Publishing Company.

Geifman, Y. 1998. *Family Law in Israel at the Era of the Family Court*. Tel Aviv: Dyonon [Hebrew].

Gerber, H. 1985. *Ottoman Rule in Jerusalem, 1890–1914*. Berlin: K. Schwarz.

______1994. *State, Society and Law in Islam: Ottoman Law in Comparative Perspective*. Albany: SUNY Press.

Gilson, R.J. and Mnookin, R.H. 1994. Disputing through Agents: Cooperation and Conflict between Lawyers in Litigation. *Columbia Law Review*, 94, 509–66.

Gluckman, M. 1961. Ethnographic Data in British Social Anthropology. *The Sociological Review*, 9, 5–17.

______1965. *The Ideas in Barotse Jurisprudence*. New Haven: Yale University Press.

Goadby, F.M. 1926. *International and Inter-Religious Private Law in Palestine*. Jerusalem: "Hamadpis" Press.

Goitein, S.D. and Ben Shemesh, A. 1957. *Islamic Law in the State of Israel*, Jerusalem: The Hebrew University, Faculty of Law [Hebrew].

Goodale, M. 2002. Legal Ethnography in an Era of Globalization: The Arrival of Western Human Rights Discourse to Rural Bolivia, in *Practicing Ethnography in Law: New Dialogues, Enduring Methods*, edited by J. Starr and M. Goodale. New York: Palgrave Macmillan, 50–71.

Greenwood, R., Oliver, C., Sahlin, K., and Suddaby, R. (eds). 2008. *The Sage Handbook of Organizational Institutionalism*. LA, London, New Delhi, and Singapore: Sage.

Griffiths, J. 1986a. What Is Legal Pluralism? *Journal of Legal Pluralism*, 24, 1–55.

______1986b. What Do Dutch Lawyers Actually Do in Divorce Cases? *Law and Society Review*, 20, 135–75.

Gulliver, P.H. 1963. *Social Control in an African Society*. Boston: Boston University Press.

______1969. Dispute Settlement without Courts: The Ndendeuli of Southern Tanzania, in *Law in Culture and Society*, edited by L. Nader. Berkeley, Los Angeles, and London: The University of California Press, 24–68.

______1971. *Neighbors and Networks: The Idiom of Kinship among the Ndendeuli of Tanzania*. Berkeley: The University of California Press.

Hacker, D. 2003. "Motherhood," "Fatherhood," and Law: A Sociological Analysis of the Field that Shapes Custody and Visitation Arrangements. PhD dissertation, Tel Aviv University [Hebrew].

Hajjar, L. 2005. *Courting Conflict: The Israeli Military Court System in the West Bank and Gaza*. Berkeley, Los Angeles, and London: The University of California Press.

Hall, M.G. and Brace, P. 1989. Order in the Court: A New Institutional Approach to Judicial Consensus. *Political Research Quarterly*, 42, 391–407.

Halperin-Kaddari, R. 1997. Rethinking Legal Pluralism in Israel: The Interaction between the High Court of Justice and the Rabbinical Courts. *Tel Aviv University Law Review*, 20, 683–747 [Hebrew].

Hammamai, R. and Tamari, S. 2001. The Second Uprising: End or New Beginning. *Journal of Palestine Studies*, 30 (2), 5–25.

Hawari, 'A. 2012. Personal Status in Civil *versus* Religious Courts: A Controversial Issue. *Jadal*, 16, 1–5. A version in Arabic may be downloaded from the website of the Working group for Equality in personal Status Issues: http://www.pstatus.org/index.php?todo=articles&aid=00000042 [accessed: 10/13/2014].

Heyd, U. 1973. *Studies in Old Ottoman Criminal Law*. Oxford: The Clarendon Press.

Hill, E. 1979. *Mahkama! Studies in the Egyptian Legal System: Courts & Crimes, Law & Society*. London: Ithaca.

Hirsch, S.F. 1994. Kadhi's Courts as Complex Sites of Resistance: The State, Islam and Gender in Post-Colonial Kenya, in *Contested States: Law, Hegemony and Resistance*, edited by M. Lazarus-Black and S.F. Hirsch. New York and London: Routledge, 207–30.

Holt, D.T., Armenakis, A.A., Feild, H.S., and Harris, S.G. 2007. Readiness for Organizational Change: The Systematic Development of a Scale. *Journal of Applied Behavioral Science*, 43, 232–55.

Hooker, M.B. 1975. *Legal Pluralism: An Introduction to Colonial and New-Colonial Laws*. Oxford: The Clarendon Press.

Ibn 'Abidin, M.A. 1966 [1820/1]. *Radd al-Mukhtar 'ala al-Durr al-Mukhtar* [The Answer to the Baffled over the Exquisite Pearl]. Cairo: al-Halabi Publishing.

Ibrahim, I. 1993. *The Status of Arab Women in Israel*. Jerusalem: Sikkuy [Hebrew].

Inalcik, H. 1991. s.v. Mahkama, 2. "The Ottoman Empire," *EI2*, 6, 3–5.Jackson, S. 1996. *Islamic Law and the State*, Leiden, New York, Koln: E.J. Brill.

Jacob, H. 1992. The Elusive Shadow of the Law. *Law and Society Review*, 26 (3), 565–90.

Kanaaneh, R.A. 2002. *Birthing the Nation: Strategies of Palestinian Women in Israel*. Berkeley, Los Angeles, and London: The University of California Press.

Karayanni, M.M. 2003. On the Concept of 'Ours': Multiculturalism with respect to Arab–Jewish Relations. *Tel Aviv University Law Review* (*Iyyunei Mishpat*), 27 (1), 71–108 [Hebrew].

Kelly, T. 2004. *Access to Justice: The Palestinian Legal System and the Fragmentation of Coercive Power*. Crisis States Program Working Paper no. 41, Development Research Center, LSE.

Khalidi, R. 2001. The Palestinians and 1948: the Underlying Causes of Failure, in *The War for Palestine: Rewriting the History of 1948*, edited by E.L. Rogan and A. Shlaim. Cambridge: Cambridge University Press, 12–36.

Khamaisi, R. 2001. Shared Space, Separate Geo-Politically: Al-Quds Jerusalem Capital for Two States. *Geoforum*, 33, 275–88.

______2003. Population and Housing, in *The Jerusalem Urban Fabric: Demography, Infrastructure and Institutions*, edited by R. Khamaisi and R. Nasrallah. Jerusalem: The International Peace and Cooperation Center, 22–35.

______2006. *Conflict Over Housing: The Housing Sector in Jerusalem: Existing Situation, Barriers, Needs and Future Policies.* Jerusalem: The International Peace and Cooperation Center [in Arabic]. http://home.ipcc-jerusalem.org/en/ipcc/1 [accessed 10/12/2014].

Khamaisi, R and Nasrallah, R. (eds). 2003. *The Jerusalem Urban Fabric: Demography, Infrastructure and Institutions*. Jerusalem: The International Peace and Cooperation Center.

Kimhi, I. (ed.). 2006. *The Security Fence around Jerusalem: Implications for the City and Its residents*. Jerusalem: The Jerusalem Institute for Israel Studies. http://www.jiis.org/.upload/the%20security%20fence%20around%20jerusalem.pdf [accessed: 10/13/2014].

Klein, M. 1996. Islamic Holy Places as a Political Bargaining Card, 1993–1995. *Catholic University Law Review*, 45 (3), 741–70.

______2001. *Jerusalem: The Contested City.* New York: NYU Press.

______2003. By Conviction Not by Infliction: The Debate Over Reforming the Palestinian Authority. *Middle East Journal*, 57 (2), 194–212.

Knauft, B.M. 1994. Pushing Anthropology Past and Posts: Critical Notes on Cultural Anthropology and Cultural Studies as Influenced by Postmodernism and Existentialism. *Critique of Anthropology*, 14, 117–52.

Kraatz, M.S. and Block, E.S. 2008. Organizational Implications of Institutional Pluralism, in *The Sage Handbook of Organizational Institutionalism*, edited by R. Greenwood et al. LA, London, New Delhi, and Singapore: Sage, 243–75.

Kraemer, J.L. 1980. The Jerusalem Question, in *Jerusalem: Problems and Prospects*, edited by J.L. Kraemer. New York: Praeger, 16–40.

Kressel, K., Hochberg, A.M., and Meth, T.S. 1983. A Provisional Typology of Lawyer Attitudes towards Divorce Practice. *Law and Human Behavior*, 7, 31–49.

Kretzmer, D. 1990. *The Legal Status of the Arabs in Israel*. Boulder, San Francisco, Oxford: Westview Press.

Kupferschmidt, U.M. 1987. *The Supreme Muslim Council: Islam under British Mandate for Palestine*. Leiden: E.J. Brill.

Landau, J.M. 1969. *The Arabs in Israel*. Oxford: Oxford University Press.

Lane, E.W. 1954 [1908]. *Manners and Customs of Modern Egyptians*. London and New York: J.M. Dent & Sons, E. P. Dutton.

La Tendresse, A. 1995. *Jerusalem: Palestinian Dynamics, Resistance and Urban Change 1967–1994*. Jerusalem: PASSIA Publications.

Layish, A. 1965. Muslim Religious Jurisdiction in Israel. *Asian and African Studies*, 1, 49–79.

______1975. *Women and Islamic Law in a Non-Muslim State*. Jerusalem: Israel University Press.

______1979. Islam as a Source of Law in the Druze Religious Courts. *Israel Law Review*, 14, 13–30.

______1996. *The Mahdi's Legal Methodology and its Application in the Sudan: A Selection from the Mahdi's Documents (1881–1885)*. Jerusalem: Akademon.

______1997. The Legal Methodology of the Mahdi in the Sudan, 1881–1885: Issues of Marriage and Divorce. *Sudanic Africa*, 8, 37–66.

______2006. Adaptation of a Jurists' Law to Modern Times in an Alien Environment: The Case of the Shari'a in Israel. *Die Welt des Islams*, 46, 168–225.

Lazarus-Black, M. and Hirsch, S.F. 1994. Introduction—Performance and Paradox: Exploring Law's Role in Hegemony and Resistance, in *Contested States: Law, Hegemony and Resistance*, edited by M. Lazarus-Black and S. Hirsch. New York and London: Routledge, 1–34.

Liebesny, H.J. 1975. *The Law of the Near and Middle East*. Albany: SUNY Press.

Louër, L. 2007. *To Be an Arab in Israel*. New York: Columbia University Press.

Lustick, I. 1980a. Zionism and the State of Israel: Regime Objectives and the Arab Minority in the First Years of Statehood. *Middle Eastern Studies*, 16, 127–46.

______1980b. *Arabs in the Jewish State: Israel's Control of a National Minority*. Austin: University of Texas Press.

Maoz, A. 1989. Jurisdictions in Matters Connected with Divorce Suits. *Tel Aviv University Law Review* (*Iyyunei Mishpat*). 14 (1), 101–34 [Hebrew].

Maoz, M. 1984. *Palestinian Leadership on the West Bank*. London: Frank Cass.

Marcus, G. 1995. Ethnography in/of the World System: The Emergence of Multisited Ethnography. *Annual Review of Anthropology*, 24, 95–117.

Marglin, J.M. 2013. In the Courts of the Nations: Jews, Muslims and Legal Pluralism in Nineteenth-century Morocco. PhD dissertation, Princeton University.

Mazzawi, M.E. 1997. *Palestine and the Law: Guidelines for the Resolution of the Arab–Israeli Conflict*. London: Ithaca Press.

McTague, J. 1983. *British Policy in Palestine, 1917–1922*. London: Rowman and Littlefield.

Meron, Y. 1970. The Mejelle Tested by Its Application, *Israeli Law Review*, 5, 203–15.

_______1982. The Religious Courts in the Administered Territories, in *Military Government in the Territories Administered by Israel 1967–1980*, edited by M. Shamgar. Jerusalem: Alpha Press, 353–66.

______2001. *Muslim Law in Comparative Perspective*. Jerusalem: The Magnes Press [Hebrew].

Merry, S.E. 1988. Legal Pluralism. *Law and Society Review*. 22 (5), 869–96.

______1990. *Getting Justice and Getting Even: Legal Consciousness among Working-Class Americans*. Chicago: The University of Chicago Press.

Messick, B. 1993. *The Calligraphic State: Textual Domination and History in a Muslim Society.* Berkeley, Los Angeles, and Oxford: University of California Press.

Meyer, J.W. and Rowan, B. 1977. Institutionalized Organizations: Formal Structure as Myth and Ceremony. *American Journal of Sociology*, 83 (2), 340–63.

Michaels, R. 2009. Global Legal Pluralism. *Annual Review of Law and the Social Sciences*, 5, 243–70.

Mir-Hosseini, Z. 1993. *Marriage on Trial: A Study of Islamic Family Law, Iran and Morocco Compared.* London: I.B. Tauris.

Misselwitz, P. and Rieniets, T. (eds). 2006. *City of Collision: Jerusalem and the Principles of Conflict Urbanism*. Basel: Birkhauser.

Molokomme, A. 1991. *Children of the Fence: The Alimony of Extra-marital Children under Law and Practice in Botswana.* Leiden: African Studies Centre.

Moore, S.F. 1973. Law and Social Change: The Semi-Autonomous Social Field as an Appropriate Object of Study. *Law and Society Review*, 7, 719–46; reprinted in Moore, S.F. 1978. *Law as Process*, London: Routledge and Kegan Paul, 51–84.

______1978. *Law as Process*. London: Routledge and Kegan Paul.

______1986. *Social Facts and Fabrications: Customary Law on Kilimanjaro, 1880–1980*. Cambridge: Cambridge University Press.

More, A. 2005. Killing with Kindness: Funding the Demise of the Palestinian State. *International Affairs*, 81 (5), 981–99.

Morris, B. 1987. *The Birth of the Palestinian Refugee Problem, 1947–1949.* Cambridge: Cambridge University Press.

______2001. Revisiting the Palestinian Exodus of 1948, in *The War for Palestine: Rewriting the History of 1948*, edited by E.L. Rogan and A. Shlaim. Cambridge: Cambridge University Press, 37–59.

Muslim, S. 1996. *Al-Nidal min Ajal Al-Quds* [The Struggle for Jerusalem]. Al-Quds: Al-Jam'iya Al-Akadimiya Lil-Shu'un Al-Dawliya.

Nader, Laura. 1990. *Harmony Ideology: Justice and Control in a Zapotec Mountain Village*. Stanford: Stanford University Press.

______2002. Moving On: Comprehending Anthropologies of Law, in *Practicing Ethnography in Law: New Dialogues, Enduring Methods*, edited by J. Starr and M. Goodale. New York: Palgrave Macmillan, 190–202.

Nasir, J.J.A. 2009. *The Status of Women under Islamic Law and Modern Legislation* (third edition). Leiden: Brill.

Natur, A. 1994. marsum qada'i Raqam 1: Tathbit Qadsiyat al-Muqadasat al-Islamiyya wa-man' Isdar Fatawa bi-Khilaf Dhalik [Affirmation of the sanctity of Islamic sanctuaries, and prohibition to issue Fatwas contradicting this]. Jerusalem: The Shari'a Court of Appeal (republished in *Al-Kashshaf*, vol. 3, 5–9).

______1995. marsum qada'i Raqam 2: Wazifat al-Mukhbirin fi Qadaya al-Nafaqa [The role of informants in maintenance cases]. Jerusalem: The Shari'a Court of Appeal (republished in *Al-Kashshaf*, vol. 3, 9–19).

______1996. marsum qada'i Raqam 3: al-Wasiyya al-Wajiba [The obligatory bequest]. Jerusalem: The Shari'a Court of Appeal (republished in *Al-Kashshaf*, vol. 3, 20–30).

______1998. Moslem Shari'a Court should be Left to its Own Creative Devices (Conversation with Qadi Ahmad H. Natur), *Justice*, 17 (June), 16–22.

Natur, M. 1996. *Al-Mar'i fi al-Qanun al-Shar'i* [Studies in Islamic Law]. Ramallah: Matba't Al-Wahda.

Naveh, I. 1997. Application of the Shari'a in Civil Courts in the Twentieth Century. PhD dissertation, The Hebrew University in Jerusalem.

Neuhaus, D.M. 1991. Between Quiescence and Arousal: The Political Function of Religion, A Case Study of the Arab Minority in Israel. PhD dissertation, The Hebrew University in Jerusalem.

Norwood, K.J. 1996. Shopping for a Venue: The Need for More Limits on Choice. *University of Miami Law Review*, 267, 50–112.

Onar, S.S. 1955. The Mejelle, in *Law in the Middle East*, edited by M. Khaddury and H.J. Libesney. Washington: Middle East Institute, 292–308.

Ortayli, I. 1990. Ottoman Family Law and the State in the Nineteenth Century. *OTAM*, I, 321–2, reprinted in Ortayli, I. 1994. *Studies on Ottoman Transformation*. Istanbul: Isis Press, 139–49.

Palestine Yearbook of International Law, 1987/1988. Leiden: Brill.

Pappé, I. 2000. An Uneasy Coexistence: Arabs and Jews in the First Decade of Statehood, in *Israel: The First Decade of Independence*, edited by I.S. Troen and N. Lucas. Albany: SUNY Press, 617–58.

Paret, R. 1978. s.v. Istihsān and Istislāh, *EI2*, IV, 255–7.

Peled, A.R. 2001. *Debating Islam in the Jewish State: The Development of Policy toward Islamic Institutions in Israel*. New York: SUNY Press.

Peletz, M. 2002. *Islamic Modern: Religious Courts and Cultural Politics in Malaysia*. Princeton: Princeton University Press.

Perrow, C. 1986. *Complex Organizations: A Critical Essay*. New York: Random House.

Peters, R. 2002. s.v. Nafaqa, *EI2*, XII, 643–5.

Porath, Y. 1974. *The Emergence of the Palestinian Arab National Movement, 1918–1929*. London: Frank Cass.

Pospisil, L. 1958. *Kapauku Papauns and Their Law*. New Haven: Yale University Press.
______1971. *Legal Anthropology: A Comparative Theory*. New York: Harper & Row.
Powell, W.W. 1996. Fields of Practice: Connections between Law and Organizations. *Law and Social Inquiry*, 21 (4), 959–66.
Powell, W.W. and DiMaggio, P.J. (eds) 1991. *The New Institutionalism in Organizational Analysis*. Chicago: University of Chicago Press.
Pullan, W., Strenberg, M., Kyriacou, L., Larkin, C., and Dumper, M. (eds) 2013. *The Struggle for Jerusalem's Holy Places*. Abingdon and New York: Routledge.
Qadri Basha, M. 1944 [1900]. *Kitab al-Ahkam al-Shar'iyya fi al-Ahwal al-Shakhsiyya, 'ala Madhhab al-Imam Abi Hanifa al-Nu'man* [Book of Shar'i Rules of Personal Status, based on Imam Abu Hanifa al-Nu'man's School], in *Kitab majmu'at al-Qawanin al-Shar'iyya*, edited by R. al-Sarraj, Jaffa.
Qur'an (trans. A. Yusufali). 1999. 14th ed., London: Tahrike Tarsile Qur'an.
Rabinowitz, D. and Abu-Baker, K. 2005. *Coffins on our Shoulders: The Experience of Palestinians in Israel*. Berkeley: The University of California Press.
Reiter, Y. 1989. An Assessment of the Reform in the Islamic Waqf Institution in Israel: Acre as a Case Study. *Hamizrah Hehadash* [the New East], 32, 21–45 [Hebrew].
______1997a. Qadis and the Implementation of Islamic Law in Present Day Israel, in *Islamic Law: Theory and Practice*, edited by R. Gleave and E. Kermeli. London and New York: I.B. Tauris, 205–31.
______1997b. *Islamic Institutions in Jerusalem*. London: Kluwer Law International.
______2009. Judge Reform: Facilitating Divorce by Shari'a Courts in Israel. *Journal of Islamic Law and Culture*, 11 (1), 13–37.
Rekhess, E. 1989. Israeli Arabs and the Arabs of the West Bank and Gaza: Political Affinity and National Solidarity. *Asian and African Studies*, 23, 119–54.
______1991. Initial Israeli Policy Guidelines towards the Arab Minority, 1948–1949, in *New Perspective in Israeli History*, edited by L.J. Silberstein. New York: NYU Press, 103–23.
______1993. Resurgent Islam in Israel. *Asian and African Studies*, 27, 191–210.
Relis, T. 2002. Civil Litigation from Litigants' Perspectives: What We Know and What We Don't Know about the Litigation Experience of Individual Litigants. *Studies in Law, Politics and Society*, 25, 151–212.
Roberts, S. 1998. Against Legal Pluralism: Some Reflections on the Contemporary Enlargement of the Legal Domain. *Journal of Legal Pluralism*, 42, 95–106.
Robinson, G. 1997. The Politics of Legal Reform in Palestine. *Journal of Palestine Studies*, 27 (1), 51–60.
Romann, M. and Weingrod, A. 1991. *Living Together Separately: Arabs and Jews in Contemporary Jerusalem*. Princeton: Princeton University Press.
Rosen, L. 1989. *The Anthropology of Justice: Law as Culture in Islam*. Cambridge: Cambridge University Press.
______2000. *The Justice of Islam*. Oxford: Oxford University Press.

Rosen, M. 1991. Coming to Terms with the Field: Understanding and Doing Organizational Ethnography. *Journal of Management Studies*, 28 (1), 1–24.

Rosen-Zvi, A. 1989. The Jurisdictional Race in Matters Connected with Divorce Suits and its Impact on Family Law. *Tel Aviv University Law Review* (*Iyyunei Mishpat*), 14 (1), 67–100 [Hebrew].

Rouhana, N. 1989. The Political Transformation of the Palestinian in Israel: From Acquiescence to Challenge. *Journal of Palestine Studies*, 18 (3), 38–59.

Rubin, Avi. 2011. *Ottoman Nizamiye Courts: Law and Modernity*. New York: Palgrave Macmillan.

Saban, I. 2000. *The Legal Status of Minorities in Democratic Deeply-Divided Countries: The Arab Minority in Israel and the Francophone Minority in Canada. LLD thesis, Faculty of Law, The Hebrew University in Jerusalem.*

Sabella, B. 1997. East Jerusalem's Elite, in *Brussels—Jerusalem: Conflict Management and Conflict Resolution in Divided Cities*, edited by A. Datent. Jerusalem and Brussels: IPCRI and VUB, 191–206.

Sack, P. and Aleck, J. 1992. Introduction, in *Law and Anthropology*, edited by idem. Aldershot, Hong Kong, Singapore, and Sydney: Dartmouth, xii–xxxi.

Salah, R. 2001. We Shall not Recourse to the Civil Courts! *Sawt al-Haqq w'al-Huriyya*, 9 November, 13.

Santos, B. De Sousa. 2006. The Heterogeneous State and Legal Pluralism in Mozambique. *Law and Society Review*, 40, 39–75.

Sarat, A. and Felstiner, W.L.F. 1995. *Divorce Lawyers and their Clients: Power and Meaning in the Legal Process*. New York, Oxford: Oxford University Press.

Sarsar, S. 2000. Jerusalem at the Millennium: The City of Unfulfilled Expectations. *The Online Journal of Peace and Conflict Resolution*, 33, at http://www.trinstitute.org/ojpcr/3_3sarsar.htm [accessed: 10/2/2014].

Sartori, P. and Shahar, I. 2012. Legal Pluralism in Muslim Majority Colonies: Mapping the Terrain. *Journal of Economic and Social History of the Orient*, 55 (4–5), 637–63.

Sayigh, Y. and Shikaki, K. 1999. *Strengthening Palestinian Public Institutions*. Washington: Council on Foreign Relations. Available online at http://www.pcpsr.org/sites/default/files/strengtheningpalinstfull.pdf [accessed: 10/13/2014].

Schacht, J. 1964. *An Introduction to Islamic Law*. Oxford: Clarendon Press.

______1995. s.v. Nikah, (in classical Islamic law), *EI2*, VIII, 26–9.

Schmelz, U.O. 1981. Notes on the Demography of Jews, Muslims and Christians in Jerusalem. *Middle East Review*, 13, 62–8.

Schultz, D.E. 2003. Political Factions, Ideological Fictions: The Controversy over Family Law Reform in Democratic Mali. *Islamic Law and Society*, 10 (1), 132–64.

Scott, R.W. and Meyer, J.W. 1991. The Organization of Societal Sectors: Propositions and Early Evidence, in *The New Institutionalism in Organizational Analysis*, edited by W.W. Powell and P.D. DiMaggio. Chicago: The University of Chicago Press, 108–40.

Scott, W.R. 1995. *Institutions and Organizations*. CA, Thousand Oaks: Sage.

Scott, W.R. and Davis, G.F. 2007. *Organizations and Organizing: Rational, Natural, and Open Systems.* Upper Saddle River, NJ: Prentice Hall.

Sezgin, Y. 2004. A Political Account for Legal Confrontation between State and Society: The Case of Israeli Legal Pluralism. *Studies in Law, Politics and Society*, 32, 199–235.

______2013. *Human Rights under State-Enforced Religious Family Law in Israel, Egypt and India*. Cambridge: Cambridge University Press.

Shachar, Y. 1995. History and Sources of Israeli Law, in *Introduction to the Law of Israel*, edited by A. Shapira and K. DeWitt-Arar. The Hague, London, Boston: Kluwer Law International, 1–10.

Shafir, G. and Peled, Y. 2002. *Being Israeli: The Dynamics of Multiple Citizenship.* Cambridge: Cambridge University Press.

Shaham, R. 2006. Shopping for Legal Forums: Christians and Family Law in Modern Egypt, in *Dispensing Justice in Islam: Qadis and their Judgments*, edited by K. Masud, R. Peters, and D.S. Powers. Leiden: Brill, 451–69.

Shahar, Ido. 1997. Trilemma in Court: The Shari'a Court in Beer-Sheva as a Convergence Point of Three Law Systems. *Jama'a* 1, 11–35 [Hebrew].

______2000. Palestinians in an Israeli Court: Culture, Control, and Resistance in the Shari'a Court of Western Jerusalem. MA thesis, The Hebrew University in Jerusalem [Hebrew].

______2001. The *Dabt* (Protocol), the *Ḥukm* (Decision) and their Context: The Politics of Court Record Production. Paper presented at the workshop "Text, Context and the Constitution of Difference," Ben Gurion University, March 28.

______2004. Modernizer and Guardian of Tradition: The Shari'a Court and Women's Status. *Hamizrah Hehadash* [The New East], 44, 195–211 [Hebrew].

______2007. Legal Reform, Interpretive Communities, and the Quest for Legitimacy: A Contextual Analysis of a Legal Circular, in *Law, Custom and Statute in the Muslim World: Studies in Honor of Aharon Layish*, edited by R. Shaham. Leiden: Brill, 199–227.

______2008a. State, Society and the Relations Between Them: Implications for the Study of Legal Pluralism. *Theoretical Inquiries in Law*, 9, 417–41.

______2008b. Legal Pluralism and the Study of Shari'a Courts. *Islamic Law and Society*, 15, 112–41.

______2013. A Tale of Two Courts: How Organizational Ethnography can Shed New Light on Legal Pluralism. *Political and Legal Anthropology Review*, 36 (1), 118–37.

______2013. Forum Shopping between Civil and Shari'a Courts: Maintenance suits in contemporary Jerusalem, in *Religion in Disputes: Pervasiveness of Religious Normativity in Disputing Processes*, edited by K. Benda-Beckmann, F. Benda-Beckmann, B. Turner, and M. Ramstadt. London: Palgrave MacMillan, 147–64.

Sharga'i, N. 1999. Netanyahu in his Weakness. *Ha'aretz*, 23 March, B6.

Sha'shu'a, S. 1981. *Islamic Courts in Israel*. Hulun: Faraj Printing [Hebrew].

Shava, M. 1998a. The Relationship between Jurisdiction of Family Court and Rabbinical Court. *Hapraklit*, 44 (1), 44–71 [Hebrew].

______1998b. Jurisdictions in Matters of Personal Status over Non-Jews. *Hapraklit*, 44 (2), 358–400 [Hebrew]; republished with an added epilogue in Shava, M. 2003. *Jurisdiction in Family Law*. Jerusalem: Israeli BAR Press, 277–326.

______2003. When a Woman's Maintenance and Property Claim is Connected with a Husband's Divorce Suit: Should the Claim be Rejected or Suspended? *Kiryat Mishpat*, 3, 145–75 [Hebrew].

Shaw, S.J. 1977. *History of the Ottoman Empire and Modern Turkey: Reform, Revolution and Republic; The Rise of Modern Turkey* (Vol. II). Cambridge, New York, and Melbourne: Cambridge University Press.

Shehadeh, R. 1980. *The West Bank and the Rule of Law*. Geneva: The International Commission of Jurists.

Shlaim, A. 1990. *The Politics of Partition: King Abdullah, the Zionists and Palestine, 1921–1951*. Oxford: Oxford University Press.

Singer, A. 1994. *Palestinian Peasants and Ottoman Officials: Rural Administration around Sixteenth-Century Jerusalem*. Cambridge: Cambridge University Press.

Smith, M.G. 1969. Some Developments in the Analytic Framework of Pluralism, in *Pluralism in Africa*, edited by L. Kuper and M.G. Smith. Berkeley and Los Angeles: The University of California Press.

Smooha, S. 1992. *Arabs and Jews in Israel: Change and Continuity in Mutual Intolerance*. Boulder, CO: Westview.

Spiertz, J.H.L. 1991. The Transformation of Traditional Law: A Tale of People's Participation in Irrigation Management on Bali. *Landscape and Urban Planning*, 20, 189–96.

State Comptroller and Ombudsman, The State of Israel. 1995. *Report no. 46*. Jerusalem: Hamadpis Hamemshalti.

Steinberg, D.E. 1990. The Motion to Transfer and the Interest of Justice. *Notre Dame Law Review*, 66, 443–98.

Suchman, M. and Edelman, L.B. 1996. Legal Rational Myths: The New Institutionalism and the Law and Society Tradition. *Law and Social Enquiry*, 21, 903–66.

Tamanaha, B.Z. 1993. The Folly of the 'Social Scientific' Concept of Legal Pluralism. *Journal of Law and Society*, 20, 192–217.

______2000. A Non-Essentialist Version of Legal Pluralism. *Journal of Law and Society*, 27 (2), 296–321.

_______2007. Understanding Legal Pluralism: Past to Present, Local to Global. *Sydney Law Review*, 30, 375–411.

Tamari, S. 2003. A Contested City in a Sacred Geography, in *Divided Cities in Transition*, edited by A. Friedman and R. Nasrallah. Jerusalem: The International Peace and Cooperation Center and The Jerusalem Institute for Israel Studies, 119–38.

Thornton, P.H. and Ocasio, W. 2008. Institutional Logics, in *The Sage Handbook of Organizational Institutionalism*, edited by R. Greenwood et al. LA, London, New Delhi, and Singapore: Sage, 1–46.

Tucker, J.E. 1996. Revisiting Reform: Women and the Ottoman Law of Family Rights, 1917. *Arab Studies Journal*, 4, 4–18.

Twining, W. 2010. Normative and Legal Pluralism: A Global Perspective. *Duke Journal of Comparative and International Law*, 20, 473–517.

Tyan, E. 1959. *Le notariat et le preuve par ecrit dans le pratique du droit musulman*. Beirut: Impr. Saint Paul.

____1964. s.v. 'Adl, *EI2*, I, 209a.

UN Office for the Coordination of Humanitarian Affairs in the Occupied Palestinian Territories (OCHA). 2009. The Planning Crisis in East Jerusalem: Understanding the phenomenon of "illegal" construction. http://www.ochaopt.org/documents/ocha_opt_planning_crisis_east_jerusalem_april_2009_english.pdf [accessed 10/12/2014].

Ursinus, M.O.H. 1993. s.v. Millet. *EI2*, VII, 61–4.

Vanderlinden, J. 1971. Le pluralisme juridique: essai de synthèse, in *Le Pluralisme juridique*, edited by J. Gilissen. Bruxelles: Université Libre Bruxelles, 19–56.

______1989. Return to Legal Pluralism: Twenty Years Later. *Journal of Legal Pluralism*, 28, 149–57.

______1993. Vers une nouvelle conception du pluralisme juridique. *Review de la Recherche juridique—droit prospectif*, 53, 573–83.

Van Maanen, J. 1979. The Fact and Fiction of Organizational Ethnography. *Administrative Quarterly*, 24, 539–50.

Vidich, A.J. and Lyman, S.M. 2003. Qualitative Methods: Their History in Sociology and Anthropology, in *The Landscape of Qualitative Research: Theories and Issues*, edited by N.K. Denzin and Y.S. Lincoln. Thousand Oaks, London, and New Delhi: Sage Publications, 55–130.

Vitta, E. 1947. *The Conflict of Laws in Matters of Personal Status in Palestine*. Tel Aviv: M. Shaham's Press.

Wakin, J.A. 1972. *The Function of Documents in Islamic Law*. Albany: SUNY Press.

Wald, K.D. 2002. The Religious Dimension of Israeli Political Life, in *Religion and Politics in Comparative Perspective: The One, the Few, and the Many*, edited by T.G. Jelen and C. Wilcox. Cambridge: Cambridge University Press, 99–124.

Welchman, Lynn. 1990. Family Law under Occupation: Islamic Law and the Shari'a Courts in the West Bank, in *Islamic Family Law*, edited by C. Mallat and J. Connors. London, Dordrecht, and Boston: Graham & Trotman, 93–115.

______2000. *Beyond the Code: Muslim Family Law and the Shari'a Judiciary in the Palestinian West Bank*. The Hague, London, Boston: Kluwer Law International.

______2003. In the Interim: Civil Society, the *Shar'i* Judiciary and Palestinian Personal Status Law in the Transitional Period. *Islamic Law and Society*, 10 (1), 34–69.

Wilson, M.C. 1987. *King Abdullah, Britain and the Making of Jordan*. Cambridge: Cambridge University Press.

Woodman, G.R. 1998. Ideological Combat and Social Observation: Recent Debates about Legal Pluralism. *Journal of Legal Pluralism*, 42, 21–59.

______1999. The Idea of Legal Pluralism, in *Legal Pluralism in The Arab World*, edited by B. Dupret, M. Berger, and L. al-Zwaini. The Hague, London, Boston: Kluwer Law International, 3–20.

Wooten, M. and Hoffman, A.J. 2008. Organizational Fields: Past, Present and Future, in *The Sage Handbook of Organizational Institutionalism*, edited by R. Greenwood et al. LA, London, New Delhi, and Singapore: Sage, 130–48.

Wurth, A. 2003. Stalled Reform: Family Law in Post-Unification Yemen. *Islamic Law and Society*, 10 (1), 12–33.

Yanow, D. 2009. Organizational Ethnography and Methodological Angst: Myths and Challenges in the Field. *Qualitative Research in Organizations and Management*, 4, 186–99.

Yildirim, S. 2005. Aftermath of a Revolution: A Case Study of Turkish Family Law. *Pace International Law Review*, 17 (2), 347–71.

Yngvesson, B. 1988. Making Law at the Doorway: The Clerk, the Court and the Construction of Community in a New-England Town. *Law and Society Review*, 22, 409–48.

Zahalka, I. 2009. The Shari'a Courts: Between Adjudication and Identity. Tel Aviv: Israeli BAR Press.

Zamir, A. 2002. The Family Court—Its Extensive Jurisdiction according to the Habas Judgment. *Hamishpat*, 7, 463–71 [Hebrew].

Ze'evi, D. 1996. *An Ottoman Century: The District of Jerusalem in the 1600s*. Albany: SUNY Press.

Zink, V. 2009. A Quiet Transfer: The Judaization of Jerusalem. *Contemporary Arab Affairs*, 2 (1), 122–33.

Index

Abu Gosh 41, 61
Abu ʿUday (aide to the chief clerk, the shariʿa court in West Jerusalem) 65–6, 77, 79, 87, 89, 153
Abu Zayd (chief clerk, the shariʿa court in West Jerusalem) 65, 65n8, 77, 77n1, 77n4, 79, 87–8, 88n7, 91, 92n13, 112n14, 113, 115, 118n31, 142n12, 152, 152n6, 153, 159–60, 193
ʿadala 111
administration, of (Israeli) shariʿa courts 1, 30–32, 56, 65, 66n11, 68, 68n15, 69n16, 68n18, 70, 70n23, 73, 77n2, 78–9, 88n7, 91, 110, 110n9, 152
ahl al-khayr 67, 130n12, *see also muhakamin*
ahl al-ʿurf 16
ʿAin Nequba 61
al-ʿAlami, Saʿad al-Din 46, 145
American Colony 63
amr himaya, *see* protection order
ʿAnata 63
annexation of Jerusalem 8, 42, 43, 43n5, 45–7, 54, 61, 63, 95, 154, 178, 181, 183
ʿArab al-Sawahrah 63
Arafat, Yasser 139
ʿAsliyya, Tawfiq [qadi] 64, 145–6, 146n22
ʿAsliyya, Ziad [qadi] xiii, 46, 46n13, 52–3, 55, 64, 64n7, 65, 75, 75n35, 77, 145–7, 162, 162n27
al-Ataune, Dugan [qadi] 33n12
al-ʿAzariyya 61

bab al-musalaha 133
al-Barghouti, Marwan 143n16
Beit Hanina 63
Beit Safafa 41
Bethlehem 63, 68
blue marriage 54n6, 163n28, 202
border police 52

connection principle 106, 123, *see also iqaron hakrikha*
Custodian of Absentee Property 23n19, 38, 38n26, 201
custody 22n16, 47n14, 97, 106n26, 113, 114, 114n20, 123, 123n2, 160–61, 202, 209, *see also hadana*

Dahiyat al-Barid 63
darb [beating (of wife)]
  mubarrihan [brutal] 129
  taʾdibi [educational] 130n12
daʿwa 79, 114, 155, 170n4
Dir Yassin 56n13
divorce 18, 22n16, 23, 35, 39, 79, 100n8, 101, 105–6, 106n26, 121n37, 123, 127, 127n8, 128–32, 132n14, 132n15, 133n16, 142, 154, 157–8, 158n20, 159, 171, 179, 181, 200, 202, 207–8, 210, 211, 214–15, 217
  by consent with mutual waiving of all financial obligations 118, 156, 157, 158n21
  certificate 73, 78, 151–2, 154, 158
  irrevocable 82
  ratification 110, 113
  registration of 158, 174n7
  sharʿi justification for 120
  unilateral 82n12, 82n13, 119, 152n5
dower 55n7, 79, 115, 142n13, 162n27, *see also mahr*
  deferred 113

fatwa viii, 104, 104n18, 104n19, 104n22, 145, 145n20, 147, 149, 173, 195, 213, *see also istiftaʾ*

Gaza Strip 41, 44n10, 89n9, 170, 209, 214
Ghandur, Izzat, *see* Abu ʿUday
Givʿat Shaʾul 56, 56n13, 57, 77n1

Haʾaretz 202
hadana 114, *see also* custody
half yamin 55, *see also* oath
hanafiyya 17n5, 18, 18n8
hanbaliyya 18n8
Haram al-Sharif 44, 72, 147, 159, *see also* Temple Mount
hardane 117, 125, 142
hasr ʾirth 152–3
HCJ (High Court of Justice) xi, 32, 32n9, 33, 38, 38n26, 89, 100n8, 123n2, 201
High Court of Justice, *see* HCJ
hijab 125
Hizme 63
hujja pl. *hujaj* 73, 77, 78n5, 91, 112, *see also muʿamalat*; *musadaqat*
Hussein, King of Jordan 138, 138n2
Hussein, Sadam 90

Ibn ʿAbidin 36, 36n21, 209
ʿidda 82, 100n8, 127n8, 156n17, 157
ijab waqabul 115
intifada
  first 138n2
  second [al-Aqsa] 66n10, 86, 142n11
iqaron hakrikha 106, *see also* connection principle
Islamic Movement, in Israel 104, 104n17, 104n18, 104n21, 105, 108n6, 170
isomorphism 168–9, 172, 174, 207
ʿIssawiyya 63
istidʿaʾ 91, 193, *see also hujja*
istiftaʾ 104, 147, 195, *see also* Fatwa
istihsan 116n25, 213
istislah 116n25, 213
ithbatat 73, 113

Jabel al-Mukkabar 63
Jaffa Street [in Jerusalem] 51–2, 57
jaha 125, 155n12
Jamil, Muhammad, *see* Abu Zayd
Jericho 63
Jilbab 64

Judicial Circular 102, 102n14, 103, 103n16, 153, 153n7, 154, 154n9, 171, 216, *see also marsum qadaʾi*

kafil 128
kashf sharʿi 86, 86n3, 87
Al-Khadr 63
Khatib, Taufiq 104n18
khulʿ 35
khuluʿ mawaniʿ 160, *see also* marriage, impediments to
Knesset xi, 9, 29–30, 31, 31n8, 32, 32n11, 34, 37n24, 38–9, 67n11, 89n9, 95–7, 99, 101–3, 105, 105n23, 105n25, 106, 107n2, 108, 151–3, 169, 171–2, 185n13

Legislation, Israeli
  Abolishment of the Majalla Law 34n16, 199
  Absentee Property Law 38, 199
  Age of Marriage Law 34, 35n18, 36, 38, 97, 199
  Basic Law: The Judiciary 32n9, 199
  Capacity and Guardianship Law 34, 36, 172–3, 199
  Civil Wrongs Ordinance 82, 199
  Court Regulations (Suspension of leaving the country) 39, 199
  Establishment of a Shariʿa Court in Jerusalem 46, 200
  Family Court Law 37n24, 39, 200
  Law and Administration Ordinance 29n2, 200
    Amendment No. 11 43, 200
  Municipality Ordinance 43, 200
  Nationality Law 89n9, 200
  Penal Law 34, 82n12, 200
  Qadis Law 30, 30n4, 200
    Amendment No. 10 32, 33n13, 34, 34n14, 200
  Rabbinical Courts Jurisdiction 106n26, 200
  Regulations Regarding Sharʿi Advocates 31, 200
  Regulations Regarding Sharʿi Court Fees 31, 200

Religious Courts (Assistance Units) Law 30, 200
Religious Courts (Prevention of Disturbance) Law 30, 200
Religious Courts (Summons) Law 30, 200
Shariʿa Courts (Validation of Appointment) Law 29, 30, 200
Spouses (Property Relations) Law 34, 36, 36n19, 39, 200
Succession Law 34, 36, 36n19, 38–9, 97, 200
Women's Equal Rights Law 34–6, 82n12, 97, 200
Legislation, Mandatory
Criminal Code Ordinance 35, 35n17, 199
Moslem Family Law Ordinance 20, 199
Palestine Order in Council 20, 20n11, 22n16, 29n2, 37, 199
Proclamation No. 42 20, 21n12, 199
proclamation regarding the Establishment of Shariʿa Court of Appeals 21n13, 34n15, 199
Succession Ordinance 20n10, 199
Legislation, Other
Egyptian Law of Testamentary Disposition 153n7, 200
Jordanian Law of Family Rights 42, 200
Jordanian Law of Personal Status 151, 153n7, 200
Jordanian Law of Sharʿi Procedure 42, 200
Syrian Personal Status Law 153n7, 201
[US] The Indian Civil Rights Act 180, 181n4, 201
Legislation, Ottoman
Law of Family Rights, *see* OLFR
Law of Succession 20n10, 199
Law of Procedure for Shariʿa Courts 29, 34, 37, 42, 66, 143n15, 199
Majalla 17, 17n5, 34, 34n16, 35, 38n27, 55, 55n10, 111n11, 199
OLFR xi, 17–20, 22, 29, 34–5, 38, 42, 54n7, 71, 71n25, 74, 86n3, 127n8, 156n15, 199
maʾcdhun 8, 67, 71, 71n24, 72, 72n26, 72n28, 73, 75, 78, 142n13, 145, 148–9, 151–2, 159–60, 180, *see also* marriage registrar
mahr 115, *see also* dower
tawabiʿ al-mahr (supplement of the dower) 142n13
maintenance vii, xiv, 9, 22n16, 54, 55n7, 79, 82, 86n3, 96–8, 100, 100n8, 101–3, 103n16, 105–6, 106n26, 113, 113n18, 114, 114n20, 116, 116n26, 117, 117n28, 117n30, 118, 120–21, 123, 123n2, 123n3, 124–5, 125n5, 126–7, 127n6, n7, n8, 128–9, 129n9, 130, 132–3, 133n17, 154, 156, 156n17, 157–8, 158n22, 159, 171–2, 213, 216–17, *see also nafaqa*
malıkiyya 18n8, 74
marriage 18, 22n16, 23, 35, 39, 45, 63, 71, 71n24, 71n25, 72–3, 78, 79, 80n9, 101, 105, 115, 123, 143n15, 148, 151, 159, 171, 179, 193, 202, 206, 211, 212
certificate 45, 72, 72n28, 73, 78, 112n14, 142n13, 147, 152
dissolution of 82n12, 132, 154n10, 156n15, 156n17, 157
[on the] initiative of the wife 121n37
judicial dissolution of 35, 74, 100, 121–2n37, 155, 158n20, 163
impediments to 159, 159n23, 160, *see also kuhulʿ mawaniʿ*
[of] minors 20n10, 35n18, 38, 38n28, 97, 151, 151n1, 163, 174n7, 180, 181
polygamous 35n17, 97, 152, 163, 180, 181
proper *sharʿi* 115n23,
ratifications 110, 112n14, *see also ithbatat*
registration of 72n28, 148, 148n25, 151–2
marriage registrar xiii, 8, 38, 58n15, 61, 67, 71–2, 72n28, 73, 73n30, 145, *see also maʾadhun*

marsum qada'i 102, 102n14, 213, *see also* Judicial Circular
Masalha, Nawaf 105
maskan shar'i 54, 55n7, 86n3, 113n18
matrimonial conciliation 66n11, 67n12, 69n19, 74, 74n32, 74n34, 83, 118, 128–9, 129n10, 129n11, 130–32, 133n16, 154, 155n13, 156, 158n20
millet 7, 15, 19–20, 23–4, 24n20, 24n22, 27, 37, 100, 218
MK (knesset member) xi, 30n5, 104n18, 105
mu'amalat 73, 77, 77n5, 78, 112, 205, *see also hujaj*
Mudlij, Zaki [qadi] 64n7, 140
muhakamin 67, *see also ahl al-khayr*
muhtasib 16n2
mukhbirun 102, 213
murafi' shar'i 31, 70, 110n9, *see also* shar'i advocate
musadaqat 112, *see also hujaj*; *mu'amalat*

nafaqa 113, 117, 213, *see also* maintenance
  ma'kal 117
  malbas 117
  mu'aqqata 127
  sukna 113, 117
nakba 22, 42
nashiz 54n7
National Insurance Institute, *see* NII
Natur, Ahmad [qadi] xiii, 32–3, 35, 36n20, 51, 91, 92n12, 101, 102, 102n14, 103, 103n16, 104, 104n18, 105n23, 117n27, 145, 145n21, 146, 146n23, 148, 153n7, 172, 174, 213
New Institutional Theory 10, 106, 167–72, 176, 207, 209
NII xi, 54, 114, 114n20, 116n26, 126, 127n6, 129n9, 158n22, 159, 163n28, 178
nikab 157n18
nikah 215, *see also* marriage
niza' wa-shiqaq 74, 121n37, 154, *see also* strife and discord
nizami courts 16–17, 42, 189, 215

oath 55, 55n8, 55n9, 55n10, 112, 126, *see also half yamin*
obedience suit 54, 54n7, 86n3, 98, 98n4, 121, 123, 123n2, 155–7, 157n19, 163
occupation of Jerusalem 8, 43–6, 53, 70, 88, 141, 144n19, 174, 181, 183, 218
organizational field 6–7, 10, 167–8, 168n2, 168n3, 169–70, 170n5, 171–6, 186–7, 189–90, 207, 219
orient house 53
Oslo II (Interim) Agreement 53, 161n26, 189n17

Palestinian Liberation Organization, *see* PLO
Palestinian National Authority, *see* PNA
PLO 138n2
PNA xi, 2, 6, 53, 85n2, 138–9, 139n4, 142, 142n11, 144, 148, 185n12
police 2, 16n2,52, 52n1, 53, 126, 128, 143, 160–61, 169
protection order 39, 118, 118n31, 119, 125, 128

qadi al-quda 42, 44, 46, 85, 138, 139n4, 145, 148, 189n17
Qadri Basha 36, 36n21, 74, 74n33, 83n16, 129, 214
Al-Quds (newspaper) 46, 202
Qur'an 55, 104, 130n12, 214
quiet deportation 54n5, 59n18, 179n2, 205

rabbinical courts 24n22, 31, 36n23, 39, 100n7, 105–6, 106n23, 127n7, 200, 209
Rabin, Yitzhak 53
ra'is al-shurta 16n2
al-Ram 63, 139
Ramallah 63, 68, 118, 142–3, 143n15, 146, 148, 213
Rayan, Kamil 104n18

Sabri, 'Akrama, Mufti 104, 104n20, 105, 139n4, 147, 195
sahib al-mazalim 16n2
Salah al-Din Street [in East Jerusalem] 140–41, 141n9, 153, 156–7, 161, 183, 193

Salah, Ra'id 104n18, 108n6
Sawt al-Haqq wa'al-Hurriyya 105n17, 202
separation barrier 184, 184n11, 206
*al-Sha*46, 202
shafi'iyya 18n8
shar'i advocate xiii, 9, 31, 47, 52, 57, 58n15, 59, 59n18, 61, 67–8, 68n15, 69, 69n21, 70, 75n35, 79, 82–3, 87, 110, 112, 114, 124, 124n4, 125, 140, 140n7, 143, 155–6, 158, 200, *see also murafi' shar'i*
Sharon, Ariel 86
Sheikh Jarrah 63
Shu'afat 64, 77n1, 143n15
SMC xi, 21, 21n15, 22–3, 23n18, 25
strife and discord 74, 121n37, 154, 154n10, 155–6, 156n14, 156n15, 157–8, 158n20, *see also niza' wa-shiqaq*
sulh 69n19, *see also* matrimonial conciliation
Supreme Muslim Council, *see* SMC
Supreme Islamic Board 44, 44n9, 45–6, 138, 207

ta'a zawjiyya 54, 98, 121, 123, 155, *see also* obedience suit
ta'dil 111
ta'rif 111
talaq 113, *see also* divorce
  bayyin 82
  bi'al-Ibra' 156, 158n21
  ta'assufi 82, 119
tazkiyya 111

Temple Mount 44, 53n4, 86, 138

United Nation Partition Plan 41

Waqf 17, 17n4, 21–3, 85n2, 105, 146–7,
  Administration in Jerusalem, Jordanian 44, 72, 74, 75n35, 138–9, 144–5, 159, 189n17
  in Israel 23, 23n19, 25, 25n24, 26, 37n25, 38n26, 39, 123n1, 125, 145n20, 170, 173, 214
War
  1948 22, 38, 41, 56n13
  1967 43, 170, 174
west bank 41–2, 44, 44n10, 45, 45n11, 60n20, 63, 63n3, 64, 68–9, 70n22, 85n2, 88–9, 138–9, 142n11, 143n16, 144n19, 154, 161n26, 163n28, 170, 174, 183, 189n17, 204–5, 209, 211, 214, 217–18
wikala 154
working group for equality in personal status issues 100–101, 101n9, 101n10, 101n12, 107n4, 205, 209

al-Za'im 61
Zibdi, Muhammad Rashid [qadi] xiii, 1–2, 33n12, 65–6, 66n10, 73, 75n35, 77, 80, 91, 113, 113n17, 114–15, 118–19, 119n32, 120, 124, 140, 146, 153, 153n7, 154, 156, 158n22, 161–2
Zini, Da'ud [qadi] 104n18